THE FRAME OF ORDER

The earliest diagram of the Copernican Universe

The Frame of Order

AN OUTLINE OF ELIZABETHAN BELIEF
TAKEN FROM TREATISES
OF THE LATE SIXTEENTH CENTURY

Edited by James Winny

NEW YORK
THE MACMILLAN COMPANY

FIRST PUBLISHED 1957

PRINTED IN GREAT BRITAIN
in 11 *point Bell* type
BY ROBERT MACLEHOSE AND CO. LTD
THE UNIVERSITY PRESS, GLASGOW

For C. S. Lewis

The diagram of the heliocentric universe used as frontispiece to this book has been reproduced from a copy of Thomas Digges' treatise of 1576 in the library of Pembroke College, Cambridge.

The illustration on page 118 is taken from a copy of the English translation of La Perrière's *Mirror of Policy*, 1598, in the University Library at Cambridge.

CONTENTS

PART THREE: THE UNIVERSE

INTRODUCTION

Reading through a catalogue of English books printed in the second half of the sixteenth century is a tedious exercise, but an illuminating experience if we have tacitly assumed that Elizabethan literature consists chiefly of poetic drama, chronicles and lyrical miscellanies. Even when we make allowance for gaps in our records of Elizabethan printed books, and in particular for the number of plays which never reached print, the work commonly regarded as expressing the characteristic spirit of the age appears as a rather humble category in the full range of Elizabethan writing. By far the greater number of sixteenth-century books would be classified by a modern bookseller as non-fictional works: lives of great men, travel-books and accounts of voyages, scientific treatises in the fields of medicine, astronomy, navigation or husbandry, legal and political studies; but above all, sermons, homilies and religious tracts. Our immediate impression must be that the Elizabethan reading public was considerably more serious-minded than we should gather from acquaintance with the popular drama alone. Donne's seemingly perverse addiction to the topics and vocabulary of scientific and theological writers appears in a new light as we grasp the weight of intellectual interests to which more thoughtful Elizabethans were exposed. The record of books reprinted, a reliable indication of public demand, confirms the impression that Elizabethans expected serious instruction rather than entertainment of their reading. This does not mean that works of fiction—using the term to include poetry and drama—usually exhausted their popularity in a single edition. Sidney's *Arcadia*, a good example of an Elizabethan best-seller, passed through one pirated and six authorised editions in a little more than three decades from 1588. It is difficult to make a fair comparison with a dramatic work, for the acting companies were understandably reluctant to sell their plays for publication; but the anonymous *Mucedorus* gratified its publisher by running into ten editions between 1598 and 1626. None of Shakespeare's plays had so distinguished a record in

A2

print, and not many of those issued before the collected edition of 1623 appeared more than three times on the stationers' stalls. But the achievement of *Mucedorus* is itself overshadowed by the resounding success of John Dod's *Exposition upon the Ten Commandments,* which ran through nineteen editions between 1603 and 1635. *The Golden Chain,* another theological work dealing with eschatological issues, was printed ten times in the five years following its first edition in 1591. Some part of Shakespeare's audience may have divided its interests between the Globe, public executions and the ballad-monger's wares; but Elizabethan playgoers certainly included those who, like Shakespeare himself, studied the more thoughtful works of contemporary literature.

It is important to make some acquaintance with the great hinterland of Elizabethan books, not only because the poetry and drama of the age do not become fully intelligible until we recognise their philosophical context, but because a single sensibility informs the current beliefs and the literature of the period in common. We shall not expect the drama to present a practical demonstration of philosophical belief, but to be generally moulded and directed by assumptions shared, with varying degrees of consciousness, by all the members of Elizabethan society. The growth of Elizabethan drama was concurrent with a sharpening of intellectual interest in the extent of man's world and in the kind of experience to which his nature committed him; and the processes of thought to which the dramatist was exposed have left their form and pressure upon his work. It is not surprising if dramatic dialogue sometimes runs so close to a familiar philosophical tenet that the poet seems to be paraphrasing from a contemporary treatise. Romei's short account of the four states of existence open to man—a commonplace of sixteenth-century thought—seems to contain the germinal ideas of at least two of Hamlet's speeches:

If a man addict himself only to feeding and nourishment, he becometh a plant; if to things sensual, he is as a brute beast; if to things reasonable and civil, he groweth a celestial creature; but if he exalt the beautiful gift of his mind to things invisible and divine, he transformeth himself into an angel.

The parallels have some critical interest, but they are less significant than Romei's ascription to man of a great span of potential
existence embracing the remote extremes of plantlike dullness
and obscurity, and the celestial splendour of a god. Elizabethan
tragedy accepts this condition as an essential premise. The reduc-
tion of a magnificent protagonist to the level of animal wretched-
ness—depicted literally in the story of Nebuchadnezzar, which
was dramatised for Henslowe about 1595—frequently forms the
core of the tragic situation. The humanist philosophers might
have protested that the arrogant superhuman figures who
thundered across the popular stages were an almost blasphem-
ous travesty of their noble ideal. Man's splendour lay in his
angelic apprehension, not in the great-hearted courage which
Elizabethan tragedy held up for admiration. The theologians
could have brought a different complaint; that the dramatist's
usual picture of man gave a ridiculously exaggerated notion of
his strength and natural capacity. The creature whom Donne
describes as 'that nothing which is infinitely less than a mathe-
matical point, than an imaginary atom' could never bestride his
earth, though that itself was contemptibly little. Yet although
Donne insists that the Renaissance giant is the shadow of a help-
less pigmy, he does not attempt to displace man from his
central position in the universal stage. Even where disparity of
opinion over man's nature and status is keenest, Elizabethan
writers agree on the fundamental issue of his importance in the
created scheme of things. In giving their protagonists heroic
dimensions the dramatists underscored this belief; for if morally
inappropriate, such a scale was proper both to man's crucial
place in the universal design and to the magnitude of his cosmic
setting. Nor is Elizabethan tragedy at odds with the theologians' view of man irremediably weakened by the contagion
of sin. Agrippa's comment after the death of Antony,

> *A rarer spirit never*
> *Did steer humanity; but you gods will give us*
> *Some faults, to make us men*

reflects the more optimistic estimate of man which the Renaissance had promoted; but its admission of a tragic predisposition

in man to yield to disastrous impulses conforms with the theological outlook of the age.

Apart from their interest as the philosophical complement of Elizabethan literature, current treatises on broadly scientific subjects have an obvious value for modern readers as a source of information about beliefs which the poets saw no need to explain. Elizabethan assumptions about the nature of the solar system, the proper form of political government or the physiological behaviour of the body have long been superseded, and the beliefs which have replaced them are largely unrelated to the earlier systems of thought. We may still speak of being cold-hearted or of expressing cordial feelings, but with the lapsing of the old philosophy the phrases have lost their lively and very specific meanings. The modern reader who wishes to understand Elizabethan literature must be prepared to adjust his beliefs; grasping the impudent paradox compressed into Donne's epithet 'unruly sun' by recalling the sixteenth-century conception of the sun as a sovereign ruling a faultlessly ordered system of spheres. Donne's scientific allusions can be especially perplexing. That curious organ

the sinewy thread my brain lets fall
Through every part

mystifies every reader who is unacquainted with the physiological beliefs which Donne shared virtually unchanged with Chaucer. None of his contemporaries would have paused over the passage. Like him they believed with the Schoolmen that

the animal or lively spirit, which hath his seat in the brain, is distributed by the sinews into every part, giving unto the same power and feeling.

So familiar a part of learning required no gloss; but fortunately for later readers those who wrote physiological treatises were not much concerned to produce original theories or to avoid repeating commonplace beliefs. Consequently, any sixteenth-century work on the subject is able to make Donne's meaning clear, and to untie the 'subtle knot' of man's nature which he draws tight in *The Extasie*. But Elizabethan beliefs do not always manifest themselves in so obvious a form, and we may lose more of a poet's meaning by missing the significance of remarks which seem either trivial or inconsequential. It is not easy for a modern play-goer to grasp the full import of Othello's descent to domestic banality:

> *I have a salt and sorry rheum offends me:*
> *Lend me thy handerchief.*

The deadly dramatic point of his remark, it could be argued, is enough; but his barbed speech contains a clear signal to the audience that Othello's habitually phlegmatic nature is on the verge of a dangerous and terrible change. The opening scenes of the play, and especially the encounter with Brabantio, reveal a protagonist temperamentally cold despite his torrid background; a man most unlikely to commit crimes of passion. But the theory of humours, as Timothy Bright explains, admitted an exception to this rule in the case of a salt phlegm:

> *then approacheth it to the nature of choler, and in like sort thereof*
> *riseth anger and frowardness.*

The 'salt and sorry rheum' beginning to annoy Othello is the warning of a disastrous breakdown of rational command to come; already foreshadowed in the great tempest raging about Cyprus before his arrival. Again, we may recognise the general poetic aptness of the storm as a symbol of disorder without appreciating its pointed relevance to Othello's later condition. Bright is again helpful, dropping an open hint in his reference to

> *those domestic storms that arise more troublesome and boisterous to*
> *our nature than all the blustering winds in the ocean sea.*

This analogy, an invariable feature of sixteenth-century treatises of the passions, was to the Elizabethan mind no mere literary figure but a statement of literal similarity: an instance of the sympathetic link which united man with the natural world.

The habit of thinking in such analogical terms is a dominant characteristic of the age. The Schoolmen whose philosophy the sixteenth century inherited, we might reasonably conclude, were more concerned to determine the occult relationships and correspondences which bound together universal creation than to ascertain the true nature of any single part of it. The engaging but unproductive task of devising degrees and categories for all created things might seem to have been forced upon the medieval philosophers by their lack of scientific instruments. But the end of the Schoolmen's enquiry was not to know the material nature of things; it was to understand their purpose in the whole scheme of Creation. God had framed the world to a design which could not be otherwise than perfectly conceived, and in which no object could be without its appointed place. Every mineral, herb and creature, as each of the celestial bodies, existed to fulfil one peculiar function in the great organism of cosmos. The task of the natural philosopher was to comprehend the form of divine will by discovering this hidden purpose in all things. When a sixteenth-century scientist, repeating what he could read in Pliny's *Natural History*, affirmed that the end of meteors was to make the earth fruitful and to set forth God's power, or that the purpose of winds was to stir up the air and so keep it wholesome, he was not indulging a quaint and irresponsible fancy but promoting a serious enquiry into the workings of the universe. We demand another kind of explanation, capable of accounting for the physical nature and behaviour of things without metaphysical assistance; and leave the scientifically irrelevant question of why they were made to purely theological speculation. Medieval science could not be so easily disengaged from religious faith. The behaviour of objects—even if, like stones, they did nothing—revealed natural qualities implanted in them by divine will, by whose operation the frame of universal order was held in place. As fire leapt upwards towards its appointed sphere, leaving earth to sink to the basest level, so creatures were attracted or repelled by reason of like or unlike qualities inseparable from their nature. The theory of sympathies linking even the most remotely related bodies was energetically exploited by the medieval physicians and their Elizabethan successors. A patient subject to melancholy would wisely avoid

sauces prepared with vinegar or verjuice, because the melan-
cholic humour was itself sharp and biting; and the phlegmatic
must refuse fish, whose cold and moist nature would aggravate
the superfluity from which he was suffering. Upon such bases of
belief the old philosophy could erect its major teleological argu-
ments; explaining that the planet Saturn had been placed furthest
from the earth so that the baleful influence of its cold and dry
nature should have less terrible consequences for sublunary life.
The unwearied delight in analogy and correspondence which
sixteenth-century literature exhibits is nourished by beliefs held
in common by theologian, scientist and poet, and deeply impressed upon the outlook of all three.

Elizabethans found little to add to the elaborate theories of
correspondence which the Schoolmen had patiently worked out.
These elaborations must have proved cumbersome in an age
without the Schoolmen's leisured seclusion, and distracted by an
increasing number of claims upon intellectual attention; and they
were not treated in great detail by later Elizabethan writers.
This generalisation does not cover Robert Fludd's great cosmo-
logical treatise, *Utriusque Cosmi*, published in the early years
of the seventeenth century, which contains some of the most
intricate diagrams of universal order which the old philosophy
produced. But taken together, works of this kind published
about the beginning of the sixteenth century, of which Elyot's
Governor is representative, tend to be far more explicit about
the implanted natures and correspondences of things than are
similar treatises published sixty or seventy years later. Writers
of these later works pass more rapidly over the great interlock-
ing fabric of order assumed by the Schoolmen, alluding to the
orderly congruence of the universe, man's political system and
his individual nature in comparatively general terms. The
graded steps of the hierarchies and the meticulous observation
of degree which they entail are never overlooked; but interest
seems to have moved from the details of the design to the simple
fact of its existence. 'If we enter into the consideration of the
nature of bees,' observes the author of a popular political treatise,

how well they are ordered in their hives; if we look into the spinning of the spider's web, if we note the members of a man's body, how well they are ordered, much more ought Reason to persuade and teach us to range and bring the subjects of a good commonweal into a decent order.

Recent critical studies have made the general reader familiar with the form of this argument; characteristic of its age in its assumption that the creatures beneath man in the chain of being, still subject to divine law, were continuing to display the harmonious order of the Creation which man, corrupted by passion, could now regain only by a great effort of will. It remained a tragic paradox that the creature for whose delight and service the world had been created should alone have brought disorder into his unblemished kingdom; but he might find some consolation and pleasure in contemplating the ordered design impressed upon the works of nature. The opening paragraph of Lodowick Lloyd's *Brief Conference of Divers Laws*, published in 1602, presents a typical picture of the well-regulated government ascribed to the natural world:

All creatures of God, as well in heaven as in earth, had laws given them after they were created, to be governed and ruled by: the sun, the moon and the stars, to keep their perpetual motions and course in their places and regiments; so the seas have their limits and bounds, how far they should rule and reign. And though one star differeth from another in glory, in greatness and in brightness, yet are they governed by one perpetual law: so the seas, although the waves thereof be so lofty and proud, yet are they shut up within doors and commanded to keep in, and not to go further than the place to them by law appointed. By law also the elements are commanded to stay within their own regiments, without trespassing one of another.

As we should expect, these remarks preface a consideration of particular laws operating within human society; a subject which no sixteenth-century writer could treat without some introductory reference to the orderly pattern of nature. Belief in the fixed and unalterable frame of universal law proved hard to dislodge. Even so radical an innovation as the Copernican theory, first published about the middle of the century, could not seriously disturb traditional outlook; and the new conception of the universe was grafted without much difficulty upon the old stock of belief. Copernicus, affirming that the Schoolmen had been mistaken in supposing the earth to be a fixed body set beneath the spheres of the incorruptible heavenly bodies, has been regarded as a main cause of the collapse of the old philosophy; but evidence of any contemporary alarm at his challenge to established belief is hard to find. Thomas Digges' *Perfect Description of the Celestial Orbs*, a Copernican treatise published six times between 1576 and 1596, helps to explain why the new theory caused no greater misgivings. Copernicus continued to regard the stellatum or sphere of the fixed stars as 'the very court of celestial angels' and its height above the earth as the measure of its spiritual purity; and his theory confirmed anew the inherent orderliness of the universe. 'In this form or frame,' Digges claims of the new cosmic system,

we may behold such a wonderful symmetry of motions and situations as in no other can be proponed.

The old framework might be modified, but not the conviction that the earth held its place within a scrupulously ordered system of spheres; a sublime witness to the nature of its Maker.

Although it would be very difficult to consider sixteenth-century outlook apart from its deeply ingrained concern with order and degree, such a concern is not peculiar to one age alone. In all ages men wish to be assured that the world of their experience is governed by more or less constant laws which stabilise the terms by which human life is lived. What distinguishes Elizabethan outlook is not merely its assumption of a meticulous universal design, but the kind of order which its philosophy envisaged. An eighteenth-century scientist would have considered that he had proved the innate orderliness of the universe when he had shown its unvarying obedience to the recently formulated laws of Newtonian physics. An Elizabethan's proof would have depended upon metaphysical argument in which exact observation or measurement played no significant part. The manifest facts that every species was ranged beneath one superior creature, as kings among men and eagles among birds, or that every animal had a natural opposite whom it hated and avoided instinctively, assured him that some ordered principle had shaped the world. It would not have occurred to him that the supposedly innate qualities of lions, hares or peacocks were no more than arbitrary and fanciful attributes, valueless as a basis of scientific inference. The nobility of one beast, the cowardice or pride of another, were as self-evident as the proverbial antipathy of cats and dogs. The belief that every creature and condition had its antithesis did not unsettle but confirmed his sense of universal design. By their mutual hostility fire and water held each other in check; each preventing the other from becoming dangerously preponderant. Moreover, the fusion or mixture of such opposites might bring into existence new and valuable properties. This point is happily illustrated by a passage in Elyot's discussion of dancing, where the author describes how the union of dancers unlike in sex and natural characteristics produces a symbol of concord:

A man in his natural perfection is fierce, hardy, strong in opinion, covetous of glory and desirous of knowledge. The good nature of a woman is to be mild, timorous, tractable, benign, of sure remembrance and shamefast. Wherefore when we behold a man and a woman dancing together, let us suppose there to be a concord of all the said qualities, being joined together as I have set them in order. And the moving of the man would be more vehement, of the woman more delicate and with less advancing of the body; signifying the courage and strength that ought to be in a man, and the pleasant soberness that should be in a woman. And in this wise, fierceness joined with mildness maketh severity; hardiness with timorousness maketh magnanimity, that is to say, valiant courage; wilful opinion and tractability, which is to be shortly persuaded and moved, maketh constancy, a virtue.

Elyot was certainly aware that not all men are fierce and covetous of glory, and that some women are neither mild nor tractable; but he is not attempting to describe the characteristics which human beings reveal in their daily behaviour. Rather, he is enumerating the qualities which human behaviour should exhibit if the pattern of universal order was to be maintained. As immobility remained the particular quality of stones despite the fact that they sometimes fell from cliffs or rolled down mountains, seeking a lower place, so effeminacy in a man or shrewishness in a wife did not disprove the Schoolmen's axiom that every creature was directed by a characteristic attribute, implanted to assure that every part of Creation was held in its appointed place and station. The fixed will of the lodestone to point north was such an implanted quality as urged every individual creature to persist in a single course of action or being; striving to fill its intended place in the macrocosm. Without a belief that the natural inclination of owls is to shun daylight, Casca's alarm at the appearance of such a bird in the market-place at noon would be incomprehensible. The greater prominence which the popular dramatists give to the reversal of natural courses may reduce our interest in the normal condition of the universe; where, ruled either by attraction or inflexible dislike, all creatures are drawn into a great system of ordered fixity. It is helpful to keep in mind Elyot's gracious image of the moving concord of dancing, resolved from the partnership of vehemence with delicacy; for if Elizabethans were particularly intent upon the antipathies which divided both man and his universal environment, they also recognised that this exactly balanced conflict of opposites was essential to the settled order of the world.

Yet it would be easy to assume that Elizabethans conceived universal order not only as fixed, but as a static manifestation of God's will; and that nothing remained to the philosopher but to admire the astonishing regularity of the divine handiwork which his studies had revealed. The settled order of things was both an assurance and a challenge. Part of the universe was indeed fixed and immutable, but the sphere of sublunary life was everywhere subject to corruption and change. The seasonal alterations in nature, like the physical growth and decline of man, warned him to expect no permanence of earthly things, whatever their size or importance. The medieval church saw in this transitoriness an irresistible argument for turning aside from the vanity of earthly life to the contemplation of heavenly felicity, despising all mortal happiness as shallow and illusory. Its attitude descended to the sixteenth century, but undergoing in its descent a shift of emphasis which made human life seem tragic rather than paltry in its brevity. The Elizabethan lover, sonneteer and tragic hero, threatened by time as by an implacable enemy, measure themselves and the integrity of their passion by a common capacity to resist or to frustrate this annihilating force:

> *This do I vow and this shall ever be,*
> *I will be true despite thy scythe and thee.*

Nothing suggests that the shadow of mortality had fallen lightly across medieval outlook, or that the terrors of the grave became apparent only when the glow of Elizabethan optimism faded. But against such terrors the medieval church had been able to oppose the unshakeable assurance of its dogma. The reformation which had given English congregations freedom of individual conscience had discredited the authority which could protect man against his individual fears. Henceforward—like Hamlet, but unlike Everyman—he would wrestle with nightmare alone. The change may be reflected in the perturbed spirit of later Elizabethan literature, and in the preoccupation with change and decay that nerves the poet to make such audacious claims for the immortality of his work. The great imaginative achievement of the Elizabethan poet rises as a defiant answer to the philosophy that sees man's lifelong struggle as a momentary scratch upon the surface of time, like the streak of a meteorite. Not the poetry alone, but the philosophical writing of the age, bears witness to a steady awareness of the ruinous process of time by which all earthly creatures are affected. It is characteristic of sixteenth-century outlook that a reflection upon vicissitude and mortality should interrupt a study of human physiology:

Forasmuch as among the outward things of Nature there is nothing of any long continuance and stability, neither that long keepeth itself at any certain state and vigour, but all subject to decay, alteration, and case worse and worse, truly the state of mankind doth specially and more than any other suffer sundry alterations, and is subject to great change and mutability.

To find the same considerations being applied in a political context may seem more surprising; but Elizabethan readers were
not disposed to challenge a suggestion that states, like animate
beings, underwent a process of growth in which maturity led
inevitably to decline:

*It is with them as with sensible creatures, which the more they hasten
to arrive at the perfection of their being, the sooner also they fail and
die. The contrary is seen in those which with a slow and measured
pace attain to a more fair maturity and perfection.*

By the second decade of the seventeenth century, the subject
of decay had developed a morbid fascination for some of the
most sensitive poets and theologians of the age. Webster's
ghastly vision of a charnel-house world is hardly separate in
mood and conviction from a theological treatise published in the
year of Shakespeare's death, *The Fall of Man*. The book consists
of a meticulously detailed exposition of the gloomy thesis
that the earth was in the last stages of physical and moral decay,
and about to reach its dissolution. 'In these latter days, when
the world is almost come to an upshot,' the author remarks
grimly, 'no wonder if God leave man to himself, neglecting the
common good.' It would be possible to indicate the source of
this despondent outlook in the previous quarter-century; but although Elizabethan writers had recognised the inevitability of
physical decay, they had not generally assumed that the world
was approaching its end. In fact, the idea had been vigorously
resisted; most impressively by a treatise published at Paris in
1579, *De la Vicissitude*. An English translation followed fifteen
years later. The author's main argument against the pessimists'
assumption of the debility of man and his world—that man's
recent achievements proved him at least as versatile and gifted
as his ancestors in antiquity, and that the progress of civilisation
followed a cyclic movement involving successive phases of
vitality and decadence—does not concern us here. We should
notice chiefly that a new interpretation of events gave man some
hope of resisting the forces which had been generally accounted
irresistible. The decay of estates, as a second French writer was
to argue, might have inscrutable causes, but it certainly was en-

couraged by specific political circumstances which man could
control. There emerges an implicit notion of a form of statecraft
whose object is to ward off the normal consequences of time by
preserving the integrity of government. A digression in this
second treatise, reprinted in this present book, enumerates some
of the conditions—the affection of the people for their prince,
equitable justice, military discipline, respect for great men—
which encourage stability and permanence in states.

Elizabethan interest in political science, manifest in the increasing number of such treatises published from *The Book of the
Governor* onwards—is sometimes obscured by an assumption
that Scholastic doctrine was still authoritative in this respect.
The notion of a hierarchical order operating within the state as
in the heavens evidently commanded at least nominal respect,
but it did not affect very deeply the practical political theory
which the later sixteenth century evolved. Those who governed,
if not those who wrote the contemporary political treatises, did
not need to read *Il Principe* to discover that man's actual behaviour, and not the ordered state of the Schoolmen's hypothesis,
was likely to prove the more rewarding study. The assertion of
an Elizabethan courtier that 'histories be no other thing but a
collection of divers experiences of all times and of all sorts of
men' may surprise us by its silence on the moral significance of
political events. Recent criticism has encouraged us to recognise
in Shakespeare's depiction of civil war God's retribution for the
usurpation and murder of a rightful king. *Henry IV* and *Henry VI*
may have carried this sense for their first audiences; and certainly the prayer of Henry V before Agincourt, 'Not today, O
Lord', admits the moral interpretation that has been claimed for
the whole sequence of Histories. Yet it would be hard to over-
look, especially in the two parts of *Henry IV*, the signs of Shakespeare's interest in man's political behaviour and in the practical
business of statecraft. Where the political theorists of the age
concern themselves with the causes of disorder and upheaval in
states it is to the material circumstances of bad government that
they turn: 'negligence, ignorance and riot of Princes . . . factions, secret practices, ambitions and desperate humours of subjects.' *Henry IV* contains an object-lesson in the resolute handl-

ing of affairs by which a monarch, however dubious his title, maintains control of an unruly kingdom lost by his politically incapable predecessor. The presentation of this theme in the play is unlikely to have been accidental. However useful the medieval theory of immutable hierarchies and disastrous consequences might prove to the poet in search of rhetorical figures, the idea of a universe animated by ceaseless activity and aspiration was more native to drama. Universal order might admit of more restless movement than Scholastic doctrine appears to suggest; its broad design settled irrevocably by divine fiat, yet allowing the creatures liberty to resolve their individual places through the force of implanted faculties. 'All creatures in general,' remarks Du Vair in a work translated in 1598,

and every one severally in his kind, with great vehemency and contention followeth and pursueth after that for which they are born and bred; and do certainly rejoice and exult in the fruition of that which they seek, when they have found it out.

From such a sense of the dynamic force impelling all living things to seek an appointed end, Elizabethan drama derives its characteristic energy and vigour.

Much has been done in recent years towards making familiar the framework of belief directing Elizabethan thought and outlook. Probably every schoolboy student of Shakespeare knows something about the four complexions and the Ptolemaic spheres, and realises that modern democratic principles can have no force in Elizabethan history plays. Scholarly summaries and commentaries on sixteenth-century outlook have helped to promote a more critical understanding of Elizabethan literature in general, and of its poetic drama especially. The usefulness of such studies is partly offset by their obvious limitations. The most serious of them is their lack of direct communication with the outlook they seek to describe. The terms in which, say, the theory of humours was defined by sixteenth-century philosophers cannot be varied without some loss of sense. Its ideas, although natural and familiar to the sensibility that informs sixteenth-century writing, are entirely alien to the outlook whose expression is modern prose. The form and vocabulary of a typical statement,

blood, of all juices and humours, is the best, and to man's life an aliment and maintainer chiefly appropriate, familiar and domestical:

are not quaint decoration but part of its meaning; for they represent the way in which a notion has been apprehended in the mind of the Elizabethan translator. In a summary or paraphrase we are denied this valuable and often enlightening contact with the process of thought behind belief. This contact appears more important when we realise that Elizabethan belief is sometimes too ambiguous or uncertain for summary to deal with it fairly. This difficulty is implicit in the attempts of sixteenth-century scientists to represent current assumptions by means of diagrams. Conceptions of universal order could be developed almost endlessly so long as the physical arrangement of the macrocosm was left to the reader's imagination, but not if it had to be illustrated. Again, different authorities provided different accounts or explanations of the behaviour of things. Lemnius judiciously skirts an ancient controversy in the first pages of his book; and the present extracts contain more than one confession of doubt about the precise nature of the relationship between soul and body. A book of extracted passages has its own shortcomings. The selection of material must be to some extent arbitrary, and still more subject to editorial ignorance. Individual extracts may break off inconveniently, leaving a topic in mid-air; and some crucial aspects of contemporary thought may be overlooked altogether. These are risks worth accepting; for where the book succeeds it will reproduce not only the substance of sixteenth-century belief but the idiom of thought that was its habitual complement.

This anthology of extracts from sixteenth-century treatises has been put together with the particular aim of providing a rudimentary handbook to Elizabethan belief for those who study the literature of the period. Partly for this reason, the extracts have been arranged in three groups under headings familiar to everyone who has noticed the Elizabethan poet's habit of drawing analogies between the microcosm of individual man and the greater organisms of state and universe. But this classification has been adopted mainly as a practical convenience. LeRoy's account of man's supposed development from savage rudeness to the exercise of civilised skills has little bearing upon the Elizabethan conception of social order, and finds a place for another reason. Elizabethan literature, philosophy and scientific belief are the related expressions of a single complex sensibility whose peculiar character is reflected in all three. In studying the scientific writing of the age we absorb some of the outlook and instinctive assumptions which distinguish that period from our own, and begin to sense the form and contour of the world in which Elizabethans were intellectually at home. Passages from Lemnius' treatise on the complexions or from Fulke's study of meteors, which set out current beliefs in a more or less workmanlike fashion, have an immediate value for literary interpretation. But beyond this, wherever a writer discloses the process of his thought or the kind of belief which seems natural to him, he carries his modern reader a little deeper inside the world where Elizabethan poetry and drama have their source.

With the exception of Bright's *Treatise of Melancholy*, of which a modern facsimile text has been issued, and of Digges' Copernican pamphlet, none of the works from which the extracts are drawn has been reprinted since the early seventeenth century. Fulke and Lemnius ran through several editions: the others—Digges again excepted—made no second appearance on the bookstalls. The standard of typesetting is generally good, and very little emendation of texts has been necessary. To cram as much useful information as possible within the covers of a modest-sized book, some liberties have been taken with the extracted passages; but omission-marks show where the text has been pruned. Elizabethan typesetters' use of i, u and v to represent the j, v and u of modern usage has been reversed; in other respects the spelling and punctuation of the original texts has been allowed to stand.

I have to thank the University Librarian, Mr H. R. Creswick, for many acts of kindness and especially for allowing photostats to be made of eight of the extracts; Mr M. J. C. Hodgart, Fellow and Librarian of Pembroke College, who permitted two rare astronomical treatises to be transcribed and their diagrams to be photographed; Mr H. M. Adams, Librarian of Trinity College, whose private supplement to the *Short Title Catalogue* enabled me to trace unrecorded copies of several works within the University; and the staff of the Anderson Room for their inexhaustible patience and helpfulness. The late Master of my College, Dr William Telfer, and several colleagues who answered technical questions claim a similar debt of gratitude. My last acknowledgment must be twofold. Miss Marie Overton, of the Local Examinations Syndicate, a source of encouragement during the preparation of the manuscript, made herself responsible for finding its publisher; and Professor C. S. Lewis undertook the tedious labour of checking the glossary when he had already acted as guide to some obscure regions of sixteenth-century literature and read the complete manuscript. I must hope that the usefulness of the book, rather than any imperfect thanks, will repay the expense of time and energy which both have so unselfishly volunteered.

JAMES WINNY

Selwyn College
Cambridge

PART ONE

Man

THE COMPLEXIONS

From *The Touchstone of Complexions*
by Levinus Lemnius
translated by T. Newton, 1565

These old Fellowes
Have their ingratitude in them Hereditary:
Their blood is cak'd, 'tis cold, it sildome
flowes,
'Tis lacke of kindely warmth, they are not kinde;
And Nature, as it growes againe toward earth,
Is fashion'd for the journey, dull and heavy.

Timon of Athens

Of a Compound Complexion

Compound Complexions consisting of two qualities apiece, are in number foure, like as the simple be: *viz.* Hot and moist: hot and dry: cold and moist: cold and dry: unto whom there belong and are appendant so many humours, diffused into every part of the whole body, blood, flegme, choler, and melancholy. These according to the nature of nourishment received, are increased or diminished, and suffering change and alteration, are easily one into another transmuted. And albeit these humours being of great force divers wayes, and sundrily affecting the body, yea the minde also with fulsome and unpleasant exhalations and sents is oftentimes greatly annoyed and encumbred, (even as ill & naughty wine bringeth to the braine affects both hurtfull and dangerous) may not bee accounted Elements, neither are able to constitute any complexion: yet are they endued with elementall quality and vertue, and helpe much to the conservation and keeping of the whole body in good plight and order.

For as we see the fire to be fed with matter combustible: and Torches, Linkes, Candles, and such like nourished with Oyle, or some other rosenny and fatty substance, so likewise the elementall qualities, and all the powers and faculties of nature derived into the vitall[1] and spermaticke feed of our Parents, doe stand in continuall need of nourishment. For if the body should not be sustained with nourishment, or if the humours (which moisten every particular member) should lack the preservatives and fomentations wherewith they be maintained, the whole frame of mans body must of necessity decay, and be utterly dissolved, and every part thereof vanish away into his like, whereof it was generated, or into that, whose nature it containeth within it selfe, whether it doe participate with Fire, Ayre, Earth, Water, or draw neere in nature, and be familiar to any of them. They depend mutually one of another, and are stedfastly maintained by the helpe and stay one of another. Neither is there any part in mans body so small, so vile, or so abject, that hath no respect to the comlinesse and conservation of the whole body, and doth orderly discharge his due office and proper function whereunto it was created. And this I would not have to be onely spoken and meant of the use and utility of every of the members and parts severally, but also of the humours, which by the helpe of nourishment, doe maintaine, support and underprop the temperament and complexion of each body: and by the helpe of naturall heat doe give encrease and growth to all the members generally.

For which cause *Hippocrates* and *Galen,* not without good reason appoint the foure naturall humours (being perfect and pure) the elements of Creatures endued with blood: for out of them commeth a secundary originall of our procreation. For they minister matter plentifully, and helpe highly in the breeding and shaping of the Infant or yongling, specially if the body be well ballassed with good wholsome meates, and now and then heated with a draught of good wine: for without these *Venus* games are

_____
[1] Q5 1633 vocall.

performed but faintly and sorily: which thing seemeth to bee meant by the yong stripling *Chremes* in *Terence*, who being sober, began to abhorre and loath his Harlot and Concubine: but being well whittled in wine, to take therein great delight and pleasure, and not scarce able to qualifie himselfe from committing further folly with her as in this proverbiall Sentence he flatly professed,

> *Take meat, and drinke, and wine away,*
> *Small is the lust to* Venus *play.*

For the members of generation draw unto them from the principall members, and convert into seed, the best and most exquisitly concocted humours: which seed having in it great store of effectuous and profitable spirit, is the worker of heat and of all the other faculties, and in the begetting and procreation of children, is the chiefe parent and causer. Into it is a wonderfull vertue and divine power (by Gods good will and appointment) infused, for the shaping and fashioning of the yong creature, within the mothers wombe: for it produceth a fruit of seemely and most beautifull workmanship, rightly shapen, and in each point perfectly proportioned, if the seed (whereof it was begotten) doe issue from a sound and wholsome body: for otherwise, if the seed be of a diseased, corrupt, and infected body, the issue and ofspring cannot chuse but be monstrous and deformed.

Somewhat therefore to recreate the Reader, and to make this argument more plausible, delightfull and popular: I will depaint and set downe the nature and condition of the humours that rule and beare sway in mans body, because they produce and bring forth their like qualities. For blood is partaker of hot and moist: Choler of hot and dry: Phlegme of cold and moist: and Melancholy of cold and dry. Therefore that Temperament which is hot and moist, may very well bee referred to a Sanguine man, hot and dry to a Cholericke: and so forth of the rest. But yet so, that we confesse the complexion and temperament of man not to grow or proceed elsewhere, then of the elementall qualities, for of them have they their names, and not of the humours.

First therefore there be foure Elements, Fire, Ayre, Earth, and Water, which of all things made, are the originall beginnings, next are the qualities, that is to say, the mixture of Heat,

Cold, Moist, and dry: of whom proceed the differences of Complexions. Last of all, the foure humours, whose force and nature, the seed comprehendeth and containeth within it: unto whom (beside the qualities which are to it in stead of an instrument and not of a worker) the chiefe cause next under God, of the forming and creation of all the parts, is truely to be attributed. These wholsome humours to the conservation of health and maintenance of life, are right necessary and profitable. For of them doe consist, and of them are nourished the entire parts of all creatures, and for this cause, so long as a man liveth, he can never want these without great detriment and danger of his health. Notwithstanding, according to the course of time and season of the yeere, according to the quality of the ayre enclosing us, according to the disposition of the place where we dwell, and according to the nature of each age, they are increased or diminished.

For blood being the best of all the humours, and endued with heat and moisture, is in his chiefe prime and force in the Spring season: namely, peculiar and proper to lusty flourishing age, which commonly is of a sanguine and ruddy colour, which neverthelesse wanteth not also in the other natures.

Phlegme, being like unto water, is of nature cold and moist, and taketh his encrease in winter, and engendreth diseases like unto it selfe.

Choler, being of quality hot and dry, resembleth fire, and hath his most force in Summer, which, although in sight and touching, it appeare moist, and of colour yellowish, like Malvesey, yet in operation, power and effect, it is hot and of ardent nature.

Melancholy, not unlike to earth, cold and dry, encreaseth and taketh force in Autumne, this is the dryer and grosser part of blood, and the dreggy reffuse thereof.

All these differences of humours, when a veine is opened (for it is not all pure blood that gusheth thereout) is plainely of all men to be perceived. First before it bee cold, it doth shew and represent to the eye, an ayrie and fomy spirit, which by and by vanisheth away: then an exact and pure liquor of most perfect and excellent ruddinesse, the which is pure and right blood: in which there swimmeth Choler, and sometime tough clammy

Phlegme, sometime liquid and thin, according to the nature, condition, and state of man.

Last of all, if you turne up the whole masse or lumpe, you shall find Melancholy, altogether of colour blacke. And thus every humour abounding in the body, bewrayeth it selfe by his owne proper colour: insomuch that sometime the blood that issueth out of the veines, liquifieth and is dissolved into Choler or Phlegme, or clottereth and thickneth into Melancholy, and retayneth either no colour or very little of blood. And if a man were disposed by taste to have further knowledge in these humours, he may with his tongue and palate as well judge and discerne the relish and tallage thereof, as he doth their colour by his eye. For blood is sweet, and in a manner of the relish and taste of milke, because it is much like and of kin unto it: Choler is bitter, of the nature of Gall: Phlegme, unsavory as water, and without all quality, so long as it is not rotten, not mixt with other humours, for then it is either salt or sowrish. Melancholy, is sharpe, egre and tart.

These tastes and relishes there is no man that perceiveth and feeleth not, when as in vomiting and perbraking he casteth up any of them: yea in sweat and even in the spettle, these tastes are manifestly descryed and perceived: for of these humours they have and participate their powers and faculties, and with their qualities are they endued.

Of a hot and moyst Complexion: and by the way: of the disposition and nature of a Sanguine man

The Second Chapter

Having heretofore set downe the description of simple Complexions and temperatures, which be so termed, for that they consist of one onely quality, bearing sway and dominion more then any of the rest: by course of my purposed worke, I am next to entreat of them that are compound. For in the very beginning and first entrance of this worke, my promise and full intent was to set downe and describe such a Complexion and state of body, as was in every point perfect and absolute: and to repulse and

B

keepe away all such harmes and inconveniences as in any wise might empaire health, or bring the body from his good state into worse case and taking. I have therefore thought it good here in this place first to insert the temperament that is hot and moist: because it is neerest and likest to the best. For no state of body (saving onely the best and chiefest) is better or more commendable then this, nor any that longer prolongeth life, and keepeth backe old age, so that the same consist and be within the limits and compasse of temperatenesse, that is, of hot and moist. Therefore sithence this state among all that bee compound, is accounted chiefest: wee must stand upon the discourse thereof the more narrowly and precisely, and the rather because sundry Physicions make no moe but foure differences, grounding their reasons (and not altogether vainely) that it is not possible (as *Galen* witnesseth) that any temperature or distemperature can long continue alone and simple: For so much as necessarily it adopteth and taketh to it another. For the hot (consuming and wasting moisture) engendreth and bringeth drynesse: Cold, consuming and wasting nothing, after a sort encreaseth humour. Semblably, the dry quality in those ages that a Creature groweth and encreaseth, maketh it hotter: but when it decreaseth and draweth toward decay, it maketh cold, and dryeth the solid parts of the body: but the receivers and conceptacles of the humours it filleth with excrements, which thing in old men is plainely to be discerned and perceived, who abound and are full of Phlegme, spitting and spattering at their mouth, with their Noses ever dropping and snevilly.

Which thing later Physicions (even of our time) as yet observing, rejecting simple temperatures (which notwithstanding may not well be so shaken off and forgotten) appoint onely foure, to wit, them that be compound: unto whom they have given names (not of their qualities, but somewhat unaptly) of those commonly termed and knowne humours, that is to say, Sanguine, Cholericke, Phlegmaticke, and Melancholicke: by the squier and leavell of whom, they would have these foure differences of complexion or temperature, to bee reduced and tried. Which dealing and reasoning of theirs, as it favoureth of popular judgement, learning to the common sort, very plausible: so standeth it not with the precise opinion and censure of them that

would have each thing skanned and measured in his right nature
and kinde.

In the meane season, I, as one desirous to reconcile Physicions
thus factiously jarring in opinion (and would God this uniformity and atonement were also brought to passe in matters of
Religion, for the better quieting of many mens consciences) both
parties shall suffer the chiefe place to be assigned and given to
the hot and moist Complexion (excepting alwaies as I said before, the temperatest of all, whereunto as at a marke we must
direct our minde and levell our whole matter, that by it every
man may try his owne nature) which so long as it is in his perfect strength, vigour and quality, produceth and bringeth forth
a Sanguine man.

And thus, there is in a manner no difference, neither prejudiciall to any party, either to call it by the name of a hot and
moist Complexion, or else by the tearme of a Sanguine man:
who by the benefit of this wholesome humour, containeth and
hath within him these qualities: albeit blood it selfe (for we will
keepe all things within their prescript limits) doth not engender
and cause heat and moistnesse, but rather heat and moisture
produceth blood.

Now, blood of all juyces and humours, is the best, and to
mans life an aliment and maintainer chiefly appropriate, familiar
and domesticall: for through the force and furtherance of vitall
spirit (which is the preserver, and sender of naturall heat into
every part of the body,) blood is conveied by the Conduits and
Vessels of the Arteries and Veines, and so both nourished, maintaineth and preserveth the whole body.

And for that, this pure, cleare, defecate, lovely, and amiable
juyce, is the speciall thing that conserveth every living creature
in his being, and wherein also consisteth the life and vigour of
every nature that liveth by breath: therefore the Hebrew Law-
maker *Moses*, by the direction and appointment of God himselfe,
forbade all manner of blood to be eaten, because the life of all
creatures consisteth in blood, and is therewith nourished and
maintained: even as the flame of a Candle is with the Oylie
wicke: as it plainely appeareth, by a man that bleedeth very
much, whose body is then in every part cold, wan and (for
want thereof) fainting, and in a manner ready to give up the

Ghost. I have knowne many, whose vitall spirit bleeding out and issuing together with their blood, have beene thereby brought into great danger of their lives. And therefore this treasure of Life, must most carefully bee conserved, because it is of all humours the most excellent and wholsome.

Now, as the Arteries (which abound more with vitall spirit then with blood) spring from the heart: so, the veines (which containe more blood then any spirit,) proceed and spring from the Liver, and are dispersed abroad in branches and fibres into every, yea, the very furthest places of the body. For the Liver is the shop and chiefe workemaster of grosse and thicke blood, although the first originall thereof be ascribed to the Heart, by whose power and faculty the blood is made and throughly wrought: and being endued with vitall spirit, convaieth naturall heat to each part of the body.

Blood and vitall spirit, are in their chiefest prime and most abound in lusty and flourishing yeeres, albeit there is no age that lacketh the same: although in old-worne age, blood beginneth to draw to a coldnesse, and the vitall spirit then neither so hot, neither so strong and effectuous: which thing as it is in them well to be observed and perceived by their frequent gestures and often mooving of the body and the parts thereof: yet specially may it bee seene and noted by their colour, which in a yong lusty Stripling and youthfull body of good constitution is ruddy and fresh: but in them that be further striken in yeeres, or further off from this temperament, is not so pure, so beautifull, nor so pleasant to behold, for that all their comlinesse and beauty is either faded away, or through some evill humours, and hidden imperfection or blemish appeareth in them worse then in the yonger sort.

So, many being affected or distempered in their Splene, Wombe, Liver, Ventricle and Lungs, are commonly either pale, yellow, tawny, dunne, duskie, or of some other ill-favoured colour.

There is no surer way (said *Galen*) certainly to know the humours and juyce in a creature, then by the colour and outward complexion. If the body looke very white, it is a token that phlegme in that body, chiefly raigneth and most aboundeth. If it be pale or yellow, it argueth the humour to be greatly Melancholique and Cholerique, and the blood to be fresh and reddy: if it be blackish, it betokeneth blacke adust Choler, specially if no outward accidentall occasion happen, as great heat or chafing, labour or wearinesse: or if the minde be not intoxicate, and perplexed with affects and passions, as anger, joy, sorrow, care, pensivenesse: for these make the humours sometime to resort unto the skin and utter parts, and sometime to hide and convey themselves farre inwardly: and for this cause, we see men that are fumish and testy, to be in a marveilous heat proceeding not of any sicknesse or discrasie, but of the motion and stirring of the humours: againe, them that be affrighted and in minde amazed, to be pale. Some to looke as wan as Lead, some white and swarfie, sometime bluish, sometime of sundry colours: all which betoken crude humours and raw juyce to beare rule and sway in the body, either of Phlegme, glasselike and tough, or of some other sort, or else many rotten humours clamped up in the body, which by outward tokens and signes bewray and shew themselves what they be, and what they signifie.

They therefore that be of a hot and moist constitution, and have great store of blood within them, are of a purple and ruddy colour, soft, warme and smooth skinned: comely of stature, and of reasonable feature, fleshy bodied, and a little rough, aburne haired, red or yellow Bearded, and comely bushed: of which feature, plight and bodily shape the Scripture witnesseth that *David* was: who being (after that *Saul* was cast off and rejected) appointed King, and anoynted by *Samuel*, was of a brownish Complexion, excellent beauty, well favoured in sight, and of countenance very cheerefull and amiable. . . .

Of a cold and moist Complexion, which setteth out and declareth the condition, state, and nature of persons Phlegmaticke

Next after the hot and moist constitution, order requireth to describe and set out the cold and moist Temperature, wherein reigneth and aboundeth phlegme: whereof (after blood) no small portion is diffused into every part of the body. And this humour draweth somewhat neere to the nature of blood, and is in affinity with it, both in respect of essence, and societie of their conceptories. For it is as it were a certaine blood unconcoct, or a rudiment and first beginning of blood, yet unperfect and not exactly laboured: a resemblance, shew, or patterne, whereof we may well behold in Must or new Wine, while it is yet hot, and newly taken and wringed out of the presse. For (as *Galen* right learnedly noteth) the subtill and ayrie part of the Wine (which is the fome or spurging thereof) boileth up to the top, and underneath, is an unsavory humour, in relish like to the nature of sweetish water, which being excoct, settled, and cleansed and fined from the dregges, obtaineth, and is brought to the nature of pure and good Wine. And albeit Phlegme be whitesh, and have no rednesse in it at all, yet being excoct, and the coldnesse thereof taken away and subdued by the force and efficacy of heat, it is reduced and brought into a ruddy and fresh-coloured liquor. . . . And this liquid and thin humour in the bodies of all Creatures is to purpose and use no lesse profitable then necessary. For being conveied every way into the veines, it qualifieth and allayeth the heat of Blood and Choler, finally, it maketh the joynts nimble and stirring, keeping them from being stiffe and lumpish through drynesse: and last of all, it nourisheth all Phlegmaticke members, and them continueth in lusty state.

And although there be commonly no certaine place assigned where Phlegme resteth, yet the greatest part is still in the stomacke or ventricle, wherein the meat is first boiled and altered into a thin juyce, or liquid substance. For we see men that have surcharged their stomackes in vomiting and perbraking, sometime to cast up great abundance of lothsome, clammy, and tough Phlegme, or to scowre and evacuate the same through the guts: those I meane that have excessively and ingluviously surfeited either in eating or drinking: Whose heads consequently being filled with moistish vapours, those fumosities striking upward as in a Stillitory, grow into a thicke, filthy, and snevelly Phlegme, whereby through coldnesse of the braine, the parties become subject and open to sundry diseases, as the Poxe, Murre, Hoarsenesse, Cough, and many others, of which sort is the Rheume or distillation of humours from the head, wherewith in the Low-countries of *Belgia* both rich and poore, high and low, in Winter

season are much troubled, and finde by experience to be true,
and yet they be people commonly healthy, and as sound as a
Bell. . . .

The head therefore and the stomacke (namely and much more
then any of the other parts) are pestered with the excrement of Phlegme, specially if a man use to eat such meats as be
cold and moist, and discontinue exercise, whereby it hapneth
that this humour being too crude, is very hardly to be concocted,
and brought into an wholsome juyce profitable and availeable
for the body. For it is a certaine uliginous moistishnesse and
superfluous excrement, which ought rather to bee sent out and
purged, that way which nature specially alloweth, and whereby
most conveniently she is wont to exonerate her selfe. For as the
originall of this inconvenience beginneth first at the stomacke,
and afterward infesteth the head (as we may plainely perceive
and observe by Wine copiously quaffed and swilled, which although it descend downe into the stomacke, yet doth it assayle
and distemper the head) it standeth us therefore upon, carefully
to foresee, that in those parts as little of this Phlegmaticke excrement as may be, be engendred: because the harme and inconvenience redoundeth to the generall harme and detriment of the
whole body.

And as it fareth in a Realme or Kingdome, in a Common-
wealth, in a civill Policy, or Corporation, in any honourable
Houshold or worshipfull Family: so likewise in the body of
man, that disease of all other is most dangerous and ill, which
taketh his originall beginning at the head and principall members. For the harme diffuseth and spreadeth it selfe into all the
inferiour parts of the body, and them greatly damnifieth. As
(for more plainenesse) let every man take an example at any
house which he enjoyeth and hath in occupation. For even as
those houses that will hold out neither winde nor weather, be
very unwholsome to dwell in, and a great back-friend to health:
or when the ridges or roofes thereof be ill timbred, and (for
want of good looking to) runne in ruine, and take water as often
as any raine falleth: So likewise as long as the head is distempered and affected with this baggage phlegme and distilling
humour, both it, and the rest of the body can never be in perfect
health. For being it selfe of a cold and moist nature, it quickly

drinketh up vapours out of a watrish stomacke, and being thereby replete with humidity, moistneth likewise those parts that be
under it: yea this distilling phlegme is as noysome and grievous
to it, as a brawling and scolding wife is to a quiet man.

For out of the head continually doe humours distill and (like
soot out of a Chimney) fall downe into the throat, eares, nose,
eyes, brest and lungs: whereupon happen rumors and swelling
of the eyes, bleare-eyednesse, drynesse of sight, whizzing and
running in the eares, hardnesse of hearing, and sometime be-
hinde the eares Impostumes, botches, and wexkernels, beside
many sorts moe: for the instruments of the tongue be affected,
the voice hindered, yea sometime stopped, that a man is not able
to utter out a plaine word. The sinewes, pellicles, Muscles,
Wesantpipe, and veines of the throat called *Jugulares*, and the
parts that serve to frame the voice, being surcharged with too
much humour (as in drunken persons is manifestly to be seene)
make the tongue unperfect, faltering and stammering, and all
the members to reele and stagger, their words double and not
intelligible, in so much that at some times they be not able to
speake one plaine word, nor in sensible termes to declare their
owne meaning. And thereby being by nature otherwise unready,
and in utterance staggering, and now also throughly whittled
and soaked in Wine, their tongue doubleth, stammereth and
faltereth a great deale more: insomuch that they bring out their
words by stops and pauses, like them that have the hicket: and
such persons cannot speake softly and stilly, because their voice
commonly is stopped and kept backe, which maketh them to
force out their words the louder. They must therefore earnestly
strive and accustome themselves roundly and distinctly to de-
liver out their words, for otherwise their tongue through default
and imbecillity, and lacking stablenesse faileth them, and fur-
thereth them nothing in their pronunciation: but chatter and
babble so obscurely, that no man can understand any thing of
that they say: For we see them to be scarce able to utter even a
few words with one straynable tenor and treatable uniformity,
but sometime slowly and dreamingly drawing them out: and
sometime powring out by lumpes the same, as fast as the tongue
can roll.

The selfsame thing which superfluity and distemperance of

drinke, bringeth unto the haunters thereof, both the distillation of Humours and defluxion of Phlegme, bring to them that be troubled with the Catarrhe, which (beside these) is accompanied also with sundry other inconveniences, to every one of sharpe judgement well known and easily perceived: For whoso is disposed exactly to sift and search out the very markes and tokens of a cold and moist Complexion, shall finde them (through abundance of that Humour and quality) to be sleepy, lazy, slothfull, drowsie, heavy, lumpish, and nothing quicke at their businesse: as they commonly be, which minde nothing else then gurmandize and belly-cheere, and use seldome exercise.

We see also among Beasts, Fowles, and other Creatures both wild and tame, that such as use little or no exercise, but lurke still in holes and Caves, and be pent up, and in franked cowpes, are neither so wholsome, neither so fit for man to eat, as others, that are greatly exercised and use much stirring. Such waxe (indeed) very fat, and grow bigger bodied (I cannot deny) but the nourishment which they give to the body, is somewhat unwholsome and excrementall: as among Fishes, Eeles, and other slippery Fishes that lye still myering themselves in mudde, using no exercise, stirring or agitation of body.

And this is the cause why Eeles being dead (contrary to the nature of all other Fishes) float not above water, by reason that they feed upon muddy and standing water.

But that every man may throughly and perfectly know the state and condition of his Body, it must bee painted out in his right colours, and is to be described by his owne proper indications, markes and tokens. All they therefore that are of this habit (if their constitution bee naturall and not accidentally happning) are gross, pursie, and fat bodied: their stature not so tall as bigge set, and strongly pitched, their skin soft, white, and unhayrie, their Muscles and Veines not appearing, but lying inwardly, insomuch that when occasion serveth to be let blood, the same Veines doe not apparantly shew out themselves. The haires of their head bee either white or dusky blacke, or else of the colour of Barly straw, which will not fall off, nor become bald, till after a long time, but they soone waxe hoary for want of heat, and imbecillity of the member, which is not of ability to excoct the nutriment into the use and comlinesse of haires.

B2

For hoarinesse is (as it were) a certaine refuse vinewed baggage of Phlegme putrefied, or a fusty darkishnesse under the skin, whereof (through want of heat) proceedeth hoarinesse and whitenesse of the haires.

Such a like hoary downe, or vinewed mouldinesse, we see to be in loaves of Bread, and Pies that be somewhat long kept unspent, and also in Vaults, Arch-Roofes, Sielings, Hoales and Cellers under ground, and other musty, fulsome, darke, filthy, and stinking places. . . .

Now, to satisfie them that are desirous to know the inward notes and tokens of a cold and moist complexion, and Phlegmaticke persons: I will heere by the way set downe the same, and declare of what nature, condition, manners, conversation and order of life they bee: howbeit, there is no cause, why any man should hope to finde in them of this constitution and plight, any store of excellent, singular, and rare giftes,[1] sith in them appeareth small quicknesse of wit, small worthinesse or excellency of minde, small sharpnesse of judgement and learning, small knowledge or skill in atchieving and compassing matters: for that the same with prudence and wisedome cannot conveniently be brought about. For as both their tallage, taste, smelling, and other objects of their Sences, bee blunt and grosse: so are they likewise in minde and wit doltish and dull, slothfull and lumpish: finally, neither by nature, neither by use, forecastfull, sharpe witted, nor crafty: by reason their naturall heat is languishing and feeble, and drowned in moist quality and cold humour: and therefore also their memory is very faileable, oblivious, and nothing at all (in a manner) retentive: Their speech (as likewise their pulses and maner of gate) slow and soft.

But this in them specially deserveth commendation, that they be gentle and quiet of nature, not greatly addicted to venerous dalliance, not fumish, testy, or soone angred; being such as although they be thereto provoked, will not lightly chafe or fret, and to be short, not given to fraud and subtilty, cogging and foisting, craft and coosinage, wrangling and quarrelling, as the Cholericke are. And because commonly they be assayled with many and sundry diseases, for that they be given to sit still, loving their ease and idlenesse: first they are to bee injoyned

---

[1] 1633 text *griefes.*

and prescribed a diet that is hot, and next they are to bee per-
swaded and pricked forward to use themselves to exercise. . . .

*Of the state and disposition of a hot and dry Body: with
a discourse of the nature, condition, manners, and inclination of a Cholericke person*

Forasmuch as among the outward things of Nature, there is
nothing of any long continuance and stability, neither that long
keepeth it selfe at any certaine state and vigour, but all subject
to decay, alteration, and case worse and worse: truely the state
of mankinde doth specially and more then any other, suffer sundry alterations, and is subject to great change and mutability.
Thus is a hot and moist Complexion, in processe and tract of
time, brought into a state hot and dry. For, heat by little and
little doth slily and closely waste and consume naturall humour,
and bringeth all the body into drinesse: which quality for pro-
longation and lengthening of life, is the greatest enemy that can
bee. For as the flame in a Torch or Taper feedeth upon the combustible matter thereof, and is therewith nourished, which being
all wasted and consumed, the same flame also quencheth and no
longer burneth: so likewise native heat by little and little
weareth away, and diminisheth the juyce and moisture, wherewith it is nourished, and finally bringeth the cause of destruction
both to it selfe, and to the whole body beside.

Now that constitution of body, which consisteth of a hot and
dry quality, and thereof hath his name, having warme humour
through these qualities encreased, maketh and constituteth a
Cholericke man, by reason of the great store of Choler which is
in him: of which humour there be two sorts and differences: the
one naturall, the other beside nature. Naturall Choler is the excrement of blood concoct, bitter in savour, and in colour and
effect fiery. When the heat of the Liver is moderate, then it is
yellow and shining: but when this viscosity is overmuch en-
kindled, then doth Choler also boyle with heat, and is of colour
darke, yellowish, like unto pruse Byer, called in Dutch *Jopen
Bier*, or like unto Oyle or melted Butter, when it is burned, and

with much frying becommeth blackish of colour: whereby it commeth to passe that the colour before yellow, changeth, and is turned into a sad black: which sometime apparantly uttreth and sheweth it selfe in the utter part of the skin, whensoever this Cholericke humour diffuseth and disperseth it selfe into the same skin.

Choler hath in the body two offices: for part of it being mixed with the blood, passeth into the veines, to make the same more conveniently to penetrate into every one of the narrow passages, and to be conveyed to such members as require and have need of the nourishment of Choler. The other part is sent to the bladder of the Gall, annexed and tyed to the nether end of the Liver, wherein the wonderfull providence of Gods Almighty handy-worke well appeareth, in that he hath appointed the same Entraile, whereunto he hath given an admirable vertue to attract and helpe digestion, to be also a receiver and receptory of superfluous and unprofitable humour: to the intent no harme or inconvenience should thereby in any wise happen to the other members.

For Choler is of that nature, that yeeldeth out a fiery force, whose motion (as it were a firebrand) stirreth up and insenceth our mindes to hasty moodes and furious rages. And for this cause Anger is defined to be a heat and certaine boyling of the blood about the Heart, wherewith the Braine also being excited by Choler, is set in a heat and testinesse, desirous of revenge, whensoever any injury is offered. And to the lower parts it serveth to provoke and irrite the guts and bowels to avoyd superfluous excrements: For which purpose, Natures providence hath devised and framed sundry passages needfull for the purging, conveiance and evacuation of all such superfluous humours: to wit, the Kidneyes and the Urine-pipes, the empty or fasting Guts, called *Intestinum Jejunum* (which through the sowrenesse of Choler flowing into it, continually driveth out the Excrements,) the Bladder, Eares, and Pores, appointed for the avoydance and expulsion of sweat. And in the most part of these, if obstructions should happen, all the whole filthy masse of noysome humour is thereby kept within the body, and then giveth violent assault to some of the principall parts. So when the Bagge or Bladder of the Gall or Receptacle of Choler, is not able to exonerate it selfe of that baggage, drosse and superfluity, which it drew from the Liver: it emptieth and casteth it either into the Ventricle, or else into the hollownesse of the Liver. And thus it commeth to passe, that Choler being diffused and spred over all the body, imparteth both his quality and colour to the blood.

Hereof commeth the Jaundice (named *Morbus Regius*, for that it requireth a most exquisite diet, and Princelike fare) which maketh all the body yellow as a Kites foot, and coloured like Saffron or as Silver, that is stroked over with Gold.

And if the small and slender Guts be therewith tainted, it putteth a man to intolerable torment and paine. This passion is called *Iliaca passio*, the wringing of the Guts, and also *Convolvulum*, for that, the Guts doe seeme to pucker and crumple together like the string of an Harpe, or any other Instrument. . . .

But I purpose now briefly by the way to shew the nature and conditions of a hot and dry Complexion, and then of a Cholericke person, and finally by what markes and tokens they are to be perceived, discerned, found out and knowne. And first to speake of the outward signe: A body of this Constitution is hot, slender, lean, musculous, of decent bignesse, and meane stature: and although some be of growth and talnesse but small and little: yet they are lively, dapper, quicke, nimble, and as little Bees, ever stirring and whisking about, and medling with many things not to them appertaining, for which sometimes those men deserve small thankes.

> *Within that little Corpes of theirs,*
> *right noble Stomackes have.*
> VIRGIL, *Georgics* li. 4

Of colour they be brownish, aburne, or somewhat ruddy, specially when their angry moode is up, or their bodies chafed and set in heat with exercise: and some be pale or yellowish. Their skin rough: their Arteries and Veines bigge and apparant, and not lying hidden under the flesh: their Urine red, Saffron coloured, or bright yellow, according to the proportion of Choler and heat: Their Pulse quicke and swift, as also their gate and manner of going is. Their tongue rolling at pleasure, ready and flowing in utterance: their haire blacke: and in some curled, and naturally frizled: whenas the heat and drynesse is very great and vehement: Neither will the same till after long time waxe hoary and gray, but yet by reason of drinesse some waxe bald. Their nose crooked like a Hawkes bill: and in many, especially Germanes, Polonians, Hungarians and Dutchmen, red Beards, and bright yellowy haire which commeth of glittering cleare shining Choler, that is not adusted with fervent heat. In the Low-countries, those that bee red haired are (of the vulgar sort) noted, as men subject to some naughty disposition, and lewd conditions, secretly harbouring within their mindes. . . .

Now, whereas some haskerdly Peizants, and rascall persons, having such coloured Beards, be prattlers, praters in keeping counsell, as close as a Sieve, setting all upon sixe and seven, without any regard or consideration of any thing, Ding-thrifts, and Spendalls, the same doe I impute to lewde education, which draweth the proclivity of their nature to untoward and peevish manners. For hereof it commeth, that such persons be found to be unconstant, crafty, deceitfull, subtle, wily, cogging, turning the Cat in the Pan, full of Leiger-du-maine, and so fickle of word and deed, that a man may not well and safely deale with them, nor trust them, as persons to whom there is no more hold then is of a wet Eele by the tayle, and in any bargaine or dealing be it never so intricate and cumbersome, can finde meanes to slip the coller, and winde themselves out of danger. Whereunto if other imperfections and defects of the body be added, they argue yet a worse nature and more given to mischiefe: whereupon the Poet *Martiall* very aptly saith:

> *Blacke hayr'd, short footed, purblind eke*
> *and Beard all over red:*
> *Take such a one in doing good,*
> *and strike me off his head.*

Which disposition is rooted in them, partly through the influence of the Planets, *viz.* of the Sunne and *Mercury*, and partly (which I rather take to be the chiefe and speciall cause) through thinnesse of Cholericke humour, and of uncleane spirits, which being endued with a subtle heat, pricke and stirre them forward to put in practice such kinde of prankes and Pageants.

Furthermore, among these kinde of persons, there be some diversly disposed, and of sundry conditions, Wranglers, Busie medlers in other mens matters, yallers, hot as a toast, Choplogicks, and Prattlers, with tongue at will, and are as *Juvenal* fitly saith:

> *Of dapper wit, and desperate bold,*
> *   fine-phrasd with gallant grace,*
> *More eloquent then* Isæus,
> *   for every time and case.*

Such commonly are Dizards, Gesturers, Stage-players, Jugglers, Tumblers, and roguish Pedlers, idly ranging about the Country, jangling Pratlers, Fortune-tellers, Minstrels, and such other like busie bragging Counterfeits, looking bigge upon the matter, and in their manner of gate, hands, countenance, eyes and speech, full of gestures, impudently presuming to shuffle themselves into every company and place of assembly, having an Oare in every mans Boate, and intermedling in other mens matters, wherein they have nothing to deale. In Sleepe, very unquiet, leaping sometime out of their beds, because their spirits be very hot, which incite and awake them up (even being asleepe) to motion and walking about. For Choler frameth and fashioneth the mindes of men many wayes, producing and causing in them divers manners, fancies, delights, and inclinations. And hereupon it hapneth that whosoever is of a hot and dry Constitution, and reckned in the number of Cholericke men, is naturally fierce, arrogant, imperious, stately, untractable and unruely: But as he is by nature very testy, and soone angry, so is his Cholericke moode soone alayed and pacified.

Of a cold and dry Complexion: wherein the nature and condition of a Melancholike person (because he is of this temperature and subject to Choler) is at large declared

Those bodies of all others are in worst case and habit, which consist and be constituted of the combination and composition of cold and dry. For considering that the maintenance and conservation of life consisteth in hot and moist: who is he that can rightly commend or allow that quality and constitution of body, which weareth away and wasteth these fomentations or cherishments of life, being the chiefe and onely stayes of health and welfare. For we see in the whole course of nature, and in all things within the universall World, Plants, Herbes, all Creatures endued with life, Man and all that live by breath, when they be once deprived, or lacke heat and moisture, quickly to decay, and grow into destruction. . . .

For all men for the most part at the beginning of the Spring or downefall of the Leafe (at which season of the yeere this humour doth most rifely abound) are subject to Melancholicke affections, namely, those that be Magistrates and Officers in the Commonwealth, or Students which at unseasonable times sit at their Books and Studies. For through overmuch agitation of the minde, naturall heat is extinguished, and the spirit as well Animall as Vitall, attenuated and vanish away: whereby it commeth to passe, that after their vitall juyce is exhausted, they fall into a cold and dry constitution.

And of this Melancholicke humour there be two differences, the one naturall, the other beside nature. That Melancholy which is naturall and familiar to a man, is milder and less hurtfull then the other. For being carried and conveied into the Veines together with the blood, it nourisheth the members that be of like nature and condition to it selfe, and unto them ministreth nourishment, as the Bones, Gristles, Ligaments, and Sinewes. For this Humour is not unlike unto Beastes feet when they be sodden and brought into a Jelly, which in eating, cleave to the fingers and lips as tough as Birdlime: whereby it causeth blood to have a good power retentive, and to bee thicker: because when it is joyned with perfect blood, and with the sweetnesse thereof tempered and alayed, as a sowre Grape with Hony or Sugar, it thereupon becommeth in taste and relish not altogether sowre or bitter, as those things that exasperate the Jawes and Palate, but somewhat tart and sowrish, and as it is commonly tearmed, Ponticke: such a relish I meane, as is in a Grape (out of which new Must is pressed) being not as yet come to his perfect ripenesse and maturity, such as in the latter end of

Autumne is brought out of Germany and France into the Low-countries, to stanch and fill the glutting desire and greedinesse of some: which being very sowre in taste (insomuch that it seemeth to take away the upper skin of the tongue,) their use is to condite it with Hony, and Hony combes: to make it (for them that have queasie stomackes) better relished, and pleasanter in taste. And as the dregs, mother, or settlings of Oyle retaine a tallage of the Oyle: and as the Lees of Wine keepe a certaine taste, relish, and smell of the nature of Wine: Even so Melancholicke juyce which proceedeth from blood, retaineth the spettle and taste thereof. . . . And as the Lees or Dregs of Wine serve to good use and purpose, for the making of *Aqua vita* withall: Even so Melancholicke juyce which (if I may so plainely terme it) is the settling and refuse of blood, hath in it an wholsome use and commodity. For one part goeth into the Veines, and helpeth blood, the other part (much like to the former) is driven by the Liver into the Splene or Milt: and having thence afterwards issue into the stomacke, (on the left side whereof it lyeth) stirreth up appetite to meate, through the sharpnesse and sowrenesse that is in it. This viscous substance[1] being soft, thin, fungous, and like unto a spunge, is the Chamber of Melancholy, and a Receptory appointed by nature, to draw out unto it, the dregs of blood: and sometimes so much swelled with abundance of excrements, as though it would oppresse and kill a man. . . . For as when a Princes Coffers bee full stuffed, and his Treasuries enriched, the common people bee wringed, pinched and em-poverished: so, when the Splene waxeth bigge and encreaseth, the body is pined away and wasted with leannesse. For so much therefore as God his carefull providence hath made and ordained this member to purifie the Liver, and to purge and scumme away the Grosse and seculent part of the blood, it standeth every man in hand, by all meanes possible, carefully to foresee, that it in-curre not any inconvenience, or take any harm. For if the Splene or Milt should suffer obstruction, or fall into imbecility and weaknesse: the Melancholicke juyce disperseth it selfe into every part of the body, making the skin to be of a sooty and dunne colour: and further disquieteth the minde, with sundry strange apparitions, and fantastical imaginations.

[1] i.e., the spleen.

But if it throughly performe the office, for which it was ordained and doe exactly drinke up the drossie seculency of blood,
it maketh a man thereupon wonderfully merry and jocund. For
when the blood is sincerely purified, and from all grossnesse
and seculency purged, the spirits consequently are made pure,
bright and cleare shining: Whose purity and clearnesse causeth
the minde to rejoyce, and among merry companions to laugh
and delight in pretty devices, merry conceits, and wanton
fancies. . . .

Contrariwise if it[1] be surcharged and overwhelmed with too
much confluxe of filthy humour, and be debarred or disappointed
of the ordinary helpe and ayde of the Liver, either through
imbecility or obstruction, then bringeth it many discommodities
and annoyances, no lesse hurtfull and prejudiciall to the minde
then to the body, as heavinesse, sorrow, sadnesse, feare and
dread of missehap to come, carefulnesse, thought, desperation
and distrust, that is to say, cleane out of hope of any better fortune. Which affections and perplexities cast a man into exceeding griefe, torment, vexation and martyrdome, wearing away
his beauty, and wasting his bodily comelinesse, and making him
to looke like silver all fustied with Chimney soot, or as bright
and handsome things in a reaky house that are besmeared,
dusked and smoaked.

For when the dregges and reffuse of humours have recourse
thither in greater abundance, then the heat and naturall power
of the member is able to wield and qualifie, the greater is the
decay thereof, and much more dangerously is it oppressed. For
as a Porter or labouring man which carrieth burdens, heavier
then his strength will allow, cannot but fall downe under the
waight, thereby many times hurting both himselfe, and spoyling
his carriage: So when greater store of Melancholicke juyce is
conveied and derived into this Entraile, then it is either able to
beare, or by concoction to overcome, it is thereby sundrywise
distempered and brought into many diseases. . . . For the fulsome vapours (which as it were out of a dampish Marsh, or
stinking Camerine,) strike upward, doe annoy the braine with
grievous and odious fumes, and distemper the spirits Animall
with strange and forraigne quality.

[1] i.e., the spleen.

Hereof commeth disquietnesse of minde and alteration of right wits, absurd cogitations, troublesome dreames, giddinesse of the head, ringing of the eares, dazeling of eyes, mournefull sighes, trembling and beating of heart, a minde sorrowfull, comfortlesse, perplexed, pensive and fearefull: insomuch that they which be in this sort affected, distrust, and be afraid, as well of their friends, as of their enemies, looking about them for feare of danger every minute of an houre, trembling at every small noyse and wagging of a leafe, and ready for feare to run into a Mouse-hole, although there be no cause of any such feare at all: and if they be demanded the cause why they so pine away themselves with needlesse care, and bootlesse sorrow, either they will make no answer at all: or if they doe, very unwillingly, and with much ado. Insomuch that thereupon they will desire to shift and convey themselves out of all company, not abiding any fellowship nor conference with friends, but peaking in darke corners, and secret solitary places, like *Timon* (sirnamed Μισαν-θρωπος, because he hated all men) and *Bellerophon*, who (as *Homer* reporteth) assayed to shake off his carefull thoughts and pensive dolours, by bestowing himselfe in some waste Wilder-nesse, or solitary corner.

> *For he, poore soule, in queachy Woods did stalke,*
> *Abroad in Fields, and waylesse Soyles alone:*
> *No sight of men, no company, no talke,*
> *Could he abide: but fret his heart with moane.*
>
> Iliad 3

By many and sundry wayes doe men fall into this ill case and habiting, who afore were cleare and free enough from it. Some by the staying of their Hemorrhoides, and stopping of their naturall Purgations or Flowers, or by the restraint of some ordinary and accustomed issue. Some be brought into it through long sorrow and heavinesse for the death of their Parents, or some great losse of worldly wealth, or finally by missing and being disappointed of some great desire and expectation, which they hoped and had, of some thing to come to passe.

Yet there be some that have fallen into this Melancholicke habit by watching in the night at their Study at unseasonable houres, by leading a peakish and solitary life, by hunger, penury, and strict fare, or else by using and accustoming some kindes of nourishments, whereby they brought themselves into a cold and dry distemperature. Many through the conscience of their former misdeeds, and remorse of their wicked and abominable life afore-time led: have plunged into these Melancholicke affects, driving themselves many times into such great inconveniences, that what with blindnesse, fury, madnesse, and want of right minde, they become weary of their lives, and suffer many horrible and bitter torments. . . .

This humour[1] is manifold, and of sundry sorts, wonderfully framing in the bodies and mindes of men divers dispositions, and in them constituting sundry habits, manners and conditions. For it may after a sort be resembled unto Iron, Seacoles, or Char-coles, which being fired, appeare glowing hot, shining like bur-nished gold, and burning the members of the touchers: but being quenched, they looke blacke, cankered and rusty. Even so Melan-choly, albeit it be cold and dry, and in colour drawing somewhat unto blacknesse, yet retaineth it some heat of the faculty and nature of that, from whence it came, that is to say, Choler or Blood. For so the dregs or mother of Oyle, the feces or vinegar of wine, Embers and Coles, retaine and have a certaine smacke or nature of the brands when they smoaked and were on fire. Therefore Melancholy is not altogether without heat, but re-taineth some deale of that quality in it. For although it be a long while ere it will be enflamed and throughly heated, like Iron which must both be mollified and tempered with force of most ardent and bituminous coles, and also with the helpe of blowing Bellowes, for the making of the same malleable and apt to the Forge and Anvile: yet being once thorowly heated, hath such an excessive glowing ardentnesse, that there cannot be any thing more adustive. And hereupon in a manner all at one instant, and without any time betwixt, doe wee see them suddenly changed from laughter and mirth, into sorrow and pensiveness. For when this humour is once heated (because from it proceed and come bright and sincere spirits) these Melancholicke per-sons are exceedingly set upon their merry pin, and (past all godsforbod) jocund, and pleasurably given to singing, dancing,

---

[1] Lemnius is now discussing unnatural melancholy, or burnt choler.

skipping and sporting, and (contrary to their accustomed wont) to every one courteous, affable, liberall, and friendly, yea altogether pleasantly disposed, and not squemish to offer a kinde kisse and imbracement unto any lusty Wench: and nothing then so much desiring as marriage, thereby to enjoy the hoped fruit of Children, and to have their name in remembrance to posterity: very earnestly bewraying their losse of former time, repenting that they had not long agone tyed themselves to the World, and married. But when this great heat is cold, and the earnest pangs of this newfangled minde settled, when the blood waxeth cold, and their spirits at rest, they goe backe from all former resolutions, and are ready to unsay all that ever they said before. They condemne and detest yesterdayes deeds, and are much ashamed of their own oversight and foolishnesse.

THE CONSTITUTION OF MAN

From *A Treatise of Melancholy*
by Timothy Bright, 1586

As our blood labours to beget
Spirits, as like soules as it can,
Because such fingers need to knit
That subtile knot, which makes us man:
So must pure lovers soules descend
T'affections, and to faculties,
Which sense may reach and apprehend,
Else a great Prince in prison lies.

DONNE, *The Extasie*

Of the Soule and the Body

i

As all naturall humours rise of nourishment, so melancholie, being a part of bloud, from thence it springeth also. Whatsoever we receave into the bodie for sustentation of this fraile life, consisteth of diversitie of partes, being it selfe compounded, although to the outward viewe it seemeth to appeare uniforme: as bread, fleshe, fish, milke, wine, beare &c., which shewe of uniformitie being taken away by the naturall furnace, which preserveth the lively heate of everie living thing, that outward resemblance vanisheth, and the diversitie manifesteth it selfe: as we see gold or silver, before it be proved with fire, appeareth no other then all alike: but afterward is discovered by the burning crucible to be much otherwise: so fareth it with nourishments, whose divers partes are layd open by so manifold concoctions, and cleansings, and straininges, as are continually without intermission practized of nature in everie mans bodie: noe gold finer more busie at the mine, or artificiall Chymist halfe so industrious in his laboratorie, as this naturall Chymist is in such preparations of al nourishment: be it meat, or drinke, of what sort soever. By this means the bloud which seemeth in al parts like it selfe, no egge liker one to another, is preserved distinct in all partes. The purest part which we call in comparison and in respect of the rest bloud, is temperate in qualitie, and moderate in substance, exceeding all the other parts in quantitie, if the bodie be of equal temper, made for nourishment of the most temperate parts, and ingendring of spirites. The second is fleume, next to bloud in quantitie, of a waterie nature, cold and moyst; apt to bee converted into the substance of pure bloud if nature faile not in her workinge, ordained for nourishment of moyster partes. The thirde is melancholie, of substance grosse and earthie, cold and drie in regard of the other, in quantitie inferiour to fleume, fit nourishment for such partes as are of like temper. The fourth choler; fierie, hote, and driest of qualitie; thinne in substance, least in quantitie, and ordained for such parts as require subtiller nourishment, and are tempered with greater portion of the fierie element. These differences nature hath so distinguished, that although in veine and place, they remaine linked together, yet in faculty, and vertue thay are diverse the one from the other: which as they fit the varietie of parts, bloud the temperate, and the rest such partes as have like declining from temperate: so by the marvelous working of nature, these varieties of humours are entertained by nourishmentes inclining to like disposition: although no nourishment can be utterly voide of all these partes; no not those that are counted most to encline to anie one humour, as beefe and veneson to melancholie: honie, and butter, to choler: and fish to fleume. . . .

Thus then as man consisteth of partes requiring this diversitie of foode, necessarie it was, and so ordained by God, such humours might aunswer in like varietie: and as humours are diverse, so likewise that matter whereof they should be wrought could

not be of one sort, and therefore all kinde of nature ordained for
nourishment, affoorde this choyce, some in greater scarcitie, this
or that, to the end no state of bodie should complain. . . . So that
the masse of bloud being the universall soile, wanteth not for the
relief & entertainment of al the members of the bodie, choise
of substance according to their variety. Hereof is the bone
nourished, as hard as mettall: and the braine as tender as a
posset curd: the kidneyes grosse and thicke: and the lights loose
and subtile: the eye as cleere as cristall: and the splene as blacke
and darke as inke.

ii

Before I declare unto you how this humour[1] afflicteth the
minde: first it shall be necessarie for you to understand, what
the familiaritie is betwixt mind and bodie: how it affecteth it,
and how it is affected of it againe. You knowe, God first created
all things subject to the course of times, and corruption of the
earth, after that hee had distinguished the confused masse of
thinges, into the heavens, & the foure elements. This earth he
had endued with a fecunditye of infinite seeds of all things:
which hee comaunded it, as a mother, to bring forth, and as it is
most agreable to their nature, to entertaine with nourishment
that which it had borne, & brought forth: whereby when he had
all the furniture of this inferiour worlde, of these creatures, some
he fixed there still, and maintaineth the seedes, till the end of al
thinges, and that determinate time, which he hath ordained, for
the emptying of those seedes of creatures, which he first indued
the earth withall. Other some, that is to say, the animals, hee
drewe wholly from the earth at the beginning, and planted seede
in them onely, and food from other creatures: as beasts, and
man in respect of his bodie: the difference only this: that likely
it is, mans body was made of purer mould as a most precious
tabernacle and temple, wherein the image of god should afterward be inshrined: and being formed as it were by Gods proper
hand, receaved a greater dignitie of beautie, and proportion, and
stature erect: thereby to be put in mind whither to direct the
religious service of his Creator. This tabernacle thus wrought, as
the grosse parte yeelded a masse for the proportion to be framed

[1] melancholy.

of: so had it by the blessing of God, before inspired, a spirituall thing of greater excellencie, then the redde earth,[1] which offered it self to the eye only. This is that which Philosophers call the spirit: which spirit, so prepareth that worke to the receavinge of the soule, that with more agrement, the soule, and body, have growne into acquaintance: and is ordained of God, as it were a true love knot, to couple heaven & earth together: yea a more divine nature, then the heavens with a base clod of earth: which otherwise woulde never have growen into societie: and hath such indifferent affection unto both, that it is to both equally affected, and communicateth the body and corporall things with the minde, and spirituall, and intelligible things, after a sort with the body: saving sometimes by vehemency of eithers action, they seeme to be distracted, and the minde to neglect the body: and the body and bodily actions common with other creatures, to refuse as it were for a moment that communitie: wherby it commeth to pass, that in vehement contemplations, men see not, that which is before their eies: neither heare, though noyse beat the aire and sound: nor feele, which at other time (such bent of the minde being remitted) they should perceave the sence of, with pleasure or paine. This spirit is the chiefe instrument, and immediate, wherby the soule bestoweth the exercises of her facultie in her body, that passeth to and fro in a moment, nothing in swiftnes and nimblenes being comparable thereunto: which when it is depraved by anie occasion, either rising from the bodie: or by other meanes, then becommeth it an instrument unhansome for performance of such actions, as require the use therof: and so the minde seemeth to be blame worthy: wherein it is blamelesse: and faultie of certaine actions imputed thereunto: wherein the body and this spirit are rather to bee charged, thinges corporall and earthly: the one, in substance, and the other in respect of that mixture, wherewith the Lorde tempered the whole masse in the beginning. And that you may have greater assurance in reason of this corporall inclination of spirit, consider how it is nourished: and with more evidence it shall so appeare unto you. It is maintained by nourishments, whether they be of the vegetable, or animall kind: which creatures, affoord not only their corporall substance, but a spirituall matter

[1] of which, according to tradition, Adam was made.

also: wherewith everye nourishment, more or lesse is indued: this spirite of theirs, is (as similitude of nature, more nighly approcheth)[1] altered more speedely, or with larger travell of nature. Of all things of ordinary use, the most speedy alteration is of wine: which in a moment repaireth our spirites, and reviveth us againe, being spent with heavinesse: or any otherwise whatsoever, our naturall spirites being diminished: which bread, and flesh, doth in longer time: being of slower passage, and their spirites not so subtile, or at least fettred as it were in a more grosse body: and without this spirite, no creature could give us sustentation. For it is a knot, to joyne both our soules & bodies together: so nothing of other nature can have corporall conjunction with us, except their spirites with ours first growe into acquaintance: which is more speedily done a great deale, then the increase of the firme substaunce: which you may evidently perceave in that we are ready to fainte, for want of food: after a little taken into the stomach of refreshing, before anie concoction can be halfe reformed, the strength returneth, and the spirite reviveth, and sufficient contentment seemeth to be geven to nature: which notwithstanding, not fully so satisfied, prepareth farther the aliment of firme substaunce, & spirits of purer sort, for the continuall supply of those ingenerate, for sense and motion, life & nourishment. Nowe although these spirites rise from earthlie creatures, yet are they more excellent then earth, or the earthy parts of those natures, from which they are drawne, and rise from that divine influence of life, and are not of them selves earthie: neither yet comparable in purenes and excellencie, unto that breath of life, wherewith the Lord made Adam a living soule, which proceeded not from any creature, that hee had before made, as the life of beasts and trees, but immediately from him selfe, representing in some part, the character of his image. So then these three we have in our nature to consider distinct, for the clearer understanding of that I am to intreate of: the bodie of earth, the spirit from vertue of that spirit, which did as it were hatch that great egge of Chaos: & the soule inspired from God, a nature eternall and divine, not fettered with the bodie, as certaine Philosophers have taken it: but handfasted therwith, by that golden claspe of the spirite:

[1] in proportion as the nature of the food resembles the nature of the spirit.

whereby one (till the predestinate time be expired, and the bodie become unmeete for so pure a spouse) joyeth at, and taketh liking of the other. Nowe as it is not possible to passe from one extreme to an another, but by a meane, & no meane is there in the nature of man, but spirit: by this only the body affecteth the mind: and the body and spirits affected, partly by disorder, and partly through outward occasions, minister discontentment as it were to the minde: and in the ende breake that bande of fellowship, wherewith they were both linked together, This affecting of the minde, I understand not to bee any empairing of the nature thereof, or decaye of any facultie therein, or shortning of immortalitie, or any such infirmity inflicted upon the soule from the body (for it is farre exempt from all such alteration:) but such a disposition, and such discontentment, as a false stringed lute, giveth to the musitian: or a rough and evill fashioned pen, to the cunning writer: which only obscureth, the shew of either art, & nothing diminisheth of that faculty, which with better instruments, would fully content the eye with a faire hand, & satisfie the eare with most pleasant and delectable harmonie. Otherwise the soule receiveth no hurt from the bodie, it being spirituall, and voyde of all passion of corporall thinges, and the other grosse, earthie, and far unable to annoy a nature of such excellency.

iii

But you wil say unto me, experience seemeth to declare a further passion of the soule from the bodie then I mention: for we see what issues, bodelie thinges, and the body it selfe drives our mindes into: as some kinde of musicke, to heavines; other some to chearefulness; other some to compassion; other some to rage; other to modestie; and other to wantonnes: likewise of visible thinges, certayne sturre us to indignation and disdayne; and other to contentednes, and good liking. In like manner certaine natures taken inward, move us to mirth: as wyne; and other to heavines; some to rage, furie and frensie; and other some to dulnes and heavines of spirite: as certaine poysones in both kinds do manifest these passions unto us; besides such as rise of our humours bredde in our owne bodies; which may be reasons, to one not well advised, so to mistake these effectes of

corporall thinges, as though the soule received farther impression, not onely in affection, but also in understanding, then I
have unto you mentioned: for satisfying of you, in which
doubtes, you are diligently to consider, what I shall declare,
concerning the severall actions of bodie, soule and spirite, and
how, each one of these performeth their actions: which must be
kept distinct, for better understanding of that I shall hereafter
in this discourse lay open unto you. And first, concerning the
actions of the soule: you remember how it was first made by
inspiration from God himselfe, a creature immortall, proceeding
from the eternall; with whome there is no mortality. The end of
this creation was, that being united to the bodely substance,
raised and furnished with corporall faculties from the earth,
common with other living creatures, there might rise a creature
of middle nature betwixt Angels, & beastes, to glorifie his name.
This the soule doth, by two kindes of actions: the one kinde, is
such as it exerciseth, seperated from the bodie; which are contemplations of God, in such measure as he is by naturall instinct
opened unto it, with reverent recognisaunce of such blessinges,
as by creation it is endued with. Next unto God, whatsoever
within compasse of her conceits is immortall, without tedious-
nes, or travell, and with spiritual joye incomparable. These
actions she is busied with in this life, so long as she inhabiteth
her earthly tabernacle; neither in such perfection, nor yet so
freely, as she doth seperated, and the knot loosed betwixt her
and the body, being withdrawen, by actions exercised with corporall instrument, of baser sort. These are the other kinde which
the soule, by the creators law is subject unto, for the continuance of the creature, and maintenance of the whole nature,
with dueties thereto belonging; animall, vitall, naturall; and
whatsoever mixed, requireth joyntly all three; as this corporall
praising of God for his goodnes, and praying unto him for
necessities, releeving our brothers want, and defending him
from wrong; with everie ones severall vocation, wherein his
peculiar charge lyeth; whether it be in peace, or in warre; at
home, or abroade, with our countrymen, or with straungers;
in our owne famelies, or with our neighbours; whether it be
superiority of commaundement, or duety of obedience: which
differ in degree, as they be nigher, or farther of the actions

peculiar to the soule; or communicate more, or lesse with them. . . .

Next ensueth the nature of the bodie, and his severall instruments, with their uses; which my purpose is here so farre to touch, as it concerneth the understanding of that ensueth of my discourse: leaving the large handling thereof to that most excellent hymne of Galen.[1] Touching the use of the parts: the bodie being of substance grosse, & earthy; resembleth the matter whereof it was made: and is distinct into diverse members, and diverse parts, for severall uses required, partly of nature, and partly of the humane societie of life: whereupon, the braine is the chiefe instrument of sense, and motion, which it deriveth by the spirit before mentioned, into all the partes of the bodie; as also of thoughtes, and cogitations, perfourmed by common sense, and fantasie: and storing up as it were, that which it hath conceaved in the chest of memorie: all which the braine it selfe with farther communication exerciseth alone. The hart is the seate of life, and of affections, and perturbations, of love, or hate, like, or dislike; of such thinges as fall within the compasse of sense; either outward, or inward; in effect, or imagination onely. The liver the instrument of nourishment, & groweth: & is served of the stomach by appetite of meats and drinkes; and of other parts, with lust of propagation: & as the hart, by arteries conveigheth life to all partes of the bodie: so the liver, by vaines distributeth her faculties to every member; thereby the body enjoying nourishment, & increase, served with naturall appetite, whereby ech part satisfieth it selfe with that, which therto is most agreable. And these actions are bodily performed of the soule, by employing that excellent and catholicke instrument of spirit, to the mechanicall workes of the grosse and earthy partes of our bodies. Thus then the whole nature of man, being compounded of two extremities, the soule, and the bodie: and of the meane of spirits: the soule receaveth no other annoyance by the bodie; then the craftes man by his instrument: with no impeach, or impaire of cunning: but an hinderance of exercising the excellent partes of his skill: either when the instrument is altogether unapt, and serveth for no use: or in part only fit; wherby actions,

[1] *De usu partium*, Lib. III. x, in which the author repeatedly hymns the wisdom of the Creator of man's being.

and effects are wrought, much inferiour to the faculty of the
worker: & as the instrument is of more particular use, so is the
soule the lesse impeached: and as more generall, so yet more
hindered: both from varietie, and perfection of action: as the
hart, more then the liver: and the liver, more then the braine:
the stomach more then the rest of the entrailles: and all publicke
parts, more then private: of which sort the spirit being disordered, either in temper, or lessened in quantitie, or enter-
mixed with straunge vapours and spirits, most of all, worketh
annoyance, and disgraceth the worke, and crosseth the soules
absolute intention: as shall more particularly appeare in the processe of my discourse. . . .

iv

Thus much shal suffice to prove the spirite and body to be
wholly organicall: by organicall I meane a disposition & aptnes
only, without any free worke or action, otherwise then at the
mindes commandement: else should there be mo beginninges &
causes of action then one, in one nature: which popularity of
administration, nature will none of, nor yet with any holygarci-
call or mixt: but commandeth only by one soverainty: the rest
being vassals at the beck of the soveraigne commander. The
kindes of instruments are of two sorts: the one dead in it selfe,
and destitute of all motion: as a saw before it be moved of the
workman, and a ship before it be stirred with winde, and hoised
of saile: the other sorte is lively, and carrieth in it selfe aptnes,
and disposition of motion: as the hound to hunt with, and the
hauke to fowle with, both caried with hope of pray: the hand to
move at our pleasure, and to use any other kind of instrument
or toole. The second sort of these twaine, is also to be distinguished in twaine, whereof the one obtaineth power in it selfe,
and requireth derection onely, as the beast, and fowle above
mentioned: and the other not only derection, but impulsion also
from an inward vertue, and forcible power: as the motion of the
hand, and the varietie of the hand actions do most evidently declare. Of these three kinds of instruments, I place the spirit &
bodye both to the mind, as the saw or axe in the workmans
hand, or to the lute touched of the Musitian (according to the
sundry qualities & conditions of the instrument of the bodie) in

the thirde sort, but so, as the spirit in comparison of the bodye, fareth as the hand to the dead instrumentes. Of the first sort they are not, because they partake of life: of the second they may not be, because of themselves they have no impulsion, as it appeareth evidently in animall and voluntarie actions, (and although more obscurely to be seene) in such as be called naturall. For the spirit being either withdrawne from the outwarde parts by vehement passion of griefe, or over prodigally scattered by joy, or wasted by paine, the outward partes not only faile in their sense and motion, but even nourishment & growth therby are hindered: and contrarily, though the spirit be present, except the part be also well disposed, not only feeling is impaired, & such actions as require sense and motion, but also concoction and nourishment. Againe, the spirit it self without impulsion of minde lyeth idle in the bodie. This appeareth in animall actions more plainly: as the mind imploying vehemently the spirit an other way, we neither see that is set before our eyes, nor heare, nor feele that which otherwise with delight, or displeasure, would vehemently affect us. In naturall actions and parts, it is more obscure: either because the spirit cannot be altogether so seperated by the order of nature, being rooted so in the part, or because the verie presence of the soule in an organicall bodie, without further facultie or action, carieth the life withal, and is not subject to arbitrement and wil: as the royal estate of a Prince, moveth silence, reverence, and expectation, although there bee no charge, or commaundement thereof given, nor such purpose of presence: so life lyeth rather in the essence or substance of the soule, giving it to a fit organed body, rather then by any such facultie resident therein, except wee maye thinke that lesse portion of spirite serveth for life only, then for life, sense and motion, & so the partes, contented with the smaller provision therof, are entertained with life, though sense and moving require more plenty. But howsoever this be obscure in naturall actions, the minde transporting the spirits an other way by sodeine conceit, study or passion, yet most certaine it is, if it holde on long, and release not, the nourishment will also faile, the increase of the body diminish, and the flower of beautie fade, and finally death take his fatall hold: which commeth to passe, not onelye by expence of spirit, but by leaving destitute the parts,

whereby declining to decay, they become at length unmeete
for the entertainement of so noble an inhabitant as is the soule,
of stocke divine, of immortall perpetuity, and exempt from all corruption. Then seeing neither body, nor spirit are admitted in the
first, or second sorte of instruments, they fall to the third kinde,
which being lively, or at the least apt for life, require direction,
and also foreine impulsion: foreine, in respect of themselves,
destitute of facultie, otherwise then disposition: but inward and
domesticall, in that it proceedeth from a naturall power, (resident in these corporall members) which we call the soule: not
working as ingens, by a force void of skil and cunning in it selfe,
& by a motion given by devise of the Mechenist: but farre otherwise indued with science, & possessed of the mover: as if
Architas had bin him selfe within his flying doves, & Vulcanne
within his walking stooles, and the moving engine as it were
animated with the minde of the worker, therein excelling farre
all industrie of art. For here the natural Apelles painteth as well
within as without, and Phydias is no lesse curious in polishing
the entrailes, and partes withholden from the viewe, then in
garnishing the outward apparance, and shew of his frame: and
which is yet more, here the craftes man entreth himselfe into all
the parts of the worke, and never would relinquish the same.
Although we place the spirit and body in the third kind of instruments, yet is there great oddes, betwixt these two. For the
spirit answereth at full all the organicall actions of the soule, &
hath in it no distinction of members: the body is of more particular uses, compounded of sundry partes, ech of them framed
of peculiar duties, as the mind & spirit emploieth them. The
spirit is quicke, nimble, and of marvelous celeritie of motion,
the bodie, slow, dull, and given to rest of it selfe: the spirit the
verie hand of the soule, the body & bodily members like flailes,
sawes, or axes in the hand of him that useth them. For as we see
God hath geven us reason for all particular faculties, and hand
for all instruments, of pleasure, of necessitie, of offence, of defence, that thereby, although man be borne without covering,
without teeth, without hoofe or horne, only with tender nailes,
and those neither in fashion, nor temper fit for fight: yet he
clotheth him selfe, both against the tempest warme, against
force of weapon with coate of steele, and maketh unto him selfe

weapons of warre, no tush, no horne, no hoofe, no snout of elephant in force comparable thereunto: so the spirits of our bodies,
and this hand of our souls, though it be but one, yet handleth it
all the instruments of our bodie: and it being light, subtile, and
yeelding, yet forceth it the heaviest and grossest, & hardest
parts of our bodies, chewing with the teeth, and striking with
the fist, & bearing downe with the thrust of shoulder, the resistance of that which standeth firme, and containing alone the force
of all the members: seeth with the eye, heareth with the eares,
understandeth organically with the braine, distributeth life with
the hart, and nourishment with the liver, and whatsoever other
bodely action is practised.

Of Humours and the Mind

Hitherto we have bene led by reason of the objection from
humors, which imported great power in them of affecting the
minde. It was answered before generally, whatsoever was done
in the body of any parte to be done organically, and that was
applied specially to certaine objections before aunswered: it
remaineth here, that the same be applyed also to our humours,
which have no other power to affect the minde, then to alter the
state of the instrumentes: which next to the minde, & soule it-
selfe are the only causes of all direct action in the body. So here
we are to consider, in what sort the humours move these perturbations above mentioned: whether as cheefe workers, instruments, or other kinde of helpers: and so how they may claime
any interest in terrifying, or soliciting the minde, this way or
that way, as the objections before mentioned would beare us in
hand. It hath ben declared before how the mind is the sole
mover in the body, and how the rest of the partes fare as instrumentes, and ministers: whereby in naturall affections the humors
are secluded from cheefe doers, and being no organicall partes
serve for no instrumentes. For whatsoever hath any constant
and firme action in our bodies, the state of health remayning
firme, is done either by soule, or by the partes of the body: of
which the humours are neither, and so utterly secluded of nature

c

from any peculiar action to any use of the body. For that they are said to nourish, it signifieth only a passive disposition, by which through our nourishing power, they receive the Character of our nature, and are altered into the substance of the same, they themselves giving over their private action, and submitting to the naturall concoctive vertue, which destroyeth all particularities of nourishment, and bringeth them to that uniformity which our nature requireth. Then while the body is in health, the humors beare no sway of private action, but it being once altered, and they evill disposed, and breaking from that regiment whereunto they should be subject, are so farre of from subjection to the disposition of our bodies, and strength of our partes, that they oppresse them, and as it appeareth in simptomaticall eventes in sicknes, dispise that government, whereto by natures law they stand bound. Thus then I hold humours to be occasions of disorderly perturbations, even as they are meanes of depraving the instrument of perturbation, and turning it otherwise, then nature hath disposed, whose government when it hath shaken of, it affecteth us two maner of wayes: the one by the corporall substance, whereby it annoyeth the corporall masse of bodies, and complexion, and breaketh out into soares, Emposthumes, or other such annoyances: the other by a spirit which it possesseth, either contrary altogether, or diverse at the least from ours, wherewith many wayes it disturbeth the orderly actions, & weakneth the vigor of the same: now both by substance, and by spirite it altereth complexion where it prevaileth, and thereby giveth greatest stroake to the organicall members. Then seing all actions are performed both by spirite and corporall instrument, and the humours exceeding the government of nature, and withdrawing themselves from subjection thereof, affect us both wayes, spirite against spirite, and corporall substance against his like, we are to consider, how by these two meanes our actions suffer through their disorder, and where their operation taketh most place in working such phantasticall perturbations wherewith we are deluded. Of all partes of the body, in ech perturbation, two are chiefly affected: first the brayne, that both apprehendeth the offensive or pleasaunt object, & judgeth of the same in like sort, and communicateth it with the harte, which is the second part affected: these being troubled carie with them all the rest of the partes into a simpathy, they of all the rest being in respect of affection of most importance. The humours then to worke these effectes, which approch nigh to naturall perturbations grounded upon just occasion, of necessity, alter either brayne or hart: if the brayne be altered, and the object not rightly apprehended then is it delivered otherwise then it standeth in nature, and so the hart moved to a disorderly passion. Againe though the brayne be without faulte, and report delyvered to the hart sincerely: yet that being distempered, or altered in complexion by faulte of humour, doth not aunswere in affection as the object requireth: but more or lesse, as the distemper misleadeth: if both partes be overcharged of humour, the apprehension & affection both are corrupted, and misse of their right action, and so all thinges mistaken, ingender that confused spirite, and those stormes of outragious love, hatred, hope or feare, wherewith bodies so passionate are here and there, tossed with disquiet. Now particularly the spirite of the humour being subtiler, thinner, and hoter then is meete, maketh the apprehension quicker then it should be, and the discretion more hasty, then is meete for the upright delivery to the hart, what to embrace or to refuse: this causeth pronenes to anger, when we are offended without cause, commonly called teastines, and frowardnes. If the humour also with his spirite possesse the brayne, then are these passions of longer continuance: humour being of a more sollid nature then the spirite, and so not easily dispersed, which causeth fittes of such passions to be of longer continuance: and thus the hart may be abused from the brayne: not much unlike as it falleth often out in communication of speach amongest us: a man of hasty disposition, ready to aunswere, and quick witted, will make reply to that which should be said, before the tale be halfe told, whereby he faileth in his replication, and aunswereth from the purpose: which if he had bene first assured, whereto to reply, he should not have missed. This appeareth plaine in Cholericke persons, or such as are disposed to anger: such are offended where they have no cause in truth, but by mistaking: and where they have cause the vehemency of the apprehension, and the suddenness of the report from the brayne unto the seat of perturbation, inforceth double the passion: especially when the hart is as flexible, as the brayne is light:

then raungeth it into all extremity. This commeth to passe, not by any power of anger in the Cholerick humour: but by reason the instrumentes are misordered, either by vapour rising from that humour, or the very substance of the same. They are disordered in this sort through Choler. The naturall spirit and complexion of these partes become subtiler, thinner, and quicker, proner to action, then of their natures they should be, through the heat which riseth of Choler, and his spirit intermixed with ours: by this mobility of vapour, our spirit (of a quieter and more stable disposition,) is either made more rare, then is expedient for the use of our bodies, or else striving as it were to subdue this bastard spirite and unwelcome ghest, cannot give that attendance upon his proper duety, which naturally it should: and so the actions thereupon rise depraved, and having wherwith it is encumbred within, admitteth the cause of displeasure more easily which riseth abroad: being an addition to that which molesteth at home: and these natures for the most parte are troubled with a Cholerick humour, or fretting, like to Choler, about the mouth of the stomach, which is of all the inward partes of quickest sense and feeling. This causeth them, especially fasting, before the humour be mitigated, and delayed with nourishment, to be most prone to that angry passion. The teasty waywardnes of sick persons, such as are vexed with payne or feaver, wherby the humors of the body become more fell maketh evident proofe hereof. We see how small matters put them out of patience, & every thing offendeth: whereas in health the same occasions would litle, or nothing move. The reason is because, they measure all outward accidents, by that they finde of discontentment within: not that the humor that discontenteth is any instrument of passion, or carieth with it faculty to be displeased: but because it disquieteth the body, and giveth discontentment to nature, it is occasion why displeasures are made great: and where there is no cause, nature troubled within, faireth as greatly displeased with that which outwardly should not displease: the griefe within, being added to an indifferent thing without, and drawing it into like felowship of displeasure, even but for that it pleaseth not: like as in a troubled sea, a great vessell is more easily stirred with smal strength, then in the calme haven, or quiet streame: so our spirites, and

organicall instrumentes of passion, the parte tossed with stormy
weather of internall discontentment, is with litle occasion dis-
quieted, yea with the shaking of a rush, that hath no show of
calming those domesticall stormes, that arise more troublesome,
and boisterous to our nature, then all the blustering windes in
the Ocean sea. For when our passion is once up by such occasion,
the common sense is also caried therewith, and distinction of
outward thinges hindered at the least, if not taken away, all
things being wayed by that which nature findeth offence at within: even as the tast altered in feavers by cholerick vapours,
maketh sweete thinges seeme bitter, and unpleasaunt, which of
themselves are most delectable to the tast, and would greatly
satisfie the same partie, the bitter relish through that taint of
choller once taken away. And in this sort in my opinion ariseth
the disorderly, & unruly passion of choler, both increased, where
some occasion is offered, and procured by inward disposition of
the bodie and spirit, when there is no pretence, or shewe of
cause. This is seene as plainly in mirth and joye, which riseth as
well upon inward harmonie of spirit, humour, and complexion,
as upon glad tidings, or externall benefite whereof we take re-
joycing. A bodie of sanguine complexion (as commonly we call
it, although complexion be another thing, then condition of
humors) the spirits being in their just temper in respect of
qualitie, and of such plenty as nature requireth, not mixed or
defiled, by any spirit or vapor, the humours in quantity &
qualitie rated in geometricall, and just proportion, the substance
also of the bodie, and all the members so qualified by mixture
of elementes, as all conspire together in due proportion, breedeth
an indifferencie to all passions. Nowe if bloud abound, and keepe
his sincerity, and the body receave by it, and the spirits rising
from the same, a comfort in the sensible partes, without doubt
then, as anger without cause externall, rose upon inward displeasure; so this spirit, these humours, and this temper, may
move an inward joy, whereof no externall object may be accompted as just occasion. This is the cause that maketh some
men prone to joy, and laughter at such thinges, as other men
are not drawne with into any passion, and maketh them picke
out, and seeke for causes of laughter, not onely to move others
to the like, but to expresse their mery passion, which riseth by

the judgement of our senses imparted to the hart, not regarding whether the cause be inward or outward, that moveth, which taketh comfort thereat, as though the object were externall. This especially commeth to passe if the bloud be such about the hart, as his purenesse & sincerenesse with sweetnesse that carieth moderation of temper doth so comfort, and mollifie it, that it easily, & aptly enlargeth it self: then such bloud or such vapor that hath this tickling qualitie, causeth a delight conceived in the braine, and communicated with the hart, procureth a comfortable gratulation, and inward joy of that whereof nature taketh pleasure. For as we have sights, tastes, smelles, noyses, pleasant objectes without us, and on the contrary part, as manie odious, and hatefull, which do force our senses: so have we also all these internall, pleasaunt or unpleasaunt: & as we have of sensuall objects internall, so in like manner pleasure & displeasure is communicated from within of the braine to the heart, of such things as we are not able directly to referre to this or that qualitie: as we see it fareth with tasts oftentimes: such mixtures may be in sauces, that something may please us we cannot expresse what, raysed of the composition. This chiefly falleth to our bodies, when that which giveth this occasion carieth force of gentle and light spirits: as wine, and strong drinke, and all aromaticall spices, which have a power to comfort the braine, and hart, and affect all our bodie throughout with celeritie and quicknesse, before their spirits be spent in the passage: then the braine giveth merie report, & the hart glad for it selfe, and all the fellow members, as it were, daunceth for joy, and good liking, which it receaveth of such internall provocations. Then as we see wine give occasion of mirth by his excellent spirit, wherewith out spirit is delighted, and greatly increased, if it be drunke with moderation; so such as are of merie dispositions, enjoy a naturall wine in their bodies, especially harts & braines, which causeth them to laugh at the wagging of a feather, and without just matter of laughter, without modest regard of circumstance, to beare them selves light & ridiculous: & this my friende *M.*[1] I take to be the cause of merrie greekes, who seeke rather to discharge them selves of

---

[1] 'a supposed frend not ignorant of good letters', to whom the treatise is addressed.

the jocond affection, stirred up by their humour, then require true outward occasion of solace and recreation. Nowe as before I have sayd that choler procureth anger, not as cause, but as occasion, so likewise bloud thus tempered and replenished with these aromaticall and merie spirits, giveth occasion only of this pleasantnesse, and is no cause thereof, the hart making just claime to these affections as the only instrument, & under the soule, chiefe author of these unruly companions: which instrument is so disposed, that obeying the mind, and those naturall rules whereby all things are esteemed, good or bad, true or false, to be done or not to be done, no otherwise then by a civill subjection ruled by counsell & no constraint, it repugneth oft times all the strong conclusions whatsoever reason can make to the contrary. Thus you understand how a man may be angrie and merie without externall object, or outward cause: now let us consider, howe sadnesse and feare, the points which most belong to this discourse, and your present state,[1] may also arise without occasion of outward terror either presently molesting, or fearing us by likelihood, or possibility of future danger. As the nature of choler is subtile, hote, bitter, and of a fretting and biting qualitie, both it selfe and the vapors that passe from it, and bloud temperate, sweet, and full of cheerefull and comfortable spirits, answerable to those we have ingenerate, especially if they become aromaticall, as I may terme them, and of a fragrant nature, by naturall temper, or by meanes of diet: so melancholie of qualitie, grosse, dull, and of fewe comfortable spirits; and plentifully replenished with such as darken all the clernesse of those sanguineous, and ingrosse their subtilnesse, defile their pureness with the fogge of that slime, and fennie substance, and shut up the hart as it were in a dungeon of obscurity, causeth manie fearefull fancies, by abusing the braine with uglie illusions, & locketh up the gates of the hart, whereout the spirits should breake forth upon just occasion, to the comfort of all the family of their fellowe members: whereby we are in heavinesse, sit comfortlesse, feare, distrust, doubt, dispaire, and lament, when no cause requireth it, but rather a behaviour beseeminge a heart upon just cause, and sound reason most comfortable, and chearfull. This doth melancholie work, not otherwise then

[1] melancholy.

the former humours, giving occasion, and false matter of these passions, and not by any disposition as of instrument thereunto. Of all the other humours melancholie is fullest of varietie of passion, both according to the diversitie of place where it setleth, as brayne, splene, mesaraicke vaines, hart, womb, and stomach; as also through the diverse kindes, as naturall, unnaturall: naturall, either of the splene, or of the vaines, faultie only by excesse of quantitie, or thicknesse of substance: unnaturall by corruption, and that either of bloud adust, choler, or melancholie naturall, by excessive temper of heate, turned in comparison of the naturall, into a sharpe lye by force of adustion. These diverse sorts having diverse matter, cause mo straunge symptomes of fancie and affection to melancholike persons, then their humour to such as are sanguine, cholericke, or flegmaticke: which fleume of all the rest serveth least to stir up any affection: but breeding rather a kind of stupiditie, and an impassionate hart, then easily moved to embrace or refuse, to sorowe or joye, anger or contentednesse: except it be a salte fleume, then approcheth it to the natur of choler, & in like sort therof riseth anger & frowardnes.

THE REASONABLE SOUL

From *A Treatise of the Immortalitie of the Soule*
by John Woolton, 1576

Our soules, whose faculties can comprehend
The wondrous Architecture of the world:
And measure every wandring plannets course,
Still climing after knowledge infinite,
And alwaies mooving as the restless Spheares. . . .
TAMBURLAINE

🜊

Hitherto have I spoken of the substances and Origine of the reasonable soule. Nowe followeth, that I speake of the powers or partes of the same: for albeit it be impermixte and indivisible in it selfe, yet it is distinct, not in essence and substaunce, but in vertue and operation. Wherein I mynde not scrupulouslye to followe the steppes of the Philosophers, the Phisitions, who with endlesse curiositie doe vexe them selves and their Readers aboute the inquisition of the same. I am content to yeelde to their division of the Organicall powers, as eyther true or probable. And let it be graunted unto them, that the soule beeing inclosed and as it were tyed to the body, cannot (so long as it remayneth in that prison) eyther behold, know, or conceyve any externall & corporal thing, beeing without the compasse of himselfe, but by the helpe and ministrie of the bodely instrumentes and senses, called of Plato, Orgaines: whereby all Objectes are powred and in-

C2

stilled into the commune Sence, as it were into a certayne
Receptacle or Cesterne: Which because they may after a sorte
be discerned in beastes, the doctrine thereof is not so obscure.
But mans soule hath other more excellent powers then the
beastes have, as it is inferred manifestly, because he is endued
with those accions and qualities which beastes can not by any
meane follow and expresse. For man counteth and numbreth,
not onely singular, but also universall thinges, he hath in him
selfe notices and knowledges naturally, he reasoneth of one
thing by another, he inventeth Artes, he examineth and judgeth
his owne argumentes, and often revoketh his untrue opinions:
he discerneth betweene thinges honest and unhoneste, and with
deepe contemplation he deliberateth of thinges that maye insue.
All whiche thinges brute beastes want, and are therefore inferior to man: whereas in the accions of externall senses, as Seeing, Hearing, and suche like, divers of them do farre excell man,
as the Eagle in seeing, the Vulture in smelling &c.

But of these Organicall powers (as they call them) or Externall accions, I thinke it not so partinent to this my purpose, to
use any long speeche. For albeit aswell the interior as exterior
senses doo serve the Reasonable soule, so long as it remayneth
heare in this body: yet all these doe issue, and as it were flowe
from that fountayne: And when the soul departeth from the body,
he reserveth still his owne moste peculier and proper accions
and mocions which they call inorganicall: Thother serve onely
in the union and conjunction of body and soule, but these abide
with the soule after his separation from the body: Of the which
I will speake as breefly and playnely as I can.

The Reasonable soule is not content with the viewe of Objectes externall, and consideration of naturall thinges, but he
ascendeth higher, apprehendeth spirituall thinges, & flieth up to
the Majestie of god, seking there his origine and offspring, beeing the Image of God, not in substaunce, but in similitude. The
whiche thing that hee may more exactly doo, he is instructed
and furnished by God, as it were with two winges, to witte,
Reason and Will, both of one substance: that, fastened and
affixed to the right side, this, to the lefte: the propertie of
Reason was to understand and know, and of Will to approve and
electe thinges understoode and knowen. Now if these two winges

did with equall force, strength, and consente, carrie and beare
uppe the soule, she shoulde keepe the right and straight Way
towarde God, and flying continually neerer and neerer heavenlye
thinges: Like the Eagle who carieth her young ones in the highe
Ayre, inuring them to beholde the brighte Sunne beames:
woulde departe very farre from hys contagious Pryson, and earnestly lothe the route of raging affections and uncleane imaginations. A rectitude and straightnesse of mans harte was added,
that it mighte as it were, beare a force and power of a cleare gale
of winde to these two winges, whiche blaste receyved into the
brayne, dyd carrie and freshly sette forwarde these powers: as
when the flight of the Larke or Nightingale, ascending on highe,
is hastened with quicke and pleasaunte winde, wherewith (as it
is written) those byrds are so much delighted, that the higher
they flye towarde the skye, the more delectably and pleasantly
they chirpe and sing.

But after the horrible fault of our first Parentes, and infective
contagion of original sinne overflowing al mankinde: not onely
many of the moste beautifull and best feathers of every wing
were plucked from us by the fraud and malice of the Devill: but
also that of Will was unjoynted and almoste knapt asunder:
Whereby mans seelye soule is caried with an unequal flight,
muche like a Goose that laggeth after her fellows with a broken
wing. Yet in this great deformitie of nature, god hath yet left in
the soule certayne sparkes and seedes, whiche doe admonishe us
of the originall excellencie of mans soule, and therewithall hath
left us medecines and salves of these sortes, that we may both
know how to have these fractures and luxacions of oure natures
cured, and also to recover our beautiful feathers which we have
lost. Al which cure is to be had out of gods worde, wherein whosoever are conversant, do recover somewhat both in reason and
wil, and because they find the Phisick holsome, they meditate
therin both day and night: And contrariwise al those that des-
pise this kind of cures, must needes be lame Criples, not able to
flye up into Gods mountaine. But let this be sufficient by the
way, to put us in remembrance aswel of the originall excellencie,
as lamentable corruption of mans soule. Let us now returne to
the inorganical powers of the same, which we named reason
and will. Reason therefore, which they also call the minde or

understanding, is that power of the soule whiche understandeth & judgeth by reasoning aswel of thinges having bodies, as having no bodies: of thinges general as several. It differeth much from imagination, memorie, senses, and other faculties or powers of the soule. For he understanding those things, also with them hath in him selfe a certen reflexion, and by ratiotination knoweth a reason of his knowledge, & that which is the greatest of al, hath in him selfe those naturall notices, whiche the Grecians call *ennoias*, wherby it perceyveth al things which have any being, even after this maner. It first receiveth thinges external, brought to the common senses, and conjoyneth them: afterward judging of them by imagination, dothe transmit them to memorie, and so conserveth them: and lastly reasoning & inquiring of the same intentively, observeth the causes & effects, collecteth by induction and singular examples, and so giveth his judgement, and, as it were, pronounceth sentence.

The seconde inorganicall power of the reasonable soule, is Will, that is to say, a natural facultie, wherby man electeth or refuseth whatsoever Inteligence or reason hath judged to be good or evill: And will is sayd to be proper unto man, but Appetite unto brute beastes. The object (as they call it) of will, is whatsoever lieth in mannes habilitie. For there are many things, which when we can not have, we covet and desire, as strength of bodye. And something we will freely, as to defende our countrey: some other things not freely, but almost by coaction, as to dye for our countrey, or in the storme & tempest to cast our goodes into the sea, the rather that we our selves may be preserved: I speake yet of external & mundayne accions, and not of heavenly thinges: wherin howe lame and blind Wil is, I have already partly declared.

But to returne to the operations of the soule, their properties & differences are sette out in this similitude. The Minde or reason is muche like unto a King, and the Will unto a privie Counselour: the hart representeth the obedient Communaltie. Nowe it is the duetie of will to impart unto the hart those thinges whiche righte reason hath appoynted, that the affections may do nothing contrarie to their allegiance: which thinges when they be omitted, the wil and the hart are ledde with corrupte mocions, as nowe and then we see it come to passe in

Politicall Regimentes, where undiscrete and wyckell councel-
lours are caried away by the sway of the wavering multitude,
agaynst the honestie and dignitie of good Lawes: according to
the verse:

Fertur equis auriga, nec audit currus habenas.[1]

For the actions and inclinations of the will are free, willing or
nilling those thinges which perfit reason propoundeth. And unto
it there are apperteyning two powers and operations, whereof
the one, that is to say the appetite sensitive, was created to be
subjecte unto reason, which they compare unto obedience in
civill regiment, where the Citizens obey willingly and not by
coaction. This Harmonie was heavenly in manne before his
faule, but is now mervelously corrupt with ignorance and disobedience. The other powers obey rather by constreynt, and
thereby are the externall members kept in awe, that they may
not be caried hedlong by the fury and rage of carnall affections.
And this they call a Masterdome over the barbarous and stub-
berne multitude, who withoute forcible meanes, will give no
dew reverence nor obedience to the magistrate. There are great
causes why we ought after this maner to make a difference betwene reason and will: And it standeth us upon to know that
naturall Notices or Knowledge is one thing, and earnest appeti-
tions another thinge: as for example sake: Saule knew David,
and that knowledge remayned all one before the battell with
the Philistians, and after.[2] But in the beginning there was love
and friendshippe in Saules will, which afterwarde was turned
into hatred & malice. And as reason and will are two thinges
and diverse, so is their place destincte and diverse: Whiche
thing we may see to be true by the Orgains or instruments
annexed to the soule. For the inferior senses are coupled with
the power intellective: but the hart is annexed and knitte with
Will and Desire. The knowledge therefore of David is in the
brayne, but goodwil and Hatred are in the hart. These notices
or seedes, & as it were sparkes of knowledge, are not gotten by

---

[1] The charioteer is whipped along by the horses, nor does the chariot obey the
reins.

[2] See *Samuel* xviii. 6–9.

little & little through education and study, as Aristotle supposed, but are together ingendred with the body and Soule. . . .

We may then by the due consideration of these things, acknowledge humaine infirmity; in that even directly against
Reason, & judgement in the power intellective, the Will & hart
do roush into al kind of mischeefe, according to the saying of
Medea, *I see good things & do like well of them: But I elect &
follow the worst,* whereunto the divil addeth his poyson, sowing
raging and furious affections in mans minde, and casting a
thicke & dim myst in the vertue intellective: Wherby many being caried astray & inflamed with suche hellish furies, doe
practise upon them selves all unnaturall & savage cruelty. So
Hercules murdered him self, his wife, & his own children. We
reade in histories that the mother of the Xanthians did hang her
selfe at the rofe of the house, with her child hanged in a cord
about her necke, holding in her hand a flaming firebrand to set
the house on fire, minding so to destroy al her goods with hir:
& yet in these tragical facts, we may not thinke that the light of
nature was altogether extinct and quenched in them: And muche
lesse in other, eyther civill or godly men: But that the divill doth
violently and tyrannously move and draw into all mischeefe, men
that are deserte and given over of God. Let such examples styrre
us earnestly and humbly to beseech the sonne of God, to direct
and guide us: who came into this worlde to destroy the workes
of the divell: that he might not utterly obscure in us the lyght
of reason and true judgement, nor altogether carrye headlong
our will against the perfitte will of God: and therfore we say
daily in the Lordes prayer, *And lead us not into temptation*: and
the lord him self saith, *Pray that you enter not into temptation.*
And thus I have somewhat shadowed and expressed the properties, and places of the powers of the soule called inorganicall,
very muche passing and exceeding the instrumentall powers,
common with man and brute beastes, as by due collation and
examination it wyll more evidently appeare.

Fyrste of all, the soule with his presence quickeneth this mortall and earthly body of ours, he so compasseth and embraceth
it, that it decayeth not: he distributeth the foode into all his
partes, he mainteyneth and conserveth the same in a juste conveniency and order, not onely in beuty, but also in augmentation

& generation. But these things are common to man with herbes
and plantes, for they in their kynde do lyve, and we see that
they are fed in the grounde, that they multiply and increase,
and bring forth young ones in their due seasons. Let us then
consider what the soule executeth in the senses, where the lyfe
is more cleere & evident. And therin it boweth or spreadeth it
self in touching colde or hotte things, rough or smoth, harde or
softe, lighte or heavy: Moreover it tryeth many diversities of
savours, odours, sounds, shapes, by tasting, smelling, hearing
and seeing. And in all these it coveteth and desireth those
thynges which are agreable unto the nature of hys bodye, but
rejecteth and sheweth the contrarye: And lastly is not onely intent in procreating yssue, but also very carefull for their sustentation and conservation: but the brute beastes are moved and
caryed with these inclinations.

We will now examine the proper and peculiar operations and
powers of the reasonable Soule: And here marke the wonderfull
gyfte of understanding and reasoning, the notable and deepe
remembraunce of manye matters. Consider also the manifolde
artes and sciences, invented and perceived by manne, the tilling
of the grounde, building of Cyties. Weighe moreover the find-
inge oute of so manye Characters in signes and letters, suche
diversitie of tunes and soundes, suche varietie in speaches and lan-
guages, such plentie and store of bookes, writynges and monu-
metes as well of Cyvill as of divine matters, for the comfort and
instruction of the posteritie. These vertues and powers of the
Soule are greate, but the bad as well as the good are partakers
thereof. We comme nowe unto those thynges which are proper
to the godly alone. The Soule therefore endevoreth to keepe the
bodye in subjection, to absteyne from fylthy luste and pleasure,
to be puryfied and clensed by faythe and the holye ghost, to
strengthen hym selfe agaynste all assaultes of wickednesse, to
imbrace all menne wyth love and charitye, to wyshe nothing to
any man, but as to hym selfe. He precisely followeth Gods holye
worde, and maketh accompt that therein hee heareth God most
lively to conferre & talke with him, in that woorde is all hys
delyte, and after the same he frameth his lyfe, and conversation.
But amongst suche notable and prayseworthy endevours he
susteyneth no small labours, for, he hath a dayly battell with the

fleshe, the world, and the divel: neither hath he rest at any time, for allarmes and assaultes: Yet beeing strengthned by Gods power, he carieth away glorious and triumphant victories. The soule is busied about these holy thinges, (the soules of holy men I meane,) for the soules of the ungodly dwelling in a foule and stinking dungeon, the wicked feende therwithall yching them forwarde, doo runne headlong into all kinde of iniquitie. As we see in the example of the riche Glotton, who abused his soule, and his whole rase of life in committing sinne and wickednesse.

Hereby is seene an apparant difference betweene the reasonable soule of man, and the sensuall soule of brute beastes. There is externally breathed into man the breath of life, into the which god infuseth his holynes, justice and wisdome, an habilitie to judge betweene honest and unhonest thinges, and other notices, which proceed not of any elemental nature: But the soule in brute beastes, is the vitall spirite in the blood, or it is *Crasis*, that is, a temperature of the whole body, or a kind of elemental matter, moving and stirring the body, which is called (but unaptly) in beastes, a soule, and beeing but a breath or vapor, it vanisheth away, much like unto a flame, with the body. For as in a Candle there is a flame, which feedeth upon the Match and Waxe: even so in brute beastes there is a vitall spirite, like a flame, ingendred of the blood by the operation of the harte, flying and breathing throughout all the body, yeelding and imparting to the body a lively heate and power to stirre motions and accions. The soule of man differeth not onely from these elementall matters, but also from the Angelicall spirites. For the Angels are absolute and perfect persons of themselves, created together in the beginning of the world to be as it were flames of fire serving God: But mans soule is no absolute person, without the body: And moreover beeing breathed into man in his formacion, is not only separable from the body, but mutable in the bodye. Whereas the spirituall essence of Angels is nowe so established and confirmed, that they cannot hencefoorth by any meanes depart from God, and fall from the state of salvation.

And hitherto you have heard of the marvelous union and conjunction of the body and soule, and of her powers and operations: Whereof a question ariseth, which hath exceedingly vexed the Philosophers and Divines, to witte in what sort the soule abideth and resteth in the body, whether it be conteined in any one parte, or els be dispersed throughout the whole body, and whether it be therein circumscribed in length, breadth, & deapth &c. Whereof I thought it not amisse to say something, not taking upon me to discide the controversie (for that were extreme follie in a doubtfull matter) but onely to set before the Reader the diversitie and difficultie of judgements, that he mighte the rather hereby be caried to a deepe consideration and a reverende admiration of Gods majestie, and of the workes of his handes. And herein I finde two opinions, the one of those that affyrme the soule not to be conteyned in any one place of the body, but dispersed, and as it were spredde throughout everye parte of the same: The other that thinke it to be settled and placed in some one place of the body (as it were in his Throne) from whence he doth extende and powre out plentifully his powers into everye externall parte and member. Concerning the firste opinion Aristotle hathe sayde nothyng in hys bookes, whiche he writ of the Soule.[1] Plato considering the Reasonable soule to be of a Simple and Incorporall substaunce, thought that it coulde not bee mingled or interlaced with the body: for that thinges corporall and spirituall can not bee compounde in one: And if they shoulde bee mingled, the Soule shoulde not bee onely infected with the contagion of the body, but therewithall bee subjecte to corruption. Wherof because the soule is voyd, if we consider the perfection of her nature: he thinketh it not to be mingled with the body, but appointed as a master & guide thereof: And calleth not that which consisteth of body & soule, Man, beeing afrayde of the absurditie which might arise by meanes of the comixion and conjunction thereof: But he sayth that the soule only is man, which useth the body as his Chariot or Carriage, & whereof he beareth rule & dominion. . . . But to say my opinion playnly, neither he nor any other seeme unto me to have approved this matter sufficiently. For whereas all men almoste consent therein, even by the authority of Aristotle, that the soule is of a differinge substance from the bodye, and cannot by any means be confounded or mingled with the same: Yet he is so affixed and coupled with the bodye, that they two

[1] *De Anima* is Aristotle's principal work on the subject.

make one person or lyving creature indued with many powers
and faculties. And therefore Galene is well liked of manye, in
that hee writeth, the soule so to followe the complexion of the
bodye, that it may seeme after a sorte to be a temperature of the
same. . . . For as we see the light in the ayre sometime to be
clearer, sometime darker, by meanes eyther of the cloudy or
faire wether, even so by meanes of the temperatures of the body,
specially those whiche are common to the whole man, the powers
of the minde alter and chaunge. Hereof it commeth to passe,
that we see some geven to anger and carnall luste, by meanes of
the whot constitution of their bodies, some ingenious, some dul-
lardes, some severe and sharpe, other some mery and curteous,
some affected this way, other that way: all whiche thinges followe
the constitution and complexion of the body. Certayne it is that
moyste and colde doo breede a dulnesse and heavinesse, as heate
and drought ingender quicknesse and nimblenesse in the bodies
of all living creatures, and suche as their constitutions be, suche
is their state and inclination. And heereunto you may adde mans
dyet, Education, the nature of the Element, ayre, and soyle, custome, and other suche like: all which have a marvelous force,
not onely in the body, but also in the minde of mortall men. Let
us not inferre hereof, that the soule is mortall: Let us rather
consider that precept of S. Paule, that we should give honour to
the body. For albeit the Masse or lumpe of these oure bodyes
be compact of earth and clay, yet it was created to this ende that
it myght be the Temple and Mancion of the holy ghost, and a
paterne and glasse of his wonderfull workes. For in this lyfe
those that beleve, are the very temples of god, wherin the
whole sacred trinitie exerciseth his workes, even the father, the
sonne, & the holy ghost. On the other side what sense of pietie
can there be in those, whose brain is astonied, overwhelmed &
oppressed as it were with a thicke cloude of dimme blastes,
whose hartes do boyle with the fire of flaming affections, and
whose appetites are kindled with burning lustes: Whereby all
mans senses must needes be amased & oppressed. Let us therefore use sobrietie in meates and drinkes, and beseche our
heavenly father, who is the fountaine and beginning of lyfe, that
hee woulde breathe into oure hartes his heavenlye spirite, and
power into oure braynes the newe and eternall light of the sonne

of God, that in the commixtion of our vitall & animall spirites
we may have motions & inclinations, consonant and agreable to
the lawe of God, and extoll hys majestie through oute all eternities.

But to returne to the question, albeit I doe thinke that the
Soule cannot be sayde properly to be in a place as a thing that
may be circumscribed & measured, yet because the soule is a
substaunce fynite, it must needes be lymited within some space
and place. For that proprietie is onely competent to the majestie
of God, to be immense and infinite. I am not ignorant of that
olde sentence: *Anima est tota in tota, et in qualibet parte tota.* All
the soule is in all the bodye, and all in every parte of the bodye,
which the scholemen woulde father uppon Aristotle. In deede I
fynde the verye wordes in saint Augustine. But touching Aristotle, we may deserne by the writing of Thomas Aquinas, that
Aristotle was of another opinion, and his owne wordes doe very
playnely expresse his judgement herein: Whiche for that they
bee verye excellent, I accompte them woorthye the putting
downe in this place. *Wee ought to conceave that the state of manne
is muche lyke a City well governed: wherin after thynges be once
well appoynted & placed, it is not needefull that the prince be at
the execution of all and singular affayres, but every one attendeth
uppon his calling, and one thinge is donne after another according
to order and custome. &c.* Nowe seeing that nature doth exactlye
observe this order, it is not needefull that the soule shoulde
be in every member: For he beeing in one certaine place,
styrreth and moveth hys actions in every member & part of
the body. Even as there commeth a certaine brightnes from
the sunne beames, which is dispersed into every part of the ayre
round about, & yet the substance of the sunne abideth in one
place. . . .

And thus you may see the varietie of mindes of this matter:
which disputation albeit it be ample & hard, wherin the Phisitions do discent altogether from the Divines, yet diligent examination is not to be blamed, specially if it be joyned with reverent
consideration of Gods great majestie & goodnes toward mankinde, & have on our behalfe thankfulnesse toward him for his
benefites. The Aristotelians marvell, not without cause, why
Galen denyeth life to have her beginning from the Harte, seeing

that he placeth the power and facultie of the vitale spirite in the
same. But let it bee graunted unto the Phisitions agaynst
Aristotle, that the Liver of Manne is first perfected, which is
the fountayne and welspring of blood, whiche receyving *Chilum*,
dothe boyle it untill the bloodde bee devyded and separated from
other humours. Whiche thing beeing done, it sendeth the humours downewarde, and imparteth unto the Harte very thinne
blood, which beeing purified, and as it were distilled with the
hotnesse of the Harte, ingendreth a most subtil breath, much like
a flame of fyre, whiche passeth from the Hart, and walking
throughout the whole body, dothe minister and yeelde unto every
member a livelye heate, whiche is called a *Vitale Spirite*. The
heate or spirite boyling from the harte, ascendeth up into the
brayne, by whose vertue it is made more cleare: Whiche maketh
mee affyrme, that the apprehension of these Notices are in the
hart, and Notices are in vayne without the consent of the harte.
Nowe seeing that the Brayne dothe drawe from the Harte that
vitale or lively spirit, why should we denie the harte to be the
fountayne of life, and the seate of the Reasonable Soule: which
thing we may almost feele and perceyve in our selves and others,
by often and dayly experience. For in sodayne feare and vehe-
mente sorowe or oppression of the soule, the Soule speedely
draweth and plucketh unto him selfe all the powers of the
spirites, that he may be strong, and defende him selfe. Heereof
it commeth now and then to passe, that such as have a faynt
Hart, doe sodenly perishe, beeing overwhelmed and strangled
with that hastie and mightie recourse of the spirites: And then
the Brayne beeing destitute and forsaken of his comforte and
vitale spirites, and altogether naked and as it were unarmed
waxeth dull & colde, and all his accions doe ceasse. The Orgaines
and instrumentes of Mocions spoyled of life and senses, doo rest
and fall on sleepe: & if the impression of that feare be very
strong and mightie, the maze or astonishment abideth longer:
and so it continueth untill the daunger be eyther averted or
mitigated, at what time the Harte easeth him selfe somewhat of
sorrowe, loseth these bondes wherewith he was stayed and tyed,
and so by little and little remitteth the vitale spirites unto the
Brayne, and all other members and partes ef the body. By whiche
consideration wee may see the Brayne too receyve her lyfe from

the Harte, whome nature her selfe chiefly and especielly of all other partes of the bodye defenceth and fortifieth, as that member wherein the moderator and governour of man, the Reasonable soule hathe hys princely place and principall mancion. . . .

Some may happely think al this ado aboute the place of the reasonable soule in mans body, to be a matter frivolous & of no moment. But because suche men eyther suppose there is no soul at all, or have not weighed this matter, according to the worthines therof, their sentence is not muche to be accompted of. For sith that all godly and honest men thinke that there is an immortall soule, resting eyther in the brayne or in the harte, or in both, or els is dispersed throughoute the whole body of man, (for I dare not pronounce any thing in so obscure a matter) the diligent vew and consideration of it must needes be very profitable to embrace vertue, to avoid vice, and to moderate and governe mans manners and conditions, in all the course and trade of lyfe. For when by the consideration of the braine and harte, we understand the fountaine of appetites and causes of senses: we shalbe moved to use great care and industrie in all our actions and motions, & direct our cogitations toward the study of vertue, and avoydance of vice. And for as much as it is moste evident that by the mixture of humours and qualitie of temperaments, there do arise alterations, not onely of the spirites in the braine and hart, but of all the actions and operations of the same: We knowing the causes of these things shall (if our natures be not to wilde) keepe our selves within an honeste measure and compasse.

An earnest consideration of our spirites, will move us to temperancy and modesty in life and conversation: For he that observeth the passages of the spirites, and knoweth their entercourse betwene the brayne and harte, will not willingly quench or weaken those flames and lights of lyfe, & motions, eyther with intemperate dyet, or with violent and raging affections. . . . For all suche as are given to disorder in their affections and actions, do destroy their bodyes and soules, beeing the beautifull houses of justice, and are violent and rebellious against their creator. And whiche is more lamentable, they doe not onelye procure diseases unto them selves, and in the ende their owne death, as Galene sayth: Those men cannot lyve long, whose delight and lyfe is in their pottes & dishes: but therewithall they destroy the handeworke of God in themselves; hindering and quenching those divine actions, whereby God hathe appointed his honour and glory to bee derived amongst mortall menne. . . .

Seeing then mannes nature is contente with fewe thinges: And if we oppresse that honeste contentation, eyther with thynges superfluous or delicious, we hurt & oppresse the body and soule: Let us perswade oure selves that the very conveniency and dignity of oure members, doe shewe and appoynt unto us a wholesome and laudable meane in all oure life, which is moste acceptable and pleasant unto God, whereby the temple of God builded in manne, may be kepte impolluted, and he celebrate and serve his creator throughoute all eternities. . . . For the reasonable soul beeing dissolved from the bodye, ceasethe not to be that whiche it was: But after that the bodye is deade, that it maye rest for a tyme, and be renewed throughe deathe, wniche unto the godly is but a sleepe of the bodye, the soule surviveth, and remayneth immortall and without corruption. For the deathe of the bodye is not a deathe of the Soule also, but onely a severing and departinge from the bodye. As if a manne take onelye a candle out of a lanterne, he taketh but the lyghte oute of the lanterne, and putteth not oute the candle: And then the lanterne is full of darknesse by reason of the light removed, but the candle casteth lighte more cleerely and brightly: Even so the soule departing from the claye and earthly bodye, lyveth and moveth afterwarde more freely and blissfully.

PART TWO

The State

THE CORRESPONDENCES:
THE INDIVIDUAL AND THE BODY POLITIC

From *A Comparative Discourse of the Bodies
Natural and Politique*
by Edward Forset, 1606

> *The Kingly crown'd head, the vigilant eye,*
> *The Counsailor Heart, the Arme our Souldier,*
> *Our Steed the Legge, the Tongue our Trumpeter,*
> *With other Muniments and petty helpes*
> *In this our Fabricke . . .*
>
> > Coriolanus

🕱

It was pithily spoken of *Pithagoras*, That man is the measure of al things: importing thereby that man by the ampliation and application of his powers apprehensive, discerneth, discusseth, and confineth the severall works of nature: with his sences hee measureth things sensible, with his understanding he perceiveth things intellectuall, with his illuminate & inspired knowledge, he comprehendeth things divine and supernaturall; yea more, by this so large and unmeasured measure, all things are made sutable to the esteeme of man, and be either great or small, light or heavy, faire or illfavored, desireable or avoydable, as by mans well or ill conceaving the same bee valued. But beyond all this, the meaning of that sage sentence extendeth yet farther, That in the very composure of man, there is manifestly discovered a summary abstract of absolute perfection, by the which as by an excellent Idea, or an exact rule, we may examine and exemplifie all other things.

The Mathematicians have found out by their observance of the beautious and uniforme proportion of the body of man, and by the symetrie of the parts therof, their true scantlines and dimensions; yea by the laying of it in his full length, & then spreading the armes and legges to their widest compasse, they have contrived both the perfect square, and the exact circle: The square, by foure right lines at the foure uttermost points of the hands and feet; the circle, by rounding a line about those points, placing the center of their compasse upon the navell. The naturall Philosophers reduceth the vastnesse of the universal (comprehending all things that hath either being, or vegitation, or sense, or reason) unto this same well compacted Epitome of mans fabrifacture.

Then much more may the politique Philosopher, having for his proper subject the compound of men civilly assembled and associate, make man the object of his discourse and contemplation, to fit his treatise with good fashion to so imitable a patterne. Therefore this measure (thus induced thereto) I have made my choice of, to trie thereby the forme of a commonweale, what therein is right or wrye, what redundant or defective, what orderly or disproportionable; the helpe of such a brief, and the trueth of such a standerd, may serve to ballance the matters of deliberation, fitly accommodating and rectifying all designements and proceedings. And sith I doe find this lyne of likenesse to bee chalked out unto us in Gods works, I will there begin my applying, where that profound wisdom hath begun his framing.

As in the creating of man God conjoined a soule for action, in a body passive: so in his ordinance of mans sociable conversing (to make the union of a body politike) he hath knit together a passive subjection to an active superioritie: and as in every man there is both a quickning & ruling soule, and a living and ruled bodie; so in every civill state, there is a directing & commaunding power, & an obeying and subjected alleageance. For as neither the soule alone, nor body alone (if they should be severed) can be a man, so not the ruler alone, nor the subjects alone, can be a commonweale. Where all will rule, there is no rule, and where none doeth rule, there is all misrule: but to rule well, and to bee well ruled, is the surest bond of humane societie. Such unruly routs, as (humourously led in dislikes) denyeth the lawfulnesse of Magistrats, may well bee likened to certayne peevish Malecontents, who overtoyled with the tediousnesse of life (and that often without any apparant cause) wisheth that they had no soules, it being all one to want in the body a soule, and in the state a governour: yet as the body sustayneth no harme or wrong, yea is infinitely benefited and graced by the powerfull working of the soule in his organs, so the people guided by a just government, not only are not therby injured, hindered or abased, but much enabled, enobled, and advanced even to the highest pitch of a welthie and safe repose. Then as the soule is the forme which to the body giveth being, and essence; and the body is the matter which desiringly affecteth his forme: so both the ruler should wholy indevour the welfare of his people, and the subject ought (as in love to his owne soule) to conforme unto his soveraigne; that both of them mutually like twinnes of one wombe, may in the neere and deare nature of relatives, maintaine unviolate that compound of concordance, in which and for which they were first combined. As the coupling of the soule and bodie, tendeth not onely to give life, but also to the attayning of a perfect and happy life: So the right temper of soveraigntie and obedience, intendeth and effecteth not only the being, but also the florishing and felicitie of a Commonweale. For the gayning of which propounded happinesse, as the soule is the worthier agent, taking the greatest care, and deserving the chiefest commendation, in so much as a man is not said to be happie for any his strength, his bignes, propernesse, or comely feature of body, but for the goodnesse, noblenesse, and vertuous endowements of his soule: So for the acquiring or framing of any perfection in the Commonweale, we are not so much to behold the largenesse, the power, or the well shewing composure thereof, as the prudencie, justice, and other vertuous sinceritie of a rightfull government. In man the soule ruleth by reason, and in the State the Soveraigne governeth by lawes; which may no lesse aptly be termed the soule of soveraignty, than reason is said to be the soule of the soule. It can never bee so much as conceaved, that the soule should be without reason, though by the unaptnes or repugnancie of the organs, his power in working is either interrupted or impugned: So government may not bee so much as imagined to be without law, though the force and life of the law, through the wayward-nesse of the subjects, cannot alwayes alike be shewed or seene in his due effects: no not the Soveraigne will infringe lawes, no more than the soule will renounce reason. Herewith the fiction of the Poets and the Paynters well agreeth, which in the description and portraiture of *Jupiter* adjoined Justice sitting on his right hand; howsoever it pleased *Anaxarchus* gybingly to tell *Alexander*, that *Jupiter* was not bound thereby to doe justly, but that the people were thereof to conceive, that whatsoever *Jupiter* did was just.

It is worthie the noting, that albeit the bodie doeth often un-thankfully rebell against the soule, yet the soule ever loveth the body, still seeking to reduce it to the better, even as a worke-man mendeth his tooles, or a Musician his Instruments: whereof good Rulers doe make to themselves this rule, That notwith-standing the subjects by their misbehaviour do often cause an incitation to wrath in their Soveraign against them, yet in the punishing of such offenders, he will discover no hatred to their persons, but to their faults, shewing himselfe grieved and un-willing to afflict them, seeking rather their chasticement with pitie, than their destruction with crueltie, and rather to hold a conjunction with them by the mutualitie of loving offices, than to weaken his owne strength by the losse and cutting off the imployable parts of the state publike. The welfare and pros-peritie of the bodie giveth to the soule sweet contentment, as secured thereby from the cares, perplexities, and griefes which want occasioneth: so the plentifull and abundant estate of the subjects, is by a good Soveraigne both maintayned and rejoyced at, sith it giveth to him assurance of supply and comfort in all necessities.

In the creating of man, God is said to have breathed into him the soule, whereby the puritie and dignitie thereof is much ex-tolled above that lump of mowlded earth his body: So is the place of preheminence of an high majestie, & of a more choice and better esteemed worth, as being more to the image of God, & participating more aptly with his greatnes, his power, his jus-

tice, his mercie, his wisdome, his goodnes and bountie, and whatsoever els unspeakable perfection in his unsearchable essence; for
if mans governing of the creatures be to the image of God, then
governing of men is much more to that image. . . .

To discourse at large, with full sailes, how the sences do
recommend their conceiving unto the fantasie; how the fantasie
delivereth them over unto the understanding; how the understanding either absolutely judgeth them by reason, or erroniously
mistaketh them by opinion; how either reason or opinion exciteth
affections; how affections either advised by deliberation, or passionate by humours, induceth the assent of the will; and how the
will commaundeth & enforceth motion and prosecution in all or
any parts of the bodie: howsoever it might amplie and excellently illustrate the powerfull operations of the soule, so orderly
lincked, cheyned, and wrapped one within another: yet least the
delightsomenesse of following the tract of so well pleasing a
theame, should drawe me too far out of my way, I will wynd
about againe, by making a second survey thereof, in the match-
ing to the same of mine applications.

The governing preeminence of the estate, though it be som-
times in like maner obscured, and wronged by inferior deriva-
tions, yet such as can surmount the vulgar thoughts, in reducing
unto one glorious and potent head of majestie, all the severall
branchings and subalternations thereof, shall easily find how
agreeablie it holdeth semblance with the soule, in this respect
also, as to be but one, yet effecting all, yea, to be all in all, and
all in every part of the bodie politique. There is not in the
Commonwealth, any the least synew for mocion, the least vaine
for norishment, the least spirite for life and action, the least
strength for defence, or offence, the least member for use and
benefit, which is not replenished with this power, and sucketh
from this overflowing cesterne, all his subsistance and performance. And (if I thought it not unfit to be over-curious in fitting
exactly the particulers of each) I would not pretermit a more
large comparing of them, even in their alike forces of vegetation
also. Who seeth not, that it belongeth to the office of Soveraignitie, to provide for the nourishing and mainteining of the state
with necessaries, to amplifie the dominions thereof, for profit and
dignitie, to spread abroad the encrease of the people by Colonies,

in the nature of generating or propagating, to cherish in the subjects an appetite of acquiring of commodities, to graunt to them places of Mart and Market for the digesting of the same unto all parts of the Realme, and so to change forme and assimulate them to their most behoofe: to give order for the holding and retaining of that which is become their well agreeing and naturall sustenance, and for the expelling as well of the hurtfull overcharge, as the unprofitable excrements of the weale publique. Will you yet see farther the soveraigne vertue of the Soveraigne power, in all and everie the parts of the State? produce me any (though a person altogether private, occupying but a roome or drawing breath in the Common wealth) that is not enforced both by foreseeing reason, and after-proving events, to acknowledge all his good whatsoever, to be first given, and then secured unto him, by the force of a well ordered government, out of the circle whereof there can be neither welfare, nor safetie, but contrariwise, all confusion, slaughter, rapine, and unjust bereaving of him of all that is or can be deare unto him.

But who so listeth to behold this Politicall soule of the State in his full royaltie and amplitude, let him looke upon his more noble parts, the sensuall and intellectuall; the according and conforming whereof to his important uses, maketh the *Gordian* knot of a powerfull and peacefull blessednes. Then the Soveraignitie (moving, working, & ruling in his three estates) matcheth well the three headed *Gerion*, whom *Justine* interpreteth to signifie the union of three loving brethren; then it seeth more than the hundreth eyes of *Argus*, and acteth more than the hundreth handes of *Briareus*. All Subjects will, as the sences, play the espials and intelligencers; as the members, be stirred and commaunded in cases of imployment; and as the spirits imaginative, propose for apprehension the true shapes and formes of things, either pleasing and eligible, or hurtfull and avoydable.

The Councellors of State like the understanding facultie, applye all their endevours to advance the glorie, and further the enterprises of this their ruling soule, being themselves also by his supreame reason to be ordered, or judged in their right or wrong conceivings.

The favorites of a Prince may be resembled to the fantasies of the Soule, wherewith he sporteth and delighteth himselfe; which to doe (so the integritie of judgement, and Majestie of State be reteyned) is in neither of both reproveable. Which of us is there that doth not (especially in matters rather pleasing than important) follow and feed his fantasies, give scope unto them, suffer them to prevaile with him, reckoning it a great part of his contentment to have them satisfied? I will refraine to presse the application farther than the well-taught Subjects will of themselves conceive. There must be no despitefull envying at the Soveraignes favorites: as they be to him the recreating comforts choicely selected, acceptablie to confort withall; so their enriching, advauncing, and gracing, with the cleerest signes of their Soveraignes love, is not onely allowable, but plainely necessarie, sith they cannot walke continually in the Sunne, but they must needs be coloured.

The will of the Soveraigne in the decreeing or enacting of Lawes, holdeth the like right as the will of the soule doth in the perfourming the resolves of reason. Allow that the Soule were now in his first cleere sighted innocencie, it could not will or affect any thing that were not absolute reason: So, were Soveraignes uncorrupted with that all-taynting canker of sinne, and free from every humane infirmitie, their will alone were undoubted law & Justice; but on the other side, when reason (whose office is to shew the right) is vanquished by the errours of misconceiving, then the will by such bad direction is driven to sinne in his designed works. So where the judgement of the Soveraigne swarveth from sinceritie of true discerning, there his will and all decrees, or executions following the same, must of necessitie be culpable and turne to wrong. Wherefore sith it will not be gainsaid, but that Soveraignes through their naturall frailties, are subject as well to the imbecillitie of judgement, as also to sensuall and irrationall mocions, rising out of the infectious mudd of flesh and bloud, (the observance of which tainte in mans nature, caused *Plato* to say, that the bodie was more in the soule, than the soule in the bodie) and that such their defects may well disable them, from either attayning unto, or retayning firmely the precise points of perfect Justice: How both prudently and lovingly do those Soveraignes governe, who, neither taking to themselves that absolutenes of sole power in law-giving, which by some (being indeed of too hard a temper) is colourably claymed to be originall and hereditarie to their places; neither trusting too much to their owne sufficiencies, either of wisedome or uprightnes, (which seldome be without some admixture of imperfections) do at the making of Statutes and ordinances, assemble for consultation and consent, a full assistance of the noblest and choisest advisours that the State affourdeth: thereby drawing supplies out of their politicall bodie, to make good what wanteth in their naturall?

From the errors of inferior sences, the conceit of the common sence receiveth much misinforming, which in the end and by degrees reacheth a seducement to the soule it selfe: So may the Soveraigne unwittingly by wrong reports of some neer about him, be misled from the knowledge of the trueth, into many misbeleevings. The humors of the bodie do often forciblie prevaile in the working and stirring of the mind; whereupon some Philosophers have tyed the soule unto the temperature of the bodie: So the customes and inclinations of the people in each Countrie, hath otherwhile no smal force in the inclyning of the Soveraignes disposition, if not to approve, yet to tollerate some imperfections. The mind must not suffer it selfe, for want of resolution, to be distracted by diversitie of undiscussed opinions, as wavering and wandering without judgement, having warre within it selfe: So the governour may not well admit or harken unto different and factious sectes, tending to the disturbing and instabilitie of his government. The affections so long as they be obedient unto reason, standeth the soule in great steede; but if they become violent and unrulie, then (of their disordering, and disturbing of the minds tranquillitie) they be rightly tearmed perturbations. Such is the Soveraignes case: If the people be tractable, and truely serviceable, with all dutious subjection, in the nature of right alleagiance, then as loving subjects, by their forwardnesse in cooperating with him, they give strength and stay unto his government: but if they turne mutinous and tumultuous, troubling the governour and State with seditious disorders, then be they as Rebels by the Justice of the law to be suppressed, even as the perturbations of the mind must be subdued by reason, which alone is that powerfull *Pallas* that bestoweth her golden bridle upon *Bellorophon*, to rule therewith that fierce and haughtie *Pegasus*. The force of these headie and giddie perturbations is tyrannously extreame, and that not onelie in the common sort of men, (whom like to a heard of Swine, they whirle headlong into a Sea of vices) but also in persons of the best qualitie, whose resistance proveth oft too faint to escape, or keepe off such violent invasions as suppresseth and vanquisheth even reason it selfe: So is the Soveraigne sometimes by Traytors and Revolters surprised and constrained unnaturally and unlawfully, to the interruption of his government, and ruinating of the State. Opinion is the forerunner (if not the father) of affections, himselfe a verie misbegotten, between Selfe-love the mother and Supposal the sire, which (like an amorous make-love) woeth at once both the virgin Truth, and the harlot Errour, yet affianced to neither, hath but unperfect notions betwixt both; from which notions notwithstanding, as the same shall apprehend a conceit of good or evill, the affections taking motion, do start forth, putting themselves in readines, to repell the imagined evill, and to embrace the seeming good. Upon the surmise of good, Appetites are excited: These be the attendants, and as it were the Courtiers of the soule, who immoderately seeking to satisfie their own desires, giveth the soule no rest, till he bestow all his faculties of understanding wit, and devise, to accomplish their requests. Princes seldome want the Apes of such appetites, that is to say, begging and flattering petitioners, pleasing and applauding Parasites, who using all cunning insinuating, are never without their varietie of sutes, to advance their owne good, howsoever their Soveraigne be thereby either impoverished or dishonored. Upon the opinion of evill ariseth that hidious & snakie head of *Medusa*, fearfull, fretfull, greeving, carefull, repining and dispairing thoughts, filling the soule with the horror of much discomfiture; such malecontents and froward cinicks the Soveraigne oft is pestered with, who never well pleased with the aucthorized proceedings, (though most approveable) doe still feed upon their owne disliking conceits, and will alwaies with the Keistrell, flie against the winde, making their opposicion (by clamorous complaints) against aucthoritie. These affections of both sorts, being in their originall altogether oppinionat, will sometimes (by reason of the neerenesse that opinion hath unto reason) make bold to alleage reason for themselves, and will seeme to be

D

judicious & just in their intendements. This wanteth not his semblance (as in the natures before described) so chiefely in some Traitors of better place, who knowing their dignities in neernesse to the Prince, and of commaund in their Countries, will take upon them (though intending their owne end) to pretend equitie & honestie, yea, and the Soveraignes authoritie also, giving out a populer pretext of publique good, onely to make way thereby to their foule treasons.

The mind hath one endowment more, which almost equalleth all the rest; which is a faithfull memorie of his fore-attained[1] knowledges, in whose good trust and custodie, he treasureth up all his rich acquirings: what semblance there is hereof also in the soule of State, it cannot be obscure. The Soveraigne is well stored with remembrancers, nothing passeth from him, or setleth in him but by record; All his seates of Judgement entereth and preserveth the proceedings in causes; and to forge, corrupt, or embezill the Recordes (whereof any good government hath a tender and strict regard) what is it else, Than as if the memorie should be cleane taken from the mind, to the which it is unseperable, or should become a lying misreporter; which nor his nature, nor his office can endure. . . .

Plato imagined man to be an heavenlie plant; his head to be the roote; his bulke, the stocke; his armes and leggs the branches; and his root to draw his sapp from the heavens to feede therewith the under parts, spreading downeward towardes the earth. Such a plantation do I conceive in the institution of a State politique: the soveraigne head to be designed, inspired, depending, and protected from above; and the body with the out-growing parts thereof, to receive nourishment, strength, florishing, and fruitfulnes from that root of a rightful regiment. If the root thrive, sucking abundantly of his heavenlie nutriment, the plant must needes prosper, and cannot do amisse: but if the root be destitute of grace, as deprived of his sapp, it induceth upon the whole stocke of the State, a withering decay and pining barrennesse. In the head is the first wheele & string of motion, giving force and order to the whole frame, the first fountaine of sence streaming from thence to the other cesterns, and the high erected pallace, where the mind keepeth his court,

[1] 1606 text *attainted*.

shining in his greatest Majestie. The head is by the order and instinct of nature, so dearely esteemed and honored of the bodie, as that every part will not onely seek his ease and health, but even expose it selfe to any perils for his sake and safetie: the inferior parts do susteine and beare him up, moving at his beck, and fast bound when he taketh rest: the hands and armes, do readily receive upon themselves the strokes and wounds, intended against the head; yea, any part doth endure paine, by incision, scarifying, ligature, or issue, to remedie the greevances of the head. These good duties of kindly subjection to kingly power, I leave to the consideration and conscience of every true subject, wishing him to make his best use thereof by contemplating and applying of the same in the performance of like offices of alleagiance, love, and loyaltie. We see the head naturally endued with a fellow feeling of any griefes in the whole bodie, in so much as there is scant any disease so weake or small in any part, as doth not affect and disturbe the head also; yea, it holdeth such a sympathie with the verie foot, as that a little wet or cold taken in the remotest place, hath forthwith a readie passage to the head. Gracious Soveraignes have the like compassions and compunctions in the distresses of their subjects, and be in the same sort deeply peirced & perplexed with any wrong or distemperatures, hapning to the meanest of their people. I have learned of the Phisitions, that most of the diseases of the head, are originally arising and caused from the bodie: and I think that I may thus thereof infer, That many of the escapes of Soveraignes by omission or comission, may thus far by this excuse be extenuated, as more imputable to the people than to them. Therefore when from the head a fluxe of humours shall annoy and enfeeble the whole, or any part, I wish it should be remembred, that such as is our offering, such should be our suffering. Many and verie dangerous be the evils, that from a distempered head be distilled into the bodie. I might laboriously enlarge what harmes he may do to his subjected members, by his several excesses or defects, the disorder and uneven cariage whereof filleth the whole with remedilesse mischiefes. Yet let us marke this withall, That in the naturall bodie, there was never any parts so far digressing from their native nature of alleageance, and their indissolluble band of obedience, forgetting as well the good which they otherwise receive, as the wrong whereby they continually infest him, as did once presume to oppose, or but repine against their head, much lesse seeke or attempt to shake him off the shoulders. How much more kind be those subjects, who out of their owne dutious love, be content to have the blame of the faults, or oversights, likely to blemmish their Soveraigne, transferred & imposed upon themselves? It may seeme by a drunkard in *Plautus*, that the head thought himselfe priviledged, as it were with a point of prerogative, to charge the inferior parts with the shame of his owne distemper; *Siccine fit hoc pedes? statin an non? Nam hercle si cecidero vestrum erit flagitium.*[1]

Here leaving the head in his unresistable right of ruling over the bodie, I will to the Soule againe, taking a farther view thereof, as sitting in his other principall seat the hart: when I behold the intricate net or curious web of vaines, spread from it over all the bodie, me thinketh I may well liken it to a little spyder, placed in the middest of her work, where she so caringly and cunningly ordereth the matter, that she presently feeleth the least shake or touch in any though the farthest part of her webb. No lesse feelingly doth the hart perceive, and partake, with any injurie done unto his veines. Sometimes hee sendeth forth the bloud and spirits with a full flush, replenishing all parts plentiously, other while he retireth them home with all speed to his little sconce, to comfort and fortifie it selfe.

It is admirable to see the swift and sudden recourse of bloud, now stirred outwardly at a start like lightning, and anon posting backe in feare of daunger to the hearts succour, leaving a palenesse and trembling in the outward parts. The heart is the well of life, the furnace of heat, the center of bloud, the first living and the last dying part. Agreeably to these vertues or efficacies of the heart, let it be confessed, that everie commonweale acknowledgeth a soveraigne power, from the which it drew his first beginning, of which it receiveth his dearest life bloud, with which it is quickened as with a living fire, to the which it wholy trusteth, and returneth for refuge, by which it is imployed and directed in all intentions, and without which it fayleth of continuance, and is incontinently dissolved. Then to such a Gover-

---

[1] 'Does it go thus, feet? Are you standing or not? For by Jove, if I fall it will be your fault.'

nour which both imparteth to al parts the vaines and artiries of their surest welfare, and hath a sence of any their griefs and wrongs as of his owne; what and how regardant thankfulnesse, service, and observance is deservedly due by the faythfull performance (with the uttermost strayne of the very heartstrings) of all obedience to his commaunds and authoritie.

The heart is of all other the firmest flesh, yet not fed with bloud by any vaynes; and from it all other flesh deriveth by veynes his borrowed living. I have heard it argued, that a King in like sort is alone firmely and absolute stated, in and to the lands of his realme, and that all other owners take from him by the veynes and conveyances which he passeth to them. That which *Aristotle* saith of the heart, That it giveth and imparteth to everie member, but it selfe receiveth or taketh not from any, is a good pattern of regall magnificence and bountie, seeing that nothing more aptly representeth the nature of the soule, or commeth neerer to God himselfe than to do good, and extend reliefs to others, with free heart and open hand, himselfe in the meane while having no need of any. The figure of the hart is shaped sharpe poynted at the lower end, and upward it is more widely spread abroad: To this forme the best princes doe conforme, they open their hearts with a full spread towards vertue, goodnesse, and heavenly things, but do make narrow and close the same against all base appetites of this unhallowed flesh. The heart is the dwelling place of the affections and inclinations of the mind, whereof (as of his owne trayne, family, or household, he alone is to have the government) if they bee let loose with scope to follow their disordered desires, not only the heart it selfe is subdued and trampled upon by their turbulent passions, but the whole bodie also fareth the worse, and taketh no small harme thereby. Right wisely doe Soveraignes hereof take this instruction, to uphold their government in a strict steadinesse, tempering all extremities with an evennesse of moderation, that none about them grow too violent or headstrong, which cannot but worke as a disturbance to their persons, so a disproportion to their states.

Where any affection predominantly reigneth, it draweth thither such humors of the bodie, as are likest and best consorteth to it selfe: as anger calleth to him choller, to further his fiercenesse; mirth cheareth it selfe with the freshest bloud; and sorrow will not bee without the company of sower and dumpish melancholike: So if the Soveraigne in the precincts of his regiment, shall suffer an overgrowing inequalitie of greatnesse to get an head, it will quickly gather to it selfe a syding faction of like disposed disturbers, which will make a shrewd adventure, both of overtopping him, and overturning of his state.

The Soule also hath made choice of some other principall parts in the body, which he needfully useth & imployeth in the ministeriall functions of life; which if they once eyther fayle in their offices, or decay in their essence, the body can neither continue living, nor performe his actions: of which sort may bee reckoned, first the lungs and lights, ordeined for the alaying of the heat in the heart, and the necessitie of respiration: Then the liver, which beginneth the concoction of our susteinance, and the same so prepared, doth recommend over to the hearts more perfect converting and accomodating: Lastly, the milt, the gall, and the kidnies, everie whereof is alotted to some good worke of dissevering the refuse and drossie remnants from the selected and purified nutriment. But for that in these the soule sheweth his weakest and meanest vertue, which is of vegitation onely, whereas in the head, or heart, he displaieth all his glorie, conversing with them as with the darlings of his love, I esteem it of no great merit, to meditate too much of their worth, or to labour the likening of them (which to do were easie and obvious) unto certaine necessarie and essentiall orders or powers in the state. . . .

From this founteine of natures so wise distribution and distinguishment of the parts, in sorting them so orderly to their severall functions, this consideration also floweth and offereth it selfe; that as there must be a proportionablenesse and a kind of unanimitie of the members, for the aiding and adorning of the publike comprehending all: so that foule daughter of darknesse and Chaos, confused and all disturbing Anarchie, is to be exiled, or rather excluded out of this compaction of the body politike. Each part is to know and administer his owne proper worke, without entermixing and entermedling in the offices of any other. Shall the foot be permitted to partake in the point of preeminence with the head? or were it seemlie for the head, leaving his state, to abase himselfe to a toyle *manibus pedibusq*; in the trading businesses? For each member to take upon him all works, as it hath in nature an impossibilitie, so hath it in governance as great an incongruitie. And for any part to neglect the duties properly to it alotted, or to run forth of the circle within the which it is fixed (as quartering it selfe into a new division, by undertaking dispatches of another nature) as it agreeth not with that so well parted, yet uniforme frame of Gods workmanship, so is it not to be suffered neither in any well contrived policie of the governing wisdome. The eye is nor ordeined nor apted to any other worke, than to make use of the light by seeing; and to every singled part there is assigned some more peculier operation or administration, from the which as if *in possessionem suam venerit excludit alios*. To the like confusion it tendeth if the parts be prodigiously dislocated or transferred from their proper to other unfitting places, whereof oftentimes the whole bodie getteth the name of a monster mishapen and distorted. The sences must hold their station like to Sentinels, and attend their generall in and about the head, where they be setled. And in briefe, no parts inward or outward can either do duties, or be indured elswhere, than where both for comlinesse and use they be by natures order placed. The civill bodie may hereby be admonished how to dispose of the severall conditions and degrees of the people, according to the difference of their breed, educations, conversation, or habitation; that imployments or advancements be not unmeet or preposterous, but properly and advantagiously accomodated.

OF POLICY AND THE GOOD ORDERING
OF ESTATES

From *The French Academy*
by Pierre de La Primaudaye
translated by T. Bowes, 1586

> *Government, though high, and low, and lower,*
> *Put into parts, doth keep in one consent,*
> *Congreeing in a full and natural close,*
> *Like Musicke. Therefore doth heaven divide*
> *The state of man in divers functions,*
> *Setting endevour in continual motion:*
> *To which is fixed as an ayme or butt,*
> *Obedience: for so worke theHony Bees,*
> *Creatures that by a rule in Nature teach*
> *The Act of Order to a peopled Kingdome.*

Henry V

❧

i

If we are able to discerne between the bodie & the soule, betweene this transitorie life and the life to come which is
eternall, we will not thinke it strange, that one part of mans
building should bee created to remaine free for ever, and to
bee exempted from the yoke of humane power, acknowledging
onely the spirituall jurisdiction, and the other part to be in servitude, and to receive commandement from those humane and
civill offices, which are to be kept amongst men. *In the kingdome
of God* (saith *Paule*) *there is neither Jew nor Græcian, neither bond*

nor free, neither Barbarian nor Scythian, but Jesus Christ is all in all. Stand fast in the libertie wherewith you are made free. And by and by after he addeth: *Onely use not your libertie as an occasion to the flesh, but by love serve one another.* And else-where he saith: *Let every soule be subject to the higher powers: for there is no power but of God. Whosoever therefore resisteth the power, resisteth the ordinance of God.* Whereby it appeereth that they which thinke that the maintenance of civil policies are the worke of man only, are greatly deceived. For we must of necessitie beleeve, that it proceedeth from the counsel of God, and from his eternal providence, without which neither the round frame of the world, nor cities and townes could in any sort abide stedfast: and so that it is very necessary for their preservation, that certaine lawes should be appointed, according unto which men may live honestly and justly one with another. As there are then two chiefe regiments and governments in man, of which one respecteth the soule, & acknowledgeth no temporall king or master, but holdeth of one onely Jesus Christ according to the ministerie of his word, and the other is to ordaine a civill justice onely, and to reforme outward maners, wherunto the body during this life is wholy subject, reserving the first estate of man in his freedome according to the divine rule of pietie, we are diligently to looke to this second estate of subjection & servitude, which is most necessarie for the maintenance of common peace and tranquillitie amongst men. Now forasmuch as we have hitherto noted the morall vertues of the soule, for the better framing of mens actions to that which is decent and honest in this life, and folowing the same order have also given rules and instructions for the government of a familie, we are now to enter into this large field of humane policie, and to consider of the parts that belong unto it, referring the chiefe scope of the handling of this matter, which otherwise would be infinite, to the ruling and preserving of our French Monarchie, for the instruction of all estates that are therein. And first we will see what civil Policie is, and intreat briefly of the divers kindes of governments among the ancients, that we may so much the better attaine to the knowledge of that under which we live.

Everie civill societie must be kept in order by some policie, which is a necessarie helpe to cause a man to walke in his vocation. But as the elements cannot be intermingled one with another, except it be by an unequall proportion and temperature: so I think that civill policies cannot well be preserved but by a certaine inequalitie which is to be seene in all countries by divers sorts of governments.

In all things compounded of matter and forme, commanding and obeying are so natural, that there is some shew thereof even in things without life: as we see in that harmonie which consisteth in voice, and in sounds, wherein the contra-tenor seemeth to command over the base. This whole inferior world obeieth the superior, and is governed thereby, through a certaine vertue accompanied with light and heate, called of many Philosophers the spirit of the world, or as *Plato* saith, the soule of the world, which descending from the celestiall nature, and intermingling it selfe throughout the whole masse of this great bodie, penetrateth, quickeneth, nourisheth and moderateth all changeable things under the moone. The chiefe minister and disposer of this vertue is the Sunne, whom we acknowledge as king among the starres, lightening the universall frame with his beams. The moone is as it were the Queene, ruling over all moistures, and among other marvels, shewing hir manifest power over the flowing and ebbing of the Ocean seas. We see among the Elements that the Fire and Aire through their first qualities are Active, & that the water and earth are Passive, as being more materiall. Amongst all kindes of birds the Eagle is president, amongst beasts the Lion. In fresh and salt waters the mightiest fishes rule, as the Whale in the sea, and the Pike in pooles. Man ruleth over all living creatures, and in man compounded of bodie, soule, and understanding, the soule commandeth over the bodie, and the understanding over the desire. We have also seene by proceeding from one particular man to a familie made of manie persons, how the head commandeth diversly over the parts of his house. Even so it is necessarie, that everie civill societie, which is made one of manie families tending to a generall good, should be kept in by some policie consisting in commanding and obeying. In many places of the world there are countries where the cities are not inclosed, where there is no use of learning, and where there are no kings. Other people there are that dwell in no houses, that use no monie, that live with rawe flesh: in a word, that seeme to hold more of the nature of beasts than of men. And yet there are none that have no kind of policie established amongst them, or that use no laws or customes, whereunto they willingly submit themselves. Neither are they without some apprehension & reverence of the divine nature, using praiers and sacrifices, although damnable: so straightly are these two things, *Divine Justice and humane Policie* joined togither, that the one cannot in any sort remaine amongst men without the other. Therefore *Plutarke* saith, that a citie will sooner stand without a foundation, than civil policie can be framed & established without any religion and opinion of God, or without the preservation thereof after it is once received. Moreover, the first agreement of people forsaking their barbarous and rusticall life, to joine in civill societie, was to this end, that they might have a place of Religion to keepe them togither. Religion surely is the foundation of all common-wealthes, of the execution of lawes, of the obedience of subjects towards their magistrates, of their feare towards princes, of mutuall love among themselves, and of justice towards others. *Lycurgus* reformed the estate of the Lacedemonians, *Numa Pompilius* of the Romans, *Solon* of the Athenians, and *Deucalion* of all the Græcians generally, by making them devout and affectionate towards the gods in praiers, othes, oracles, and prophesies, through the meanes of feare and hope of the divine nature, which they imprinted in them. *Polybius* governor and lieutenant to *Scipio Africanus*, and taken for the wisest Politician in his time, saith, that the Romans had never any greater meanes than religion, to extend the borders of their empire, and the glorie of their famous acts over all the earth. Desiring therefore that religion, the truth, and the lawe of God, all which are one, and published by the mouth of God, may continue and dwell amongst us, let us see what Policie is, whereunto it ought chiefly to tend, and what sundrie sorts there are of establishing it, by the contrarie kinds of government used among the ancients. Policie is a word derived of this Greeke word πολιτεία, which signifieth the regiment of a citie or commonwealth: and that which the Græcians cal Politicall government, the Latins call the government of a common-wealth, or of a civill societie. This word *Policie* hath been taken in manie significations amongst the ancients:

somtime it signifieth a Burgesie, that is to say, the participation and enjoying of the rights and privileges of a towne: somtime the maner of life used by some politicall person: as when one commendeth the policie of *Pericles*, or of *Bias*, that is, their kind of government: somtime also when they would note some woorthie deede in the government of the common-wealth, they said, *That man hath wrought an act of policie this day*. But the cheefe signification of this word, and that which answereth to our present discourse, is *The order and estate whereby one or many townes are governed, and publike affaires well managed and administred*. But before wee begin to speake of the divers sorts of Policies, that is to say, of governments of townes, of which all Common-wealthes and Monarchies are compounded, let us speake a word of the end of the policie, and of that marke whereat it ought especially to aime. As all Cities and civill societies are appointed for the obtaining of some *Good*, so all policie respecteth the same, and tendeth to no other thing, than to unite and frame us to the companie of men so long as we live amongst them: to conforme our maners to a civill justice, to set us at agreement one with another, and to maintaine and preserve common peace and tranquillity, by procuring that everie one may have his owne. It is the cause that men do communicate togither without fraud or hurt, that the insolencie of the wicked is brideled and punished: briefly, that not onelie all duties of humanitie are used amongst men, but also that some publicke forme of religion appeereth, and that blasphemies against the divine nature, and other offences which trouble common quietnes are not openly broched. For although it falleth not within the compasse of mans power, as wee said, to prescribe and appoint by their authoritie any regiment and government over soules, yet every one is not to be suffered to forget at his pleasure lawes concerning religion, and the maner of serving God. But civill ordinance must carefully provide, that the true service of God be not publikelie violated and polluted through an uncontrolled libertie, especially considering that the conservation of every well ordered policie dependeth therupon. But we shal understand this matter more at large heerafter in the particular handling of the parts of an estate, which we will divide into three principal & general heads, following therin the ancient

Politiks, namely, into the Magistrate, the Law, & the people. Now to go on with that which was propounded unto us, let us speake of those kinds of governments which were amongst the ancients. The ordinance of a citie, or order among magistrates, especially amongst them that had the soveraign rule over al, was called of the ancients, *Common-wealth*, or as some others wil have it, *Weale-publike*, which in hir kind of government was named according to the qualitie of the chiefe rulers therof. And those Common-wealths that tended to common benefit were said to be right, and simply just: but if they respected the profit of the superiors onely, they were said to be corrupt, and were called transgressions of right Common-wealths, these being the cause of as much evill to the whole bodie of the citie, as the others are of *Good*. For as the good or evill of an house dependeth of the father of the familie, the safetie or losse of a ship, of the Pilot or master, the goode or ill successe of an armie, of the generall thereof: so the happines or unhappines of townes and peoples dependeth of the magistrates, and yet so that God ruleth over all. Common-wealths then are either good or bad, right or corrupted. That is a good Common-wealth, wherin the governors seeke the publike profite of the citizens, and the benefite of the whole civill societie. It is called right and just, bicause it hath such an end, and seeketh after the same, taking no counsell about any thing, but onely about the preservation of justice. A corrupt common-wealth is that which repugneth and is directly contrarie to that which is good and just, and chiefly to the ende thereof. For it seeketh onely the increase of private commoditie, having no care of publike profit. There are three kinds of good common-wealths, and three of bad, whose government alwaies consisteth in the superiors of the estate, taking their appellation and name of them, as hath beene said. The first kinde of good common-wealths is a Monarchie, which taketh place when the soveraigntie is in one alone. This respecting publike profite onely, and preferring common benefit alwaies before hir owne private and particular commoditie, taketh upon hir the name of a kingdome, or of kingly power. . . . This forme of regiment by the common consent of the woorthiest philosophers and most excellent men, hath been alwaies taken for the best, happiest, and most assured common-wealth of all others, as that wherein all the lawes of nature guide us. Among all creatures, both with and without life, we alwaies find one that hath the preheminence above the rest of his kind. Among all reasonable creatures, Man: among beasts, the Lion is taken for chiefe: among birds, the Eagle: among graine, wheate: among drinkes, wine: among spices, baulme: among al mettals, gold: among all the elements, the fire. By which naturall demonstration we may judge, that the kingly monarchicall government draweth neerest to nature of all others. But if she looke unto his particular benefit that ruleth, seeking to raigne by an absolute will without any observation of just lawes, then she hath the name of tyrannie, which is the first bad kinde of common-wealth. . . .

The second kind of a right & good common-wealth is of a Greek word called an *Aristocratie*, which in our language we may interpret, *the power of the best men*, whom we cal in Latin *Optimates*, bicause they are accounted for the best & most vertuous men. This form of government taketh place when a few tried and approoved men for manners & learning have the soveraigntie jointly togither, and make lawes for the rest of the people, whether it be generally or particularly, directing their thoughts to no other marke than to publike utilitie and profit. This was seen most excellently among the Lacedemonians, whose common-welth surpassed al others of hir time, as wel for hir policie and establishment, wherof there was never the like, and wherein she continued about 500 yeeres, as also for the glorie of hir warlike acts, whereby she helde the empire of Græcia a long time, under the lawes of that happie Aristocraticall goverment, which *Lycurgus* established there. This man seeing their estate to incline one while to tyrannie, when the kings had too much power, and another while to popular confusion, when the common people began to usurpe too great authoritie, devised with himselfe to give them a counterpoize, that should be healthfull for the whole bodie of the Commonwealth, by establishing there a Senate, which was as a strong barre, holding both the extremities in equal ballance, and giving firme and stedfast footing to their estate. . . . That policie then is truly Aristocratical, wherin vertue onely is respected in the distribution of magistracies, and the benefit of the subjects is chiefly considered in the government thereof. *Oligarchie* is op-

posite and contrarie to this, and is the second kinde of a corrupted common-wealth. This is when a few noble or rich men
occupie the authoritie and administration of the common-wealth,
rejecting the poorer and baser sort, and aiming at nothing but at
their owne private and particular profit, without all care of publike commoditie. These men alwaies use to take part with their
like in nobilitie or riches, to the treading downe and oppression
of the meaner sort of people. Moreover, they rule all matters
according to their affections, and through ambition and covet-
ousnes take them into their own hands, until some one that is
mightiest amongst them, find the meanes to rule absolutely, and
to change the Oligarchie into a tyrannie.

The third kind of a good and right common-wealth is of a
Greeke word called Timocratie, which we may cal *The power of
meane or indifferent wealth*. This kinde of government was after
a peculiar sort called of the Ancients by the name of *Common-
wealth*: bicause this policie tended most of all to publike profit,
and was guided by lawes, and compounded of an Oligarchie and
a Democratie, which are two extremes, and of themselves vici-
ous and corrupt. For of their mediocrities this forme of common-
wealth was instituted after three sorts. First, by taking the lawes
and institutions of both: secondly, by holding the mediocritie of
things commanded by them: thirdly, by following the constitutions, partly of the one, and partly of the other. *Aristotle* speaketh
of this kind of Common-wealth when he saith, That civill
societie consisting of meane persons is very good, and that those
cities are well governed wherin there are many of the middle
sort, who have more power than both the other parties, or at
least than any one of them. For whereas manie are passing rich,
or extreme poore, there followeth either an extreme Democratie, or an intolerable Oligarchie, or else through their excesse,
a tyrannie.

Now the last kind of corrupt common-wealths remaineth to be
seene, which is called Democratie, where free and poore men
being the greater number, are lords of the estate. There were
five sorts of them: the first, where the government was equally
communicated to all: the second, where regard was had to
wealth, although it was but small: the third, where all the
citizens were partakers of the government under the ruling of

the law: the fourth, where everie one might attaine to the magistracie, so that he were a citizen, and the law ruled: the fift,
where other things being equall, the multitude commanded and
not the law: and then the people onely governed, according to
their fansie by decrees and provisoes, which they gave out daily,
oppressing the vertuous, rich & noble, that they might live in all
libertie. This kind is not to be called a Common-wealth, seeing
the lawes beare no sway, but being answerable to a tyrannie, it
is passing ill, and unwoorthie to bee numbred among Common-
wealths. *Plato* and *Xenophon* wrote, that the Democratie of
Athens was such a one, where the people was given over to all
licentiousnes without either feare of Magistrates, or observation of lawes. Now of the three kindes of good Common-wealths
mentioned by us, *Aristotle*, *Polybius*, *Dionysius Halicarnassæus* and
Cicero, compound another, that is partaker of all three: saying,
that everie kinde of Common-wealth established simply, and
alone by it selfe, soone degenerateth into the next vice, if it be
not moderated and kept back by the rest. Therefore they say
that a Common-wealth erected with a right government to continue long, must have the vertues and properties of the other
Common-wealths, joined togither in hir, to the ende that nothing grow out of proportion, which may cause hir to degene-
rate into hir next evil, and so consequently overthrow hir. Likewise many ancient and late Politikes have maintained, that the
Common-wealths of the Lacedemonians, Carthaginians, Romans,
and others that are famous, as that of the Venitians, were compound and mildly intermingled with the royall, Aristocraticall,
and popular power. But this subject deserveth well a severall
discourse, which being needlesse for the understanding of the
matter heere propounded unto us, wee will not stay any longer
in the curious searching out of sundrie other kindes of estates
and policies, which the ancients have drawen out of these alreadie
described. We will note therefore for the conclusion of our
speech, that the reason why so manie kinds of Common-wealthes
are mentioned by the ancients is this, bicause everie citie is compounded of many parts, the diversitie of which, according as they
were in greater number and power, caused them to varie the
names of governments. But to avoide confusion and obscuritie,
we may say, that if the soveraigntie consisteth in one onely

prince, the Estate is Monarchicall: if all the people have interest in it, the Estate is popular: and if onely the least part of them have the chiefe power, the Estate is Aristocraticall. But if their forme of government be contrarie to their nature, they take another qualitie but change not their essence. Moreover we say, that the preservation of everie publike societie dependeth of the policie well ordained, without which there can bee nothing but disorder and confusion among men. We say, that policie is the order of a citie in the offices of magistracie, namely, in the chiefe of all, in whose government the whole Common-wealth consisteth: which if it be in the peoples hands, is called Popular, in the Cantons of Switzerland, and leagues of the Grisons, in manie free townes in Germanie, and in olde time was in Athens: if in the hands of certaine persons, as of the gentlemen of Venice, and of some families in Genes, it is called Aristocraticall: if it dependeth of the will of one alone, it is called a Monarchie, as in France, Spaine, Portingale, England, Scotland, Sweathland, Polonia. Further we say, that the diversitie of government among cities and peoples, dependeth of their end: if they tende to a good ende, which is to publike benefite, they are good and just: but if to an ill ende, namely, to the particular profite of such as commaund, they are evill and unjust.

ii

As we see that in the body of this universal frame, there is (as the Philosophers say) matter, forme, privation, simplicitie, mixture, substance, quantitie, action and passion, and that the whole world being compounded of unlike elements, of earth, water, aire and fire, is notwithstanding preserved by an Analogie and proportion, which they have togither: and as we see in a mans bodie, head, hands, feete, eies, nose, eares: in a house, the husband, wife, children, master, servants: in a politike bodie, Magistrates, Nobles, common people, artificers: and that everie bodie mingled with heate, colde, drie and moist, is preserved by the same reason of analogie and proportion which they have togither: So is it in every common-wealth well appointed and ordred, which consisting of many & sundry subjects, is maintained by their unitie, being brought to be of one consent & will, and to communicate their works, arts and exercises to-

gither for common benefit and profit. For every one is best in his
own art, neither can all men do all things. And if it be a very
hard matter to be excellent in any one vocation, it is impossible
to excell in all, and to exercise them duly. Now we say that sixe
things are necessarily required to frame a happy citie & civil
societie, namely, sacrifices, judgements, armes, riches, arts, and
Aliments: unto which sixe things and works, sixe sorts of men
are answerable, Pastors, magistrates, nobles, burgesses, artificers and husbandmen. Therefore to begin the particular handling of the dutie and office of these callings, & that as briefly as
I can, we are first to note, that never any nation in al the world
was so barbarous, or so far estranged from civilitie, that did not
acknowledge and adore some divine nature, and use some kinde
of sacrifices, and so consequently that had not some priests to
exercise them, and some proper ceremonies. *Aristotle* in his
Politickes saith expresly, that it is a necessarie thing to have
priests in every citie, to take care of the worship of the gods and
of sacrifices. . . . So that if sacrifices and priests alwaies tooke
place among the Barbarians, much more carefull ought they be
to maintain this divine mysterie, that adore and perfectly know
God. And as men have lived under three lawes, the law of
Nature, the written law, & the law of Grace, so there were
sacrifices and priests under every one of them. . . .

The second thing that is necessarie in everie Common-wealth
and citie, are judgements, and consequentlie magistrates to
execute them. But bicause wee discoursed at large of this
matter before, we will not stande long upon it, but comprehende
in fewe words the whole duetie and office of a good magistrate,
which consisteth in foure things: In taking nothing unjustly
from any body, in giving to every one his owne, in despising his
owne profite, in in preserving publike profite. He performeth
these duties perfectly by the distribution of justice into seaven
parts: *by procuring that God may bee worshipped, that reverence be
given to superiours, that concord be amongst equals, that discipline be
used towards inferiours, patience towards enimies, mercy towards
the poore, and that integritie of life proceed from himselfe.* Now let
us consider of Armes, and of Nobles. Armes (as *Varro* saith)
are all warlike instruments, serving both to set upon our enimies,
and to defende our selves from their assaults and enterprises.

They are necessarie in a Common-wealth and citie for these three causes, to resist the outward force of enimies, and to keepe them in feare: to repres naughtie citizens, both by compelling them to obey magistrats and lawes, and by punishing the guiltie: and last of al, to defend the libertie of subjects. The exercise and use of armes, warres and battels, hath from all antiquitie beene committed to the noble men. Nobilitie (as *Aristotle* saith) is a glittering excellencie proceeding from ancestours, and an honour that commeth from an auncient linage and stocke. Or, (according to *Boetius Severinus*) nobilitie is a praise that proceedeth from the deserts of our Elders, and forefathers. Manie make three kinds of Nobilitie: one that is bred of vertue & of excellent deeds: the second that proceedeth from the knowledge of honest disciplines and true sciences: and the thirde that commeth from the scutchions and Armes of our auncestors, or from riches. But to speake truelie, there is no right Nobilitie, but that which springeth of vertue, and good conditions. For as hee is a theefe that stealeth, and he unjust that doth unjustlie: so he is a vile and base person, that dealeth vilanouslie. He boasteth in vain of his great linage, and seeketh to bee esteemed for the nobilitie and vertue of his auncestours, that hath no goodnes in him, nor commendable qualitie of his owne to joine with those of his predecessors. Let no man please himself too much (saith *Agapetus*) in the nobilitie of his auncestors, for all men have dung for their stocke from whence they come: both they that are pricked up in purple and fine linnen, & they that are afflicted with povertie and sicknesse: as well they that are decked with crownes, as they that lie naked upon the strawe. Let us not therefore brag of our earthlie race, but let us glory in the integritie of maners. Although vice be in one that commeth of noble bloud, yet it is alwaies lothsome and infamous: yea it doth so much the more appeer shameful and odious, as it is joined with greater nobilitie. But vertue is the verie lively colour and ornament of nobilitie, & causeth it to be honored for love of it selfe onely. . . . The brier and the rose came of one and the same roote: so noble men & vile persons came of one masse and lumpe. The brier is rejected bicause it pricketh, and the rose for hir good smell is esteemed & held in mens hands. So he that maketh himself vile through vice, ought to be rejected, and he that is odoriferous

and smelleth sweetly by good vertues and noble actions, ought
to be esteemed, honored and accounted noble of what race and
stocke soever hee commeth. True it is, that ancient nobilitie
joined with excellent vertue, is verie commendable among men,
especiallie in everie monarchie well established, of which the
nobilitie is the chiefest pillar, being appointed by God, and approoved by the lawe of man, for their fidelitie towardes their
kings, and defence of their subjects, wherein the true dutie and
office of noble-men consisteth. Riches are the fourth thing necessarie in everie common-welth, and consequently Citizens, who
commonly possesse them, and are setled from all antiquitie in
townes, having rents, revenues and possessions, & being as it
were the strong pillars of cities, & of the whole politicall body.
Cicero saith, that riches are the sinews of battels. For as the
whole bodie of a man feeleth and mooveth by the sinews: so the
body of the common-welth receiveth strength & power by riches
to gather men of war togither in defence of hir liberty. For this
cause *Aristotle* in his plat-form of a happy common-welth requireth abundance of wealth and money to helpe publike affaires
at home, & warlike matters abroade. And in another place he
saith, that a happy life consisteth in the perfect use of vertue,
assisted with bodily & external goods, as with instruments that
serve to execute honest actions wel & vertuously. It is certaine
that gold & silver in respect of the soule, are neither good nor ill,
but by good usage they are made profitable for this life, & the
abuse of them is hurtfull both to the body & soule. And in deed
riches of their own nature are not to be condemned.

Therfore if the citizens of the common-wealth possesse riches,
if they imploy them upon good works, and that liberally for the
tuition, defence and setting foorth of their countrey, they behave
themselves like good citizens, borne to do good, and to profite
the Common-wealth. The fift thing necessarie in every good
Common-welth and citie, are occupations and consequently
craftsmen. An art is a habite of working according to right
reason, as *Aristotle* saith. Or else an arte is the knowledge of
some certaine thing gotten by use, instruction or reason, tending to necessarie uses for mans life. Some arts consist in Speculation, and others in practise. We call Speculation Theoricall, that
is to say, Speculative: and Action practical, that is to saie, Active.

This worde Artificer is derived of the worde Arte. Nowe bicause that nature is most perfect next to God, the neerer that arte approcheth to nature, the better and perfecter it is, as appeereth in images and pictures: so that arte is nothing else but an imitation of nature. Those Artes that are commonly called Mechanicall, or handy-craftes, whereby they differ from liberal artes, of which we have already discoursed, are of divers sortes. For the better understanding of them we will presuppose that man hath need of three temporall things for the maintenaunce of this life, namely, of *Aliments, Houses*, & *Clothing*. He standeth in need of Aliments to restore the consumption of radical moysture, wasted away by naturall heate, (as the weeke consumeth the oyle in the Lampe) I say to restore it againe by moist nourishment, as by breade, wine, flesh, and other aliments, without which a man could not live. These nutriments are provided and prepared by men of Occupations, as by Butchers, Fishmongers, Bakers, Cookes, Vintners, and other handy-crafts-men, which serve and looke to the provision of victuals. Next, men have need of houses, that every one may have his private place of refuge to keepe his body, family, & goods under covert: and these are edifices and frames erected by the arte of building, & made by Masons, Carpenters, Geometricians, Sawyers, Joiners, & other handy-crafts that are occupied in carving. Likewise a citie, in respect both of ornament and of defence, standeth in need of wals, towers, bulwarks, rampires, & other things of defence, as also of temples and other common places: all which cannot be made without the artes of building and of Masonry. The third thing which men stand in neede of, are garments to cloth themselves withall, to preserve natural heate, & to keepe out external cold; & these are provided by Mercers, Drapers, Tailors, Hosiers, & such like. Besides the above-named things we stand in need of armour & of horses to defend our liberty, & for our greater commodity: and so consequently Armorers, Glazers, Sadlers, Spur-makers, Smithes and such like, are necessarie. Likewise for the preservation & recovery of our health, we must honour the Physition, Chirurgion, Apothecarie, Drug-seller and such like. The duty and office of al artificers, is to avoid idlenes, sloth, and negligence, & especially to use no deceit in their artes, but to refer the end of their labors more to common profit

In

than to their private gaine. And for the avoiding of Ingrossers, it is very expedient that the crafts-men shoulde bee divided into divers parts of the city, and not placed all on a rowe in one quarter therof, as they do in the towns of Afrike, and in many cities of Europe. For besides the discommodities in great towns, when everie quarter hath not in it such artificers as are commonly necessary, it is to bee feared that there will be amongst them Ingrossers to forestall the merchandise and wares: or else jelousie & quarels are to be feared, if one sell better cheape than another, even before his eies that refused to take that mony. It is tru, that such artificers as are least required, as men that live by the hammer may be ranged in one quarter, that therby they may be separated from men of learning and quietnes. The sixt & last thing necessary in a Commonwelth remaineth to be considered of, namely, Aliments, & consequently laborers. We have already spoken of Aliments: but as for that which concerneth husbandry especially, there is no other arte, that doth more awaken the mind of man, that ravisheth his senses more, that affordeth greter pleasure, or is more necessarie & profitable for the life of man, than husbandry. Moreover nothing savoureth of greater antiquitie, nothing doth better discover the greatnes of the works of God, nothing doth cast foorth more lively marks and beames of a woonderfull divinitie, than husbandry. For most of other artes were invented long time after man was created of God, & augmented since by the industry of many. Onely husbandry gave sufficient testimonie of it selfe, and of the incomprehensible power of God, when presently after the creation of the elements there came out of the bowels of the earth al kinds of herbs and plants garnished with their proper vertues for the service and commodity of man. Man himselfe also by a divine & natural instinct hath been from the beginning more enclined and disposed to the tillage of the earth, than to any other study & vocation whatsoever: as we read of our first fathers who commonly called themselves Laborers of the earth, and feeders of cattel. Husbandry & the countrey life were so much commended & esteemed of the ancients, that many of them have written sundry books therof in Greek & Latin: and many monarches have heertofore left their great palaces, & contemned their purple robes & diademes, that they might give themselves to the

manuring of the countrey commodities. *Cyrus* was never better
pleased and contented, than when hee might be dressing of som
goodly peece of ground, & setting of a certain number of trees
checkerwise. *Dioclesian* forsook the scepter of his empire, that he
might withdraw himselfe into the fields, & trim with his own
hands, trees, graffs, several plots of ground, & gardens. Besides
in husbandry and the countrey life, profite aboundeth with pleasure, and gaine with delight. As for profit it is very evident. For
a good husbandman is alwais provided of bread, wine, flesh,
fruit, wood, and other aliments. And concerning pleasure, it is
incredible to one that hath skill and will to consider of the marvels of nature, besides a thousand delights, with exercises as
pleasant and profitable for his health as can be. And that benefit
which is most excellent and chiefest of all, I meane tranquillitie
of minde may more easily be obtained by the Muses darlings,
and lovers of knowledge in the midst of the open fields and pleasant sound of waters, than amongst the noise of suits and dissen-
tions wherewith cities are replenished. It belongeth to the dutie
of labourers to live in their simplicitie, and to do their endevor
in tilling the fields. For the performing heerof they stand in
neede of three things: of skill to knowe the nature of the soile,
and the seasons of sowing and gathering; of wil to be diligent
and carefull to continue in their countrey labor: & lastly of
ability to provide oxen, horses, cattel, and other instruments of
husbandrie. By this discourse therfore we may see what things
are most requisite and necessary for the institution of a happie
common-wealth, & that no man is so industrious, witty or prudent, that of himselfe without the helpe of another hee can live
without societie, and minister to himself al necessary things.
For this cause the fellowship of many togither was found out,
that by teaching, judging, defending, giving, taking, changing,
serving & communicating their works and exercises one with
another, they might live well and commodiously togither. Which
thing will undoubtedly come to passe in every common-wealth,
when every one walking in his vocation, directeth his will and
worke to the service of God, his prince and countrey.

THE INVENTION OF ARTS

From *Of the Interchangeable Course of Things*
by Louis LeRoy
translated by R. Ashley, 1594

> *Now Man, that erst hail-fellow was with beast,*
> *Wox on to ween himself a god at least.*
> *No airy fowl can take so high a flight,*
> *Though she her daring wings in clouds have dight;*
> *Nor fish can dive so deep in yielding sea,*
> *Though Thetis' self should swear her safety;*
> *Nor fearful beast can dig his cave so low,*
> *All could he further than Earth's centre go;*
> *As that the air, the earth, or ocean,*
> *Should shield them from the gorge of greedy man.*
>
> JOSEPH HALL, *Virgidemiarum*

*P*lato a most renowmed Phylosopher amongest all that
ever were celebrated for the knowledge of learning, representing under a fable the first estate of mankinde,
fayneth, that at the beginning the Gods were alone afore
there were any mortall Creatures: but that the fatal destiny of
generation being come; they framed them in the bowels of the
earth, and made them of fire, and of earth, with other thinges
mingled with them; And that being willing to bring them into
light, they gave the charge to Prometheus, and Epimetheus to
distribute to every one his forces, and proprieties. Then Epimetheus prayed Prometheus to let him make the distribution in his
presence; And so goeth about it alone, giving to some, force

without lightnesse, to others lightnesse without force: he armed
some, and for those which were without armes he invented other
succour: Those which he had inclosed in a little body, he lifted
them up into the aire with feathers; or commaunded them to
craule on the earth: He fortifyed such as were growen into a
great Masse with their Masse it selfe: And likewise he proceeded with the rest giving to every one his vertues. After he
had so furnished them, to the end they should not distroy one
another, he gave them meanes to defend them the one from the
other; and to remaine abroad without covert. Clothing some of
them with thicke heare, little houses, or shells and skales of
divers sorts, with feathers, or hard skinnes, against the untem-
peratenes of Winter, & Sommer: and of the same things made
them beds, and natural couches: joining to their feet, clawes,
nailes, and callosites: to their heads, hornes, teeth, and tronks:
then distributed to them food, making some to eate grasse on
the earth; others to feed on fruits, & roots of trees, & others
more greedy to devoure one another. Provided that they which
lived on pray should be in some sort barren, and the others that
were subject to be devoured, more fruitful: to the end that the
kind should continue. For the divine providence hath bin wise
therin, making al fearful beasts, and such as are good to feed on,
very fruitful, lest by being often eaten there should faile of the
kind: even as hurtfull, and harmeful beasts are of small increase.
Therefore the hare is very fruitfull, and alone of al kind of venison, surchargeth the burden in his belly, because that men,
beasts, and birds, do prosecute him to death. Likewise the Cony
is found so ful of rabets that some of them are yet without heare,
others somewhat riper, and others going out of the belly. But
the Lyonesse which is the strongest, and hardiest of all beastes,
never bringeth but one; and but once in her life. But Epimetheus
being not very wise, he gave all to the brute beastes, reserving
nothing for man, whom he left alone without force, without
power, without propertie, starke naked, without armour, without clothing, unhosed, and unshood, without convenient food,
and wanting all things: In such sort that he could not resist
other creatures being then more excellent then himselfe. For the
staggs ran swifter; the beares, and Lions were stronger; the Pea-
cock was fairer; the fox was craftier; the Emmet more diligent;

and the snayle better lodged then he: Every beast found a medicine fit for his malady and hurt; whereof man was ignorant. Of
this came such a confusion that men perished by little and little
thorough divers sorts of crueltie: In such sort that their kind had
soone bin consumed, without the advise of prudent Prometheus;
who seeing so great a fault, to redresse it, stole from Vulcan,
and Minerva the artificial wisedom, togither with the fire: being
not possible to obtaine it, or to use it without fire; and so did
distribute it to mankind: by meanes whereof men began for their
common commoditie to assemble togither for feare of the beastes,
and to the end to resist them, helping one another, and seeking
here and there after safe places for their habitation, they learned
to make houses, and garments to avoid the sharpnes of cold, and
the force of heate; to reserve fruits for their necessitie; to pre-
pare armes for their defence; and to finde out other commodities
for their life. Which finally necessity it selfe, being inventour of
all things, maketh known particularly to the understanding of
men; unto whom were given for helpes, their hands, speach and
reason; Reason to invent, speach to communicate, the hands to
accomplish that which they should either invent themselves by
reason, or learne of others by speach: for no other creature doth
speak in deed, for as much as speach proceedeth of reason; nor
hath hands; though peradventure somewhat like unto handes.
Wherefore man hath first found out by reason the most necessary thinges; as food, clothing; and armes: and afterward such as
serve for pleasure, ornament and magnificence: he hath imposed
names on every thing, invented letters of divers sorts, and sundry kinds of writing; made all arts both mechanical and liberal:
proceeding so farr as to measure the earth, and the sea; to reduce
by instruments the mighty masse of heaven, scarse to be comprehended by understanding, and to propose it before our eyes.
Moreover the same Plato affirmeth that before men lived in company, and spake togither, or that they had begun to invent and
exercise arts; for as much as they alone of al other creatures did
participate of the divine nature, being indewed with an immortall soule; that they by reason of this divine affinitie, did thinke
first that there were Gods, and so honoured them; and prayed to
them: from thence, had religion her beginning, publicke government, judgement, negotiation and traficke by Sea, and by land,

lawes were established, magistrates created, innumerable trades invented, houses, villages, and townes builded, consequently cities, castles, and fortresses; and then kingdoms, and Empires erected. Wherehence hath succeeded, the greatnes, and excellency of mankind such as we see it at this day. From thence I say began religion which is more natural to men then all their other arts, and inventions: no nation in the world having bin found so rude, so cruel, & barbarous; but that it had some appearance of religion. For howbeit that the greater part is ignorant, what God, & how they ought to worship him; yet al notwithstanding do agree that we ought to honour, pray, and feare one God the authour of all things: which is confirmed not only in the first, and most auncient nations, as the Ethiopians, Indians, Armenians, Chaldees, Hebrewes, Assyrians, Egyptians, Greekes, Romains, and Gaules: but also in the Goths, Vandales, Sarazens, Tartarians, Turkes, Persians, Cathayans or Chinoys: And not onely in our hemisphere; but also amongst the Antipodes; and Savages of the new found lands: of whom heretofore we never had any knowledge. They which have navigated thither, have found many people living yet as the first men, without letters, without Lawes, without Kings, without common wealthes, without arts; but yet not without religion: who beleeve, that the soules of the dead go into other places according to such workes as they have done in this life. To intertaine it, have bin appointed cerimonies, praiers ordained, temples edifyed, oratories, chapels, hospitals, almeshouses, cloisters, and covents: Sacrificers or priests have bin instituted, and much respected in all Countries. And if it pleased God that hee woulde be worshipped thoroughout all the world in one selfe same maner, men shoulde be delivered of great hatred, and cruel discorde, happening amongst them thorough the diversitie of Religions.

At the beginning men were very simple and rude in all thinges, little differing from beastes. They did eate in the fieldes and mountaines, the raw fleshe of beastes, or herbes, with their rootes, stalkes, and leaves, which the earth brought foorth of his owne accorde; and in the woodes the fruictes of wilde trees; or venison: on the bankes of the Sea, Rivers, Lakes, Pooles, and Marishes, they fedd on fishes and birdes: They clad them selves with skinnes, in steede of garments; to bee defended from heat

and colde, from winde, raine, and snow, they withdrewe themselves into great holow trees; or under their thick leaved
branches; or into low dyches, hideous caves, holow vautes,
cabins, and lodges made of great logges of wood, and lightly
covered with boughes, stalkes, canes, and reeds. Then having
strong bodies, they nourished themselves with strong meates,
and also lived longer. They abode ever almost in the open aire,
in continuall travaile, and lying on the hard ground, whereso-
ever sleep overtooke them. When they waxed weaker, and
could not digest such meates, nor dwell in the open aire naked,
and uncovered, they were constrayned to seeke by little and
little, to soften this wild and savage maner of lyving, which they
could no longer endure: learning to sow Corne, which before
grew up unknowen amongst herbes and weeds; and to dresse the
vines, which likewise the earth brought forth amongst other
plants; to transplant, and to graffe fruict-trees, to the end to
make the fruicts better; and to dresse and season both flesh and
fish: and then to build, and to assemble themselves in companies,
that they might live the more safely, and commodiously. In such
maner were they reduced, from that brutish life which they led,
to this sweetnes, and civilitie; beginning from that time forward,
to feed, cloath, and lodge themselves in better sort, and more
commodiously.

Now whereas men have taken nourishment, first of tame
beastes, before either of graine, or of fruits: there is no doubt
but that pasturage, grasing, & shepheardrie, were before husbandrie and tillage; as it appeareth by the most auncient nations,
who having so lived from the beginning, have taken their names
there hence, as the Hebrewes, and the Italians, which is to say
shepheards, and that many Nations use it even at this day, exercising (as may be said) a kind of livelie tillage. The tilling and
planting of the earth have bin both invented after pasturage, and
unto both have bin added hunting, fouling, and fishing. On the
one side they have found out the use of Wheat, which in these
partes is found the best and most commodious nourishment: as
also Barley, Millet, Rye, and all other knowen kind of graine.
On the other side, they have found Ryce, Mahiz, and Juca: the
maner to sow, and gather them, to thresh, fan, and winnow, to
boult and sift flower, to knead it, and to make dowe, to mould it,

and raise past, to make loaves, and to bake them in the oven: whereunto are appointed and doe serve, the Millers and Bakers. Then have they added pease and beanes, and other sortes of pulse, both new and old: Herbes of diverse sorts, and rootes; as persley, lettice, spinage, tyme, pepperwort, marjoram, buglosse, maloes, beetes, endive, succorie, purslain, sage, colworts, melons, cucombers, gourds, artichocks, sperage, mugwort, onyons, garlick, leekes, chibols, carrets, parsnebbs, navets, radishes, and turnepps, mingling with them salt, oiles, butter, and suet, to give them a better tast, and make them the more savorie. Moreover the fruits of trees, cheries, plums, peares, apples, peaches, apricocks, mulberies, medlers, quinces, raisins, figgs, olives, citrons, orenges, dates, chestnuts, and marrons. And not content with graine, fruits, herbes, and rootes, they have bin given to eat the flesh, first of themselves, which they have left for the most part with horrour; then of other creatures both tame and wild; of the land, of the water, and flying in the aire; neither leaving inward nor outward part of them, which they have not found mean to season, boile, & seeth, roast & frie, or put in past & bake with saulces, and spices, brought from the fardest parts of the earth, making puddings, saulciges, haggasses, tripes, and chitterlings, which they serve at the beginning of meales with potages, broathes, and sallets; and at the end therof cheeses, tarts, and creames; wafers, junkets, and march-panes, prepared and dressed by Cookes and pybakers: Neither hath their pompe and riot bin any lesse with fishes, both of the sea, and of freshwater. In somuch, that Plutarch in his Symposiacke proposing this question, whether that the Sea or the Earth brought forth most delicate and delicious meates, findeth businesse, and difficultie enough in the decision therof. Moreover being not pleased with milk, nor faire water to drink; they found out a way to brew Beere, and Ale; to draw and presse out Syder of apples and peares; wyne out of grapes, and palmes; and to make sweet drinkes, compounded with honie, as bragget, meath, and metheglem, which they call Medons in Moscovia, and Polonia; and infinite other artificial drinks, which they have dronk in cuppes of gold, silver, cristall, and glasse, spicing them in divers maners. Besides, to make their drink fresher, they have found meanes in some places to keepe snow, and yce, all the yeare. At the first

sitting on the ground they tooke their repast on the grasse, &
under the shadow of leaves: after they made stooles, formes,
benches, tables, and tressels: Table clothes, table napkins,
trenchers, saltsellers, cupbords, vessel, and utensiles of divers
sorts, and fashions; appointing officers fit for these charges: as
Stewards of the house, pantlers; cellerers, carvers, cupbearers,
cookes, boylers, and rosters. Salust blameth the Romains, which
sought in his time by sea and by land, after all sorts of delicacies,
not expecting hunger, nor thirst, nor cold, nor wearinesse; but
preventing all these things by disordinate appetite. Livie telleth
how after the Conquest of Asia, all sorts of superfluities and
delicacies came unto Rome, and that then the Romains began to
make banquets with more curiositie, and cost: And a Cooke,
which before was held amongst them for a servile drudge, began
to come in reputation. Seneca complaineth, that the kitchins were
more celebrated, then the Schooles of Philosophers, & Rhetori-
cians. Who would not wonder to heare tell of the excessive
feasts of Anthonius and Cleopatra? or of the Emperour Caligula,
who consumed on one supper the revenues of three provinces? of
Heliogabalus; of Lucullus; or of the prodigalitie of Esope, and
Apicius, who shortned his life, fearing least goods would faile
him to the maintayning of his sumptuousnes? In one feast made
to Vitellius his brother, were served two thousand dainty fishes,
and seven thousand birds. Good God, how much paine hath bin
procured unto men by their insatiable gluttonie and gurmandise!
how manie sorts of workmen, and their servants hath it set on
work! But their curiositie in apparell hath not bin lesse; to the
furnishing whereof many occupations have bin applied: as the
spinner, carder, tucker, weaver, clothworker, fuller, sherman,
dyer, taylor, cutter, hosier, doubletmaker, linnen draper, sem-
ster, capper, and feltmaker, feathermaker, lacemaker, embro-
derer, felmonger, skinner, furrier, leatherdresser, tanner, currier, cordwayner, and shoomaker. They have spon and woven
flaxe, hempe, woll, cotton, silke, made of wormes, and of it have
made Velvet, Satin, Damaske, Taffeta; and of goats haire, and
camels haire, Grogram, and Chamlet: whereunto have bin added
fustians, bombasies, sarges, cloth of Gold, and Silver, purple,
and skarlet, with other infinite colours: making of these stuffes,
shirts, rochets, wimples, doublets, caps, hats, hoods, gowns,

coats, cloaks, cassocks, jerkins, & jackets, enriched with ornaments, trimmings, embroideries, and laces, after divers fashions,
whith change from Countrie to Countrie, and from day to day,
thorough the lightnes of persons. Of tanned and coried leather
they have made Jerkins, buskins, bootes, shooes, and pantofles,
and lyned and faced them with velvet. They have applied Car-
canets and Chaines to their necks, brasselets to their hands,
rings to their fingers, spectacles to their eies, paynting to their
cheekes, jewels to their eares, tyres and borders of gold to their
heads, and garters to their leggs: distinguishing by the habits,
the Princes from the subjects; the Magistrats from private men;
the noble from the base; the learned from the ignorant; and the
holie from the prophane. What shall I say of the skinns of
Wolves, Sables, Martins, and other precious furres, set from the
farthest parts of the North, which they buy for excessive prices.
Plinie telleth it for a wonderfull strange thing, and full of great
superfluitie, that he had seen Lollia Paulina a Romain Ladie,
widow of the Emperour Caligula, at a wedding banquet, having
her head, necke, and bosome covered, and her handes likewise, with pearles, and Emeraudes, joyned together, and enter-
laced: which jewels were esteemed to bee worth a Million of
crownes.

The Queene Cleopatra comming to meete Antonius in Cilicia,
put her selfe on the ryver Cydnus, into a boate, whose sterne was
all of gold, the sayles of Purple, the oares of Silver, which kept
stroke in rowing with the sound of Musicke: Touching her person, shee was laied under a pavilion of gold tyssued, decked like
the Goddesse Venus, and round about her were marvailous odoriferous and sweet smells, and perfumes. Heliogabalus slept on
a tyke full of hares heares, and partridge-feathers. The bed of
Darius the last King of the Persians, was sumptuouslie garnished, and covered with a vine of golde, in maner of a grate or
lettice, enriched with raisins and grapes hanging in it, all of
precious stones: And at his bedds head, there was in Treasure
five thousand Talents of golde; at his bedds foote, three thousand Talents of Silver: So much and so deerely he esteemed and
valued his nights pleasure, that he would have his head rest on
so great chevisance.

But yet, the excesse in buylding hath bin more outragious, for comming out of hollow trees, hovells, bowers, cabins, and lodges, covered with straw, and reedes, and going into houses buylded with brickes, stones, and marble, cut, squared, and fastened with morter, plaister, lyme, and varnish, hanged with Tapistrie and painted, covered with slattes and tyles, the roofe hollow with arches and vaults, and the flower curiouslie paved and wrought, divided by halles, upper and lower chambers, utter chambers, inner chambers, with-drawing-chambers, bedchambers, wardrobes, cabinets, closets, staires, entries, galleries, and terrasses. They have accomodated arts and artificers for the buylding and furnishing of them: as Architects, masons, plaisterers, tylers, carpenters, smithes, glasiers, tapisters, painters, gravers, cutters, carvers, melters, casters of Images, goldsmithes, gilders, locksmithes, and others: buylding pallaices, castles, townes, cities, bridges, conduicts, pyramides, sepulchers, theaters, amphitheaters, bathes, and porches; turning the course of streames, and raising of mounts, and throwing downe mountains, with prodigalitie exceeding all bounds of reason; hoping thereby to make their names immortall. And whereas it was necessarie for them, intertayning that varietie and magnificence, to trafique by sea and by land, and to have Cariers on them both; to the end to receive from other places, such commodities as they wanted, or to send abroad such things as abounded with them; to navigate, they hollowed first the bodies of trees after the maner of the Indian Canoes, and afterwards made boates, schiffes, pinacies, and gallies, with three, fower, five, sixe, seaven, eight, and ten Oares on a side, yea; to thirtie on a side: foistes, brigantines, barkes, carvels, ships, hulks, gallions, galliasses, armadoes, and argosies, with their tackling, and furniture, of anchors, cabels, mastes, sayles, artillerie, ordinance, victuals, and compas, or boxe: To receive, keepe, and repaire them, arsenals, portes, and havens; To guide, and to man them were appointed Pilots, mariners, sailers, rowers, and gallyslaves: even as carters, wagoners, coachmen, and horse-keepers were ordayned for trafick, and travaile by land. And for both cariages, cursitours, regraters, porters, balencers; Masters of ports, customers, controllers, revisitors, and serchers. To serve which turne with more ease, it was needfull to coine money of gold, silver, brasse, and copper, defined in value by the quantitie and waight; marked with diverse

E

figures, according to the diversitie of the Countrie where it is made: being not possible to use permutation in every thing: and therefore were brought in money-tellers, and changers. Moreover it was necessarie to have Notaries or Scriveners, to passe the contracts of Markets, sergeants, huissiers, solicitors, proctors, informers, auditors, judges, counsailors, presidents, registers, criers, and executours of sentences. For the expedition of roiall letters, Secretaries, Maisters of requests, Chauncelors, or Keepers of seales. The Physicians, Chirurgians, and Apothecaries do serve for health, using druggs, comming for the most part out of strange Countries: as Rheubarbe, Cassia, Aloe, Agarike, and such others. Gymnasts, pedotribes, athletes, fencers, wrastlers, runners, swimmers, leapers, and tumblers, for the exercise of the bodie. For pleasure, and recreation, singers, minstrells, musicians, plaiers on instruments, organists, dauncers, and ballad-makers, rymers, jesters, juglers, barbers, perfumers, drawers of flowers, and curious workes. Also not contented with stickes, and stones, which the simplicitie of nature furnished unto their Choler, they have invented infinite sorts of armes, and weapons, both offenssive and defensive; long-bowes, and crosse-bowes; with arrowes and quivers, slings, darts, javelins, lances, pikes, partysans, halbards, swords, bucklers, rapiers, and daggers, shieldes, targets, cuyrasses, brigandines, headpeeces, helmets, caskes, morions, and salads: gorgets, pauldrons, vantbrasses, tasses, gauntlets, cuisses, and greves: engines to shoote in the field, or to batter wals, catapults, and ramms in old time; and of late canons, double-canons, demy-canons, basilisks, colverins, sakers, faulcons, minions, and chambers: and for smaller shot, and maniable, muskets, calivers, harquebuzes, daggs; and pistols: Serving for the warres, armorers, furbishers, spurriers, sadlers, ryders, horsebreeders, horsekeepers, smithes, and farriers, founders, and mounters of great ordinance, saltpeter-men, powder-makers, canoniers: Colonels, Captains, souldiers, with their Ensignes, trumpets, drummes, and other Officers. Going farther yet, they have found out other estates, offices, and exercises, imploying some about conducting and managing the publick revenewes: as Receivours, Treasorers, Masters of accompts, Auditours, Controllers: Others about the counsaile of Princes, and of States: Others to the establishing and preserving of the

Lawes, seeing to the publick government, to discipline, and correction of maners.

Then amongst so many commodities, idlenesse increasing with ease, and wealth, they applied themselves to the studie of learning; by reason that all naturally desire to know new things, strange, admirable, faire, and variable, and to understand the causes therof; cherishing principally amongst all their senses, their sight and hearing, which do helpe them to have knowledge, but the sight most of all, where hence hath begun this knowledge by admiration; for seeing the Heaven, the Sunne, the Moone, the Starres; and having knowen by their eyes the difference of daies, and nights, the revolutions of the monethes, and the yeares; they applied themselves to contemplate the disposition of the world, and to seeke out the secrets of nature: First, necessitie (as hath bin said) taught them the arts necessarie unto life; after followed those which serve for pleasure, ornament, and magnificence: And after they had gotten opportunitie and leasure, they began to consider all things contayned in the world, being innumerable in multitude, and admirable in beautie; inquiring after their properties, agreements, and differences, whereof they were made, what they became, when, and how they perished, what in them was mortall, and corruptible, and what divine, and perpetual. They were so desirous to learne, that dwelling and living here on earth so little while, they durst undertake to know, not onely what is above, under, and in the earth; as the nature of all sortes of living creatures, and qualities of mettals: but also the nature of the Ocean, and of all waters, and fishes that live therein: Then mounting into the aire, they inquired of the winds, of the raines, haile, snow, thunder, lightning, and other accidents appearing in the middle Region thereof, they ascended by understanding and by art even into Heaven, which they have indevoured to compasse round, imagining two Poles, and one Axeltree to sustain it, distinguishing the planets from the fixed starres, inventing the Zodiack, observing the Solstices, and Equinoxes; the causes of the equalitie, shortnes, and length of daies, and nights; the reasons of shadowes; the maner of discribing, and measuring the world; of sayling out of one Countrie into an other, guiding the way by the windes, and starres: whose movings, conjunctions, and oppositions they have diligently observed; their greatnes, quicknes, or slownes, colours, shinings, serenities, heats, colds; and the power which they have on theis inferiour things, and the good or ill which they signifie: And wholie and altogether the agreement, and sympathie of heaven, and earth; from whence as from a perpetuall spring floweth this universall aboundance, by which this world is uncessantly restored, and renewed. Their industrie hath pierced thorough all; neither the thicknesse of the earth, nor the depth of the Sea, nor the varietie of the aier, neither the heat and brightnes of the fire, nor the spacious largenesse of Heaven, could amaze their understanding. Moreover, they which were most speculative, considering the feeblenes of the senses, the multitude of the sensible things, so small that they can not be perceived; or so moveable, that they are without certaintie; that our life is short; all full of opinions, and customes; and all environed with darknes, and hidden; have thought that by humane discourse, nothing could be certainly knowen, nothing understood, and comprehended: but that, separating our selves from sight, and hearing, and from the whole bodie, we ought to take the thought of the mind, and by the understanding (which is in the Soule, as the sight is in the bodie) to endevour to know the reason every thing, and that which is in it pure and cleane, alwaies simple, and uniforme, without ever being changed by generation, and corruption. These have passed the vault of heaven, so far distant from the earth, and came to the place above; with-drawing themselves by contemplation from the world towards God, from darknes to light, from corruption to eternitie, from ignorance to wisdom, satisfied (as they say) of all their desire; and injoying the knowledge of the trueth: which is of things that are alwaies alike, not receiving any mutation; wherefore they have called this inferiour part of the world, (where there is almost nothing certain, and few things certainly knowen) the region of falshod, and opinion: and the other superiour knowen by reason, and intelligence (where are the formes, and exemplaries of things) the seat of trueth. In this progresse of knowledge, they have knowen some things by natural instinct, without learning; others by observation, use, and experience: others by reasonable discourse, and demonstrations; and others by divine inspiration. But there is such pleasure in this contemplation, that they which with a good will give themselves to it, do easily forgo all other delights, and are so constant, and perseverant, that they admit them not at any time; neither fearing domage, nor losse of goods, nor the blame of the people, and ignominie; but are readie to endure all kind of crosses, and calamities, even to the suffering of voluntarie povertie: which gave occasion to people in times past to say, that Atlas sustained heaven on his shoulders; and that Endymion had long time slept with the Moone; and that Prometheus was tied to the high mountain Caucasus, with a Vulture feeding on his liver: Meaning by such tales to signifie unto us, the great and marvailous studie, which these excellent persons bestowed, in contemplation of celestiall and naturall things. Democritus having begun to withdraw his mind from his senses, put out his owne eies. Anaxagoras forsook his patrimonie. What exceeding pleasure had Aristotle, teaching not onely Athens, and all Greece, but also the universal world, discovering the secrets of nature, before unknowen, and hidden in profound obscuritie, magnifying and boasting himself with good reason, that he had attayned thither, where no other Greeke nor Egiptian had ever come? What contentment received Plato, who did write at 90. yeares of age, and even the verie day that he deceased; who was for his excellent knowledge honoured in Greece, Sicile, and Italie, above the common estimation of men, esteemed by Kings, admired of people: and hath alwaies bin reverenced by all such as desired to have knowledge of divine and humaine things. So men moved by nature with a desire of knowledge, and of the pleasure which is found therein, have invented Grammer, Rhetoricke, and Logicke; for speach, Oration and disputation: Poesie for composition of verses, and rimes: Arithmeticke to number; Geometrie for measure and weight: And passing farther have come to Musicke, consisting in concord of voices and sounds; and in observation of due proportions; Astrologie which serves for consideration of celestiall things; Physicke of naturall things; and Metaphysicke of supernaturall: Theologie of divine things; Ethicke for institution of private maners; Economicke for houshold; Politicke for governments, and states; and Nomotechnicke for knowledge, exposition or interpretation of Lawes. Such hath bin their dexteritie in the inventing of liberall, and mechanicall sciences.

But although there are every where found people, capable of knowledge, so that they be duely instructed; yet notwithstanding, there are some more ingenious, and inventive then the rest, and more apt to certaine sciences, either by naturall inclination, and influence of the heavens, or by the situation of the Countrie wherein they are borne, or by exercise which they use while they are young, or by honour which is nurse of all arts whatsoever, and the rewards which are proposed for the learned and expert therein.

The Babylonians dwelling in spacious plaines, and having nothing to hinder them the whole sight of the heavens, they placed all their studie in observing of the Starres: The like hath bin done by the Egiptians, who have alwaies their aire cleare without cloudes: And by reason of the yearely overflowing of the river Nilus, which covereth and watereth their Countrie, they were constrained to bestow some time on Geometrie. The Phenicians being given to marchandize, invented Arithmeticke; and dwelling neere the Sea, began first navigation; which the Castilians, Portugals, and Englishmen, bordering likewise on the sea, have brought to perfection. It was unseemly amongst the Arcadians not to be skilfull in Musick; which they learned not for pleasure and delight, but for necessitie, to the end to make sweete and gentle by custome, that which was rude in them by nature, by reason of the coldnes of the aire, whereof we participate in our birth, and by their continuance of travaile, in tillage, pasturage, and brutishnes of life. Eloquence flourished at Athens, and at Rome, because that by means therof they were advanced to honours and wealth. In Augustus time, who took pleasure in Poetrie, every one made Verses: and all were Musitians, under Nero. The nations which desired to be great, and grow up by armes, have directed their Lawes and exercises to dominion, honouring and recompensing valiant men, and dishonouring and punishing the cowardes: Such were the Scythians, Egiptians, Persians, Thracians, Lacedemonians, Candians, Gaules, Iberians, Macedonians, and Indians, accounting all noble and gentle that made profession of armes; and the artisans base, and servile. At this day in Turkie, where all is reduced unto force, every one applieth armes, being assured, that in well doing they shall be advanced in pay, revenew, and publick charge: as also the punishment is certaine there for cowardize. The greatest part of good witts in France applie themselves to the Civil Law, and to the practize of it, for the profit which they find therein; and for the honour of innumerable offices of judgement ordayned both in the soveraigne, meane, and inferiour jurisdiction; being both profitable and honourable. The Hetrurians, which had their aire grosse and thicke, subject to thunders, invented the divination of lightning. The Arabians, Cilicians, and Phrygians, being great shepheards, invented that divination which is made by entrailes of beastes, or by the voice of birdes. Philosophie hath bin professed in Greece, full of subtle and sharpe witts. Architecture began in Asia, by the abundance of wealth, and leasure of the great Kings there, having neede of large and ample houses for intertainment, and magnificence of their Courts: Afterwards it flourished in Greece, whence it was banished; and from thence passed into Italie, recovering his ripenesse there: namely, under the Emperours; who as they had subdued the rest of the world by armes, would also surmount them in wonderfull buildings with incredible expences. The Ethiopians, by the abundance of all good herbes, and vigorous simples, which grow in their Countrie, invented the naturall Magick, observing by it, the wonders hidden in the secret proprieties of thinges; their agreements, and contrarieties. Plato in his Charmides, and his first Alcibiades maintayneth, that Zoroaster the Bactrian, and Zamolsis the Scithian, made profession thereof: Then it was transported into Persia, where it remayned long; as we will declare hereafter when we speake of the Persians, and of their Mages.

But as following the generall disposition to vertue, there have alwayes bin heere and there some making profession of wisedome, as the Druides in Gaule, and in great Britayne; the Chaldees in Assyria; the Brachmanes, and Gymnosophistes in the Indies; the Mages in Persia; the Priestes in Egypt; the Philosophers in Greece; the Pharisees in Jurie; the Theologians or Divines in Christendome: yet antiquitie hath given the first praise of Letters to the Ethiopians, attributing the invention to them, which they communicated with the Egiptians their neighbours; where they have bin augmented: from thence they came to the Libians, Babylonians, and Chaldeans; consequently to

the Greeks; then to the Romains; the Arabians, Italians, French-
men, Almains, Englishmen, Spaniards, and Polonians. On which
course of letters, if we think attentively as far forth as is possible
to consider all the time past, and to call to mind againe the
memorie of so many yeres overslipped, repeating from thence
where in histories, beginneth the age of people, and of Cities;
that is to say, about three or fower thousand yeares since men
began to write bookes; we shall find that there hath not bin any
Authour amongst the Gentiles, more auncient then *Homer*: And
that letters have not bin sithence with like earnestnes followed;
nor in all times and countries equally esteemed: but onely in certaine famous ages, which we may tearme Heroicall. In the which
(humaine power and wisdom, keeping companie one with the
other) men have commonly seen, the art Militarie, Eloquence,
Philosophy, the Mathematicks, Physick, Musick, Poetrie, architecture, painting, carving, and graving, to florish together, and
to fall together: as it hath especially hapned in the kingdoms of
Sesostris, Ninus, Cyrus, Alexander; of Augustus and Trajan; of
the Arabians and Sarazens; and in this age, in the which after
they had bin long time a sleepe, they have bin wakened againe,
and have recovered their former strength: which is not to say,
that there have not hapned many other admirable events in other
seasons; but these are most notable: in the which many extra-
ordinarie marvailes have met together in matter of armes, and
of letters; and which have most similitude betweene them; as it
will appeare in reciting of them.

Wherfore is it so come to passe, rather at these times then
at others? and what reason can we give thereof? to the end
the better to understand the present consideration, being of so
great waight, and long deduction: It seemes to some, that we
ought not to marvaile, that in an infinite space of time, as fortune turneth, and varieth diversly, there hapneth by casuall
chance, some accidents like unto others. For be it that there is
no certaine number set downe of accidents that may fall out;
fortune hath fruitful matter enough to produce effects resembl-
ing one an other: or else be it that humaine chances are comprehended in a determinate number, there must needs sometimes
happen like cases, considering that they are brought to passe by
the same causes, and by the same meanes: Others say, that in

length of yeares are certaine periods of the whole world; and in the one, that all arts do grow in reputation, and in the other do fall, and come to be neglected. Others attribute it to honour, and to rewards, which are more proposed at one time then at an other: for asmuch as by good intertainment all men are induced to vertue. And assaying to render a reason wherefore many notable personages meete in the same seasons, or little distant the one from the other, and travayling in divers exercises do obtaine alike excellencie, and reputation; they thinke that mens wits are nourished by emulation, and that sometimes envie, sometimes admiration, doth stir them up, and maketh them mount by little and little to the highest; where it is hard to remaine, since every thing that can not go forward, or upward, doth naturally discend, and retire, yea commonly much faster then it ascended. And as they are provoked to follow or imitate the first, so after they dispaire of going beyond them, or attayning to them, they lose their courage of travayling, and labouring with their hope; leaving the matter as alreadie possessed: which falleth after by negligence, and commeth to contempt. Aristotle, who affirmeth the world to be eternall, and Plato, who said that it had a beginning, but that it should have no end, do both affirme, that infinite things have bin in one, and the same kind, and should bee infinitely; that there is nothing whose like hath not bin; that there should be nothing which had not bin; and that nothing hath bin, but should be againe: That in this maner the Arts and sciences, and other humaine inventions can not be perpetual (those Nations being distroied where they flourished) by reason of extreme heats and inundations, which must needes happen at certaine times by the moving, and progresse of the starres: either by the fire and water, discending from above in exceeding quantitie; or fire breaking out of the earth; or the sea forcibly overflowing his bankes, or by the increase and swelling of rivers, which can not runne into the sea; or that the earth trembling and quaking open it selfe, and violently cast forth the water before inclosed in his entrailes.

But howbeit the Starres have some power towards the disposing of inferiour things; the situation of places, and temperature of the seasons of the yeare do helpe, concerning understandings and maners; the reward and honour proposed unto mans indus-

trie; the learned ages, and liberall Princes, give great advance-
ment unto Arts; and emulation serveth for a spur thereunto:
Notwithstanding for my part, I thinke that God being carefull of
all the parts of the world, doth grant the excellencie of Armes
and of Learning, sometimes unto Asia, sometimes unto Africk,
sometimes unto Europe; establishing the soveraign Empire of
the world, once in the East, another time in the West, another
time in the South, another in the North: and suffering vertue
and vice, valiancie and cowardize, sobrietie and delicacie, knowledge and ignorance, to go from countrie to countrie, honouring
and diffaming the Nations at divers times: to the end that every
one in his turne might have part of good hap and ill; and that
none should waxe proude by overlong prosperitie: as it will appeare to have fallen out unto this present, by particuler recitall
of the Nations accounted the first or chiefest of the world.

THE RUIN OF ESTATES

From *The Beginning, Continuance and Decay of Estates*
by René de Lucinge
translated by I. Finet, 1606

But all things have their end:
Churches, and Citties (which have diseases like to men)
Must have like death that we have.

The Duchess of Malfi

❧

The causes of the fall and ruine of estates

The order that nature observeth in all things created
doth plainly enough teach us that whatsoever is borne
passeth and hastneth towards death; and that all things
which have a beginning necessarilie and interchang-
ably roule towards their end. This proceedeth either of an ordinarie and naturall course, or of the violence and alteration of
compound bodies. Hence we drawe this construction, that
estates change, monarchies faile, and the ruine of one serveth as
the raising of the other.

Againe, as of humaine bodies some are more strong, vigorous,
and of a better composition then others, and so are of a longer
continuance; so we see the same difference in kingdomes and
estates: in as much as some preserve themselves longer, either
because by their nature they are more surely founded (as for
example the Signory of Nobles is more lasting then the popular

estate, and a Monarchal estate more then a common-weale, because a Monarchy keepeth the causes of corruption more aloofe
from her; or is policed with better lawes) or because of the situation which is naturally more strong then the other, as we see at
this day in the Signorie of Venice.

But because this assertion is subject to divers objections, we
will divide it only into two propositions. First then of principalities, some are small, some great, some indifferent, either in
regard of their subsistence or first essence, or of the comparison
which may be made betweene them and their neighbours:
Secondly, the efficient causes of the utter ruine of estates are
either inward, or outward, or mixt: The inward are to be
fetched and conceived in respect of the negligence, ignorance
and riot of Princes which give themselves over to all voluptuous-
nesse; whereto may be added the factions, secret practises, ambitions, and desperate humors of subjects, with sundrie other occasions, all fit to bring estates to their utter ruine. The outward
causes are the stratagemes, armes and force of the enemie. The
mixt are such as participate of both, as are the rebellions of the
people, treasons of particular men, put in execution by forraine
ayd and force. Since then it is so that all principalities are subject to ruine by one of these three causes; we are now to unfold
what maladies may infect, as well great and indifferent, as small
estates; and draw all within the compasse of inward, outward,
and mixt causes.

Now like as in naturall things naturall corruption is more
tolerable then violent, so must we consider whether the alteration and impairing of estates and common weales chance by
reason of age, or by the violence of some not forseene cause.

Returning then to our former division and well examining it,
wee shall finde that small Estates come to their ends rather by
meanes of outward causes (brought in by force and violence)
then otherwise: In as much as their power being insufficient to
withstand their mighty neighbours ambitious attempts, they are
at the first incounter overset with the storm of his conquests; in
this maner the several Signories of Lombardy fel in subjection
either of the Duke of *Milan*, or the Venetians; the free cities of
Thoscany became a pray to the Duke of *Florence*: The Princes
of *Africke* to the King of *Fez-Marocco*, and *Algiers*.

On the contrarie, great Empires are usually subverted by meanes of inward causes; either by ease & plenty, which customarily makes Princes to swell with insupportable pride; by voluptuous riot (whereto people amidst their abundance are most prone) or else by insolency and presumption seazing the great ones of the country when they see themselves much followed and reverenced, all fit inticements to dispose a hart (but indifferently generous) to plot for his own raising.

> *Nec quenquam iam ferre potest Caesarve priorem,*
> *Pompeiusve parem.*

Then is it (as one saith) that *Caesar* cannot brooke a superior, and that *Pompey* stomaketh an equall.

Meane estates undergoe danger as well as the two former, yet far lesse, since they hold the meane as the other the extreams, for they are not so unfurnished of strength, as that it would be easie for every one to invade and oppresse them, neither are they of that greatnesse and wealth, as to afforde matter to particular men to growe mighty, or else abandon themselves immoderatly to delights & pleasures, or to transport themselves beyond the limits of reason. This is it that so long preserved the common weales of *Sparta* & of *Venice*, which evermore respectively intertained a meane and equality.

The mixt causes of the ruine of Estates are inward treacheries and outward force. Treason hatched within an Estate much more indammageth a great then a small or meane Empire. For a monarke is not able to turne his eie upon every corner of his Kingdome; and sturring spirits are fortified in their attempts either with the hope of impunity (the nourse of vices in all Estates and Governments) or with the opinion they have conceived of not being discovered till such time as their projects meete with some good successe. These things happen sooner, when the Prince is far off then at hand. Spaine can witnesse it, which was so unhappily betraied by *Count Julian*, as it thereby fell into the hands of the Moores. So was the Empire of the Mamelucks by the treason of *Caierbeius* possest by *Selim* Emperour of the Turkes. Who would search more narrowly into Christendome shall finde that the civill wars of France minister more examples for proofe of this then is necessary. Thus wee see that small estates are most to stand in feare of forraine force, since they have not wherewith either of or in themselves to be able to resist or to take breath: That the meane estates are alwaies lesse offended by outward force then the smallest, and more free from outward treason then the greatest.

From what conjectures the continuance of estates may be gathered

I will no farther extend the discourse of the former chapter, nor dive into the other efficient causes of the ruine of estates: for should I handle what might be farther said of this matter, I should wander too far from the propounded subject, and perhaps racke the argument beyond his due pitch. I will then tie my selfe only to the conjectures of the continuance or fall of estates, omitting other causes, as also all that may be referred to the judgement of the heavens, the influence of the stars, and to their vertue; sithence this knowledge is fraught with so many obscurities and contrarieties in what is written thereof, as I will spare to search too far into it: Though otherwise we are to imagine that nothing is made in vaine, and that those celestiall bodies move not by chance, but rather by divine order and disposition. Againe, the errors of their Ephimerides and the different supputation of the first masters of their profession, make the knowledge to be uncertaine and their so surely grounded maximes to afforde contrarie resolutions. Let us not meddle then with the aspects of the stars, or the nativities of estates, but regard and consider the effects of what is at our owne home without taking so high a flight. We say then that estates suffer either by the unremoveable ordinance of God, or by the naturall course of time, wherewith in time they grow feeble, and change: or else by the wils of men, so unstable and light, as they ordinarily breede an universall alteration thorowout a whole estate and common-weale. We will only drawe our conjectures from naturall causes (not to meddle with the judgement of the divine Majesty or mans inconstancy) nakedly and simply to speake of them as neere and familiar, to the end we may not enter into the chaos of causes heavenly and most remote.

So then we are to thinke that the continuance of estates is proportioned to their beginning. It is with them as with sensible creatures, which the more they hasten to arrive at the perfection of their being, the sooner also they faile and die: the contrarie is seene in those which with a slow and measured pase attaine to a more faire maturity and perfection: as for example, among beastes the horse, amongst trees the willow are of no long indurance: but those that (as the Hart and Olive) make by degrees and slowly towards their ripenes, are likewise more lasting. We may say the like of Empires and Estates: for as we see them slow or swift in their increase, so are they more swift or slow in their ruine. Have not the French more then once conquered the duchy of *Milan* and the kingdome of *Naples*, and that as a man may say almost in a moment? so have they many times lost it and all in a moment: such conquests resemble Torrents tumbling downe the mountaines, which in lesse then an hour, by reason of the great shoutes of water they bring with them, become fearefull and dangerous; when soone after in an instant, we see them fallen and shallow, so as a childe may wade thorow them without trouble or danger. Now not to leave this conquest of *Milan* and *Naples*, we must to this purpose by examples contrary to the former make good the ground of our proposition: which to performe, I will set before you the manner how the Spaniards conquered and held these provinces.

I finde it hath been by a long course of time, and infinite travaile accompanied with all the paines and troubles, which those who set up their rest upon a conquest and resolve to abide out the wars, ordinarily indure. Hence their labour hath taken such roote, as nothing since hath been able to escape their hands, howsoever they have been oft times galled and put to their plunges. It is requisite then that Empires have their rootes to sustaine them, which must be deepe and sound, otherwise it is impossible they should long continue. Now that they may be such, there is an especiall wisedome and many yeeres required.

The true rootes of an estate are the love of the people towards their Prince, the sincere and holy distribution of Justice amongst the subjects; military discipline well policed and observed by the souldiours; honours, rewards, and benefits bestowed according to vertue and merit: that great men be not slightly set by, abased, or contemned: that the common sort of people be intertained with all honest satisfaction: necessary provisions for the maintenance of places of strength; well husbanding of the treasure; friendly intelligence with neighbour Princes; uncorrupt election of officers; modesty in their proceedings: these are the very true rootes able to fortifie and make monarchies to flourish and raise them to eternity: which rootes can never prove setled spring, or send foorth worthy fruit, unlesse they be planted in the soil of wisdome, advice and industrie, and husbanded by the continuance of time.

It is often seene that great conquests and victories attained without losse of labour, so blinde the Conquerour, as they make him become like one of those long reeds or canes which carry outwardly a good apparence, but are inwardly hollow and of fraile substance. They cause him to contemne his companions, and those who assisted him in obtaining his victories, but more the subdued people, when ordinarily followeth, that the higher is his fortune, the neerer is his fall. Wee have straied sufficiently. It is now high time to returne to our principall discourse: and as we have heretofore made it appeare that there are three sortes of estates; so wee are now to unfold in what ranck of the three the Turke is to be bestowed.

PART THREE

The Universe

THE COPERNICAN SYSTEM

From *A Perfit Description of the Coelestiall Orbes, according
to the most ancient doctrine of the Pythagoreans: lately revived
by Copernicus, and by Geometricall Demonstration approved*
by Thomas Digges, 1576

> *As new Philosophy arrests the Sunne,*
> *And bids the passive earth about it runne,*
> *So wee have dull'd our minde, it hath no ends;*
> *Onely the bodie's busie, and pretends.*
>
> DONNE, *Letter to the Countess of Bedford*

Although in this most excellent and difficile part of
Philosophie in all times have been sundrie opinions
touching the situation and moving of the bodies celestiall, yet in certaine principles, all Philosophers of any
account of all ages have agreed and consented. First that the
Orbe of the fixed stars is of all other the most high, the farthest
distant, and comprehendeth the other Spheres of wandring
starres. And of these straying bodies called Planets, the old
Philosophers thought it a good ground in reason, that the nighest
to the Centre should swiftliest move, because the circle was least
and therby the sooner overpassed: and the further distant, the
more slowly. Therefore as the Moone being swiftest in course,
is found also by measure nighest, so have all agreed that the
Orbe of *Saturn* being in moving the slowest of the Planets, is
also the highest: *Jupiter* the next, and then *Mars*: but of *Venus*

and *Mercury* there hath been great controversie, because they stray not every way from the Sun, as the rest doe. And therfore some have placed them above the Sun,[1] as *Plato* in his *Timaeo*: others beneath, as *Ptolomie*, and the greater part of them that followed him. *Alpetragius* maketh *Venus* above the Sunne, and *Mercury* beneath, and sundrie reasons have been of all sides alleaged in defence of their opinions. They that follow *Plato* (supposing that all starres should have obscure and darke bodies shining with borrowed light like the Moone) have alleaged that if those Planets were lower than the Sunne, then should they sometime obscure some part of the bodie of the Sunne, and also shine, not with a light circular, but segmentarie, and that variable as the Moone: which when they see by experience at one time to happen, they conclude with *Plato*. On the contrarie part, such as will maintaine them beneath, frame a likelihood by reason of the large space between the Orbes of the Sunne and the Moone. For the greatest distance of the Moone is but 64. semidiameters of the earth: and to the nighest of the Sunne are 1160. so that there remaineth betweene the Moone and the Sunne 1905.[2] semidiameters of the earth. And therefore that so huge a space should not remaine emptie, there they situate the Orbes of *Mercury* and *Venus*. . . . They therefore will not confesse that these Planets have any obscuritie in their bodies like the Moone, but that either with their owne proper light, or else being throughly pierced with solar beames, they shine and shew circulare. And having a straying course of latitude, they seldome passe betweene the Sunne and us: or if they should, their bodies being so small could scarcely hide a hundred part of the Sun, and so smal a spot in so noble a light could hardly be discerned. And yet *Averrois* in his *Paraphrasis* on *Ptolomie* affirmeth, that he saw a little spot in the Sunne at such time as by Calculation he had forecast a corporal Conjunction. But how weake this their reason is, it may soone appeare if we consider how from the earth to the lowest of the Moones Orbe there is 38. semidiameters of the earth, or by the truer computation according to *Copernicus* 52. and yet in all that so huge a space we know nothing but the ayre or firie Orbe, if any such be. . . . Againe, the

---

[1] *i.e.*, beyond the fourth sphere of a geocentric universe.
[2] *sic;* for 1096?

reason of *Ptolomie*, that the Sunne must needes be placed in the
middest of those Planets that wander from him at libertie, and
those that are as it were combined to him, is proved senselesse
by the motion of the Moone, whom wee see no lesse to stray
from the Sun, than any of those other three superiour Planets.
But if they will needes have these two Planets Orbes within an
Orbe of the Sunne, what reason can they give why they should
not depart from the Sunne at large, as the other planets doe,
considering the increase of swiftnes in their whole motion must
accompanie the inferiour situation, or else the whole order of
Theoricks should be disturbed?

It is therefore evident, that either there must be some other
Centre, whereunto the order of these Orbes should be referred,
or else no reason in their order, nor cause apparant, why we
should rather to *Saturn* than to *Jupiter* or any of the rest attribute the higher or remoter Orbe. And therefore seemeth it
worthie of consideration that *Martianus Capella* wrote in his
Encyclopedia, and certaine other Latines held, affirming that
Venus and *Mercury* do run about the Sunne in their spheres
peculiar, and therefore could not stray further from the Sunne
than the capacitie of their Orbes would give them leave, because
they encompasse not the earth as the others doe, but have their
Absides after another maner conversed. What other thing
would they hereby signifie, but that the Orbs of these Planets
should environ the Sunne as their Centre. So may the Sphere of
Mercury being not halfe the amplitude of *Venus* Orbe, bee well
situate within the same. And if in like sort wee situate the Orbes
of *Saturn*, *Jupiter* and *Mars*, referring them as it were to the
same Centre, so as their capacitie be such as they containe and
circulate also the earth, happily wee shall not erre, as by evident
Demonstrations in the residue of *Copernicus* Revolutions[1] is
demonstrate. For it is apparant that these Planets nigh the
Sunne, are alwaies least, and further distant, and opposite, and
much greater in sight, and nigher to us: whereby it cannot be,
but the Centre of them is rather to the Sunne, than to the earth
to be referred: as in the Orbes of *Venus* and *Mercury* also.

But if these to the Sunne as to a Centre in this manner be
referred, then must there needs between the convexe Orbe of

[1] *De revolutionibus orbium coelestium*, Nürnberg, 1543.

Venus and the concave of *Mercury* an huge space be left, wherein the earth and Elementarie frame, inclosed with the Luminarie Orbe, of dutie must be situate. For, from the earth the Moone may not be farre removed, being without controversie of al other nighest in place and nature to it: especially considering betweene the same Orbes of *Venus* and *Mercury* there is roome sufficient. Therefor neede we not be ashamed to confesse, this whole globe of Elements enclosed with the Moones sphere, together with the earth as the Centre of the same, to be by this great Orbe, together with the other Planets about the Sunne turned, making by his revolution our yeere. And whatsoever seeme to us to proceede by the moving of the Sunne, the same to proceede indeede by the revolution of the earth, the Sunne still remaining fixed and immoveable in the middest. And the distance of the earth from the Sunne to be such, as being compared with the other Planets, maketh evident alterations, and diversitie of aspects: but if it be referred to the Orbe of starres fixed, then hath it no proportion sensible, but as a point or a Centre to a circumference, which I hold far more reasonable to be granted, than to fall into such an infinite multitude of absurd imaginations, as they were faine to admit that wil needes wilfully maintaine the earths stabilitie is the Centre of the world. But rather herein to direct our selves by that wisedome, we see in all Gods naturall workes, where we may behold one thing rather endued with many vertues and effects, than any superfluous or unnecessarie part admitted. And all these things, although they seeme hard, strange, and incredible, yet to any reasonable man that hath his understanding ripened with Mathematicall demonstration, *Copernicus* in his Revolutions according to his promise, hath made them more evident and cleere than the Sunne beames.

These grounds therefore admitted, which no man reasonably can repugne, that the greater Orbe requireth the longer time to runne his period: the orderly and most beautifull frame of the heavens doth ensue. The first and highest of all is the immoveable sphere of fixed starres, containing it selfe and all the rest, and therefore fixed: as the place universall of rest, whereunto the motions and positions of al inferiour spheres are to be compared. For albeit sundrie Astrologians finding alterations in the declination and longitude of starres, have thought that the same also should have his motion peculiar: yet *Copernicus* by the motions of the earth solveth al, and utterly cutteth off the ninth and tenth spheres, which contrarie to all sense the maintainers of the earths stabilitie have been compelled to imagine.

The first of the moveable Orbes is that of *Saturne*, which, being of all other next unto the infinite Orbe immoveable, garnished with lights innumerable, is also in his course most slow, and once only in thirtie yeeres passeth his period. The second is *Jupiter*, who in twelve yeeres performeth his circuit. *Mars* in two yeeres runneth his circular race. Then followeth the great Orbe, wherein the Globe of mortalitie inclosed in the Moones Orbe as an Epicycle, and holding the earth as a Centre by his owne waight resting alway permanent in the middest of the aire, is carried round once a yeere. In the fifth place is *Venus*, making her revolution in nine moneths. In the sixt is *Mercury*, who passeth his circuit in eighty daies. In the middest of all is the Sunne.

For in so stately a Temple as this, who would desire to set his lampe in any other better or more convenient place than this, from whence uniformely it might distribute light to all: for not unfitly is it of some called the Lampe or light of the world, of others the minde, of others the Ruler of the world.

> *Ad cuius numeros et dii moveantur, et Orbes*
> *Accipiant leges, praescriptaque foedera servent.*

Trismegistus calleth him the visible God. Thus doth the Sun like a King sitting on his throne, governe his Courts of inferiour powers: neither is the Earth defrauded of the service of the Moone: but *Aristotle* saith, that of all other the Moone with the Earth hath nighest alliance, so heere they are matched accordingly.

In this form or frame we may behold such a wonderfull Symmetry of motions and situations, as in no other can be proponed. The times whereby wee the inhabitants of the Earth are directed, are constituted by the revolutions of the Earth: the circulation of her Centre causeth the yeere, the conversion of her circumference maketh the naturall day, and the revolution of the moon produceth the moneth. By the onely view of this Theorick, the cause and reason is apparant, why in *Jupiter* the progressions and Retrogradations are greater than in *Saturn*, and lesse than in *Mars*, why also in *Venus* they are more than in *Mercury*: and why such changes from direct to retrograde, Stationarie, and so on happeneth, notwithstanding more rifely in *Saturne* than in *Jupiter*, and yet more rarely in *Mars*: why in *Venus* not so commonly as in *Mercury*. Also why *Jupiter* and *Mars* are nigher the earth in their Acronicall, than in their Cosmicall or Heliacall rising: especially *Mars*, who, rising at the Sunne set, sheweth in his ruddie fierie colour equall in quantitie with *Jupiter*, and contrariwise, setting little after the Sunne, is scarcely to be discerned from a starre of the second light. All which alterations apparantly follow upon the Earths motion. And that none of these doe happen in the fixed starres, it plainly argueth this huge distance and immeasurable altitude, in respect whereof this great Orbe, wherein the Earth is carried, is but a point, and utterly without sensible proportion, being compared to that Heaven. For as it is in perspective demonstrate, every quantitie hath a certaine proportionable distance whereunto it may be discerned, and beyond the same it may not be seene. This distance therefore of the immoveable Heaven is so exceeding great, that the whole *Orbis magnus* vanisheth away, if it be conferred to that Heaven.

Herein can wee never sufficiently admire this wonderfull and incomprehensible huge frame of Gods worke proponed to our senses, seeing first this ball of the Earth wherein wee move, to the common sort seemeth great, and that in respect of the Moones Orbe is very smal, but compared with *Orbis magnus* wherein it is carried, it scarcely retaineth any sensible proportion: so marveilously is that Orbe of annuall motion greater than this little darke Starre wherein wee live. But that *orbis magnus*, being (as is before declared) but as a poynt in respect of the immensitie of the immoveable Heaven, we may easily consider what little portion of Gods frame our Elementarie corruptible world is, but never sufficiently be able to admire the immensitie of the rest: especially of that fixed Orbe garnished with lights innumerable, and reaching up in Sphericall Altitude without ende. Of which lights Celestiall it is to be thought, that we onely behold such as are in the inferiour parts of the same Orbe: and as they are higher, so seeme they of lesse and lesser quantitie, even till our sight, being not able further to reach or conceive the greatest part of the rest, by reason of their wonderfull distance invisible unto us. And this may well bee thought of us to bee the glorious Court of the great God, whose unsearchable works invisible we may partly by these his visible, conjecture: to whose infinite power and Majestie, such an infinite place surmounting all other both in quantitie and qualitie only is convenient. But because the world hath so long a time beene carried with an opinion of the Earths stabilitie, as the contrarie cannot but be now very imperswasible, I have thought good out of Copernicus also, to give a taste of Reasons Philosophicall alleaged for the earths stabilitie, and their solutions: that such as are not able with Geometricall eyes to beholde the secret perfection of *Copernicus* Theorick, may yet by these familiar and natural reasons be induced to search farther, and not rashly to condemne for phantasticall, so ancient doctrine revived, and by *Copernicus* so demonstratively approved.

What reasons moved Aristotle, and others that followed him, to thinke the earth to rest immoveable as a Centre to the whole world

The most effectuall reasons that they produce to proove the Earths stabilitie in the middle or lowest part of the world, is that of Gravitie and Levitie. For of all other the Element of the earth (say they) is most heavie, and all ponderous things are carried unto it, striving (as it were) to sway even downe to the inmost part thereof. For the earth being round, into the which all waightie things on every side fall, making right angles on the superficies, pass to the Centre, seeing every right line that falleth perpendicularly upon the Horizon in that place where it toucheth the earth, must needes passe by the Centre. And those things that are carried toward that *Medium*, it is likely that there also they would rest. So much therefore the rather shall the earth rest in the middle, and (receiving all things into it selfe that fall) by

his owne waight shall bee most immoveable. Againe, they seeke
to proove it by reason of motion and his nature: for of one and
the same simple bodie, the motion must also be simple, saith
Aristotle. Of simple motions there are two kindes, Right and
Circular: Right are either up or downe: so that every simple
motion is either downward toward the Centre, or upward from
the Centre, or Circular about the Centre. Now unto the earth
and water in respect of their waight, the motion downward is
convenient to seeke the Centre: to Aire and Fire in regard of
their lightnesse, upward and from the Centre. So it is meete to
these Elements to attribute the right or straight motion, and to
the Heavens onely it is proper circularly about this meane or
Centre to be turned round. Thus much *Aristotle*. If therefore
(saith *Ptolomie* of Alexandria) the Earth should turne but onely
by that daily motion, things quite contrarie to these should happen. For his motion should be most swift and violent, that in
foure and twentie houres should let passe the whole circuit of the
Earth: and those things which by sudden turning are stirred, are
altogether unmeet to collect, but rather to disperse things
united, unlesse they should by some firm fasting be kept together. And long ere this, the Earth being dissolved in peeces,
should have been scattered through the heavens, which were
a mockery to think of: and much more, beasts, and all other
waights that are loose could not remain unshaken. And also
things falling should not light on the places perpendicular under
them, neither should they fall directly thereto, the same being
violently in the meane while carried away. Cloudes also and
other things hanging in the Ayre should alwaies seeme to us to
be carried toward the West.

The solution of these Reasons, with their insufficiencie

These are the causes, and such other, wherewith they approve
the Earth to rest in the middle of the world, and that out of all
question. But he that will maintaine the Earths mobilitie, may
say that this motion is not violent but naturall. And these things
which are naturally mooved have effects contrarie to such as are

violently carried. For such motions wherein force and violence
is used, must needes bee dissolved, and cannot bee of long continuance: but those which by nature are caused, remaine still in
their perfite estate, and are conserved and kept in their most
excellent constitution. Without cause therefore did *Ptolomie*
feare least the Earth, and all earthly things should bee torne in
peeces by this Revolution of the Earth, caused by the working of
Nature, whose operations are farre different from those of Arte,
or such as humane intelligence may reach unto. But why should
he not much more think and misdoubt the same of the world,
whose motion must of necessitie bee so much more swift and
vehement than this of the Earth, as the Heaven is greater than
the Earth? Is therefore the Heaven made so huge in quantity
that it might with unspeakeable vehemencie of motion bee
severed from the Centre, least happily resting it should fall, as
some Philosophers have affirmed? Surely, if this reason should
take place, the magnitude of the heaven should infinitly extend.
For the more this motion shoulde violentlie bee carried higher,
the greater should the swiftnesse be, by reason of increasing of
the circumference, which must of necessitie in 24. houres be past
over, and in like manner by increase of the motion, the Magnitude must also necessarilie bee augmented: thus should the
swiftnesse increase Magnitude, and the Magnitude the swiftnesse infinitly. But according to that ground of nature: whatsoever is infinite can never be passed over. The Heaven therefore
of necessity must stand and rest fixed.

But say they, without the heaven there is no body, no place,
no emptinesse, no not any thing at all whether heaven should or
could farther extend. But this surely is very strange, that nothing should have such efficient power to restraine some thing,
the same having a very essence and being. Yet if wee would thus
confesse that the Heaven were indeede infinite upward, and only
finite downeward in respect of his sphericall concavitie: much
more perhaps might that saying bee verified, that without the
heaven is nothing, seeing every thing in respect of the infinite-
nesse thereof had place sufficient within the same. But then must
it of necessitie remaine immoveable. For the chiefest reason that
hath mooved some to thinke the Heaven limitted, was Motion,
which they thought without controversie to bee indeede in it.

But whether the world have his bounds, or bee indeede infinite
and without bounds, let us leave that to bee discussed of Philosophers: sure we are that the Earth is not infinite, but hath a
circumference limitted. Seeing therefore all Philosophers consent that limitted bodies may have motion, and infinite cannot
have any: why doe we yet stagger to confesse motion in the
Earth, being most agreeable to his forme and nature, whose
bounds also and circumference wee knowe, rather then to imagine
that the whole world should sway and turne, whose ende wee
knowe not, ne possiblie can of any mortall man be knowne? And
therfore the true motion indeede to be in the Earth, and the
apparance onely in the Heaven: and that these apparances are
not otherwise then if the Virgilian *Æneas* should say:

Provehimur portu, terraqua urbesque recedunt.[1]

For a ship carried in a smooth Sea with such tranquillitie doth
passe away, that all things on the shores and the seas, to the
saylers seeme to move, and themselves onely quietly to rest with
all such things as are aboord with them: so surely may it be in
the Earth, whose motion being naturall and not forcible, of all
other is most uniform and unperceivable, whereby to us that
sayle therein, the whole worlde may seem to roule about.

But what shall we then say of Clowdes and other things hanging or resting in the ayre or tending upward, but that not onely
the Earth and sea making one Globe, but also no small part of
the ayre is likewise circularly carried, and in like sort al such
things as are derived from them, or have any manner of alliance
with them: either for that the lower Region of the ayre being
mixt with earthly and watrie vapours, follow the same nature of
the Earth: either that it be gained and gotten from the Earth by
reason of Vicinitie or Contiguitie. Which if any man marvaile at,
let him consider how the olde Philosophers did yeeld the same
reason for the Revolution of the highest Region of the ayre,
wherein wee may sometime beholde Comets carried circularly
no otherwise than the bodies Celestiall seeme to be, and yet hath
that Region of the ayre lesse convenience with the Orbes Celestiall then this low part with the Earth. But we affirme that part

[1] *Æneid* iii. 72, where Vergil has *terraeque*.

of the ayre in respect of this great distance to be destitute of this motion terrestriall, and that this part of the ayre that is next to the Earth doth appeare more still and quiet, by reason of his uniforme naturall accompanying of the Earth, and likewise things that hang therein, unlesse by windes or other violent accidents they bee tossed to and fro. For the winde in the ayre is nothing els but as waves in the Sea.

And of things ascending and descending in respect of the world we must confesse them to have a mixt motion of right and circular, albeit it seeme to us right and straight: not otherwise then if in a ship under sayle a man should softly let a plummet down from the top along by the mast even to the deck: this plummet passing alwayes by the straight mast, seemeth also to fall in a straight line, but being by discourse of reason weyed, his motion is found mixt of right and circular. For such things as naturally fall downward, being of earthly nature, there is no doubt but as parts they retaine the nature of the whole. No otherwise is it to those things that by fiery force are caried upward. For the earthly fire is chiefly nourished with earthly matter: and flame is defined to bee naught els but burning fume or smoke, and the propertie of fire is to extend the subject whereinto it entereth, the which it doth with so great violence, as by no meanes or engines it can be constrayned, but that with breach of bands it will performe his nature. This motion extensive is from the Centre to the circumference: so that if any earthly part be fiered, it is carried violently upward. Therefore whenas they say, that of simple bodies the motion is altogether simple, of the circular it is chiefly verified so long as the simple body remayneth in his naturall place, and perfite unitie of composition: for in the same place there can bee no other motion but circular, which remaining wholy in it selfe, is most like to rest an immobilitie. But right or straight motion onely happen to those things that stray and wander, or by any meanes are thrust out of their natural place. But nothing can be more repugnant to the forme and ordinance of the world, then that things naturally should be out of their naturall place.

This kind of motion therefore that is by right line, is onely accident to those things that are not in their right state or perfection naturall, while parts are disjoyned from their whole bodie, and covet to returne to the unitie thereof againe. Neither doe these things which are carried upward or downeward besides this circular mooving make any simple uniforme, or equall motion, for which their levitie or ponderositie of their bodie, they cannot be tempered, but alwayes as they fall (beginning slowly) they increase their motion, and the further the more swiftly, whereas contrariwise this our earthly fire (for other wee cannot see) wee may beholde as it is carried upward to vanish and decay, as it were confessing the cause of violence to proceede onely from his matter terrestriall. The circular motion alway continueth uniforme and equall, by reason of his cause which is indeficient and alway continuing. But the other hasteneth to the end and to attaine that place where they leave longer to be heavie or light, and having attained that place, their motion ceaseth. Seeing therefore this circular motion is proper to the whole, as straight is onely unto parts, we may say that circular doeth rest with straight, as *animal cum aegro*.[1] And whereas *Aristotle* hath distributed *simplicem motum* into these three kinds, *A medio ad medium*, and *circa medium*, it must bee onely in reason, and imagination, as wee likewise sever in consideration Geometricall, a poynt, a line, and a superficies, whereas indeede neither can stande without the other, ne any of them without a bodie.

Hereto wee may adjoyne, that the condition of immobilitie is more noble and divine than that of change, alteration, or instabilitie: and therefore more agreeable to Heaven than to this Earth, where all things are subject to continuall mutabilitie. And seeing by evident proofe of Geometricall mensuration, wee finde that the Planets are sometimes nigher to us, and sometimes more remote, and that therefore even the maintainers of the Earths stabilitie, are enforced to confesse, that the earth is not their Orbes Centre, this motion *circa Medium*, must in more generall sort bee taken, and that it may bee understand that every Orbe hath his peculiar *Medium* and Centre, in regard whereof this simple and uniforme motion is to be considered. Seeing therefore that these Orbs have severall Centres, it may bee doubted whether the Centre of this earthly gravitie, be also the Centre of the world. For gravitie is nothing else but a certaine proclivity or naturall coveting of parts to be coupled with the whole:

---

[1] since a disease could not exist by itself.

which by divine providence of the Creator of all, is given and impressed into the parts, that they should restore themselves into their unitie and integritie, concurring in Sphericall forme. Which kind of proprietie or affection, it is likely also that the Moone and other glorious bodies want not, to knit and combine their parts together: and to maintaine them in their round shape, which bodies notwithstanding are by sundrie motions, sundrie waies conveied. Thus, as it is apparant by these naturall reasons, that the mobilitie of the Earth is more probable and likely than the stabilitie: so if it be Mathematically considered, and Geometricall mensurations every part of everie Theoricke examined: the discreete student shall finde, that *Copernicus*, not without great reason did propone this ground of the Earths mobilitie.

METEORS

From *A Goodly Gallery*
by William Fulke, 1563

Sometime we see a clowd that's Dragonish,
A vapour sometime, like a beare, or Lyon,
A toward Cittadell, a pendant Rocke,
A forked Mountaine, or blew Promontorie
With Trees upon't, that nodde unto the world,
And mocke our eyes with Ayre.

Antony and Cleopatra

For as much as wee entend in this Treatise, to declare the causes of all those bodies, that are generated in the earth, called *Fossilia*, as well as those other *Impressions*, named of their height *Meteors* (which no writer hitherto hath done, that we have seen) the common definition given by the most Writers, in no wise will serve us, and whether we may borrow the name of *Meteoron*, to comprehend the whole subject of our worke, we are not altogether out of doubt, although the Philosopher deriving it from doubtfulnes,[1] giveth us some colour so to take it, and peradventure we might be as well excused to apply it to *Minerals*, as other authors are to use it for earthquaks: yet to avoid all occasions of cavilling at words, we shall both define and also describe the subject of our matter on this maner: it is a body compound without life natural. . . .

[1] The literal meaning of μετέωρον is floating or hovering, but the word has also the metaphorical sense of uncertain.

The Meteors are devided after three maner of wayes: first, into bodies perfectly and imperfectly mixed: Secondly, into moist impressions and drie: Thirdly, into fiery, ayry, watry, and earthly. According to this last division, we shall speak of them in four bookes following: but first wee must be occupied a little in the generall description of the same, that afterward shall be particularly intreated of. . . .

Of the general causes of all Meteors; and first of the material cause

The matter whereof the most part of Meteors doth consist, is either water or earth: for out of the water proceed vapors, and out of the earth come exhalations.

Vapor, as the Philosopher saith, is a certain watry thing, and yet is not water; so Exhalation hath a certain earthly nature in it, but yet it is not earth.

For the better understanding of Vapors, understand that they be as it were fumes or smokes warm and moist, which will easily be resolved into water, much like to the breath that proceedeth out of a mans mouth, or out of a pot of water standing on the fire. These vapors are drawn up from the waters and watery places by the heat of the Sun, even unto the middle region of the air, and there after divers manner of meeting with coldness, many kind of moist *Meteors* are generated, as sometimes clouds and rain, some-time snow and hail; and that such *Vapors* are so drawn up by the Sun, it is plain by experience: for if there be a plash of water on a smooth and hard stone, standing in the heat of the Sun, it will soon be drie; which is none otherwise but that the Sun draweth up the water in thin Vapors: for no man is so fond to say, that it can sink into stone or metall; and it is as great folly to think it is consumed to nothing: for it is a generall rule That that which is once a thing, cannot by changing become nothing: wherefore it followeth, that the water on the stone, as also on the earth, is for the most part drawn up when the stone or earth is dryed.

Exhalations are as smokes that be hot and dry, which because

F

they be thin, and lighter than *Vapors*, pass the lowest and middle Region of the air, and are carried up even to the highest Region, where for the excessive heat, by nearness of the fire, they are kindled, and cause many kind of impressions. They are also sometimes *viscous*, that is to say, clamy, by reason whereof they cleaving together & not being dispersed, are after divers sorts set on fire, & appear sometimes like Dragons, sometimes like Goats, sometimes like candles, sometimes like spears.

By that which is spoken of *Vapours* and *Exhalations*, it is evident, that out of the fire and aire, no matter whereof *Meteors* should consist, can be drawn, because of their subtilty and thinnesse. For all *Exhalation* is by making a grosser body more thinne: but the fire (we mean the elemental fire, and not the fire of the Kitchin chimney) is so subtil and thinne, that it cannot be made thinner; likewise the aire is so thinne, that if it be made thinner, it is changed into fire; and as the fire, if it were made thicker, would become aire; so the aire being made grosser, would be turned into water. Wherefore to conclude this part, the great quantity of matter, that causeth these Meteors, is taken out of the earth and the water. As for the aire and the fire, they are mixed with this matter as with all other things, but not so abundantly, that they may be said the material cause of any Meteor, though without them none can be generated. The efficient cause of all Meteors, is that caus which maketh them; even as the Carpenter is the efficient cause of an house. This cause is either first or second.

The first and efficient cause is God the worker of all wonders, according to that testimony of the Psalmist, which saith, Fire, hail, snow, ice, wind, and storm, do his will and commandment; he sendeth snow like wool, &c. Almighty God therefore being the first, principall and universall cause efficient of all natural works and effects, is also the first cause of these effects, whose profit is great, & operation marvelous.

The second cause efficient, is double, either remote, that is to say, farre off, or next of all. The farther cause of them as of all other naturall effects, is the same; the Sun with the other Planets and Stars, and the very heaven it self in which they are moved; but chiefly the Sun, by whose heat all or at least wise the most part of the vapors and Exhalations are drawn up.

The next cause efficient as the first qualities are heat and cold, which cause divers effects in Vapors & Exhalations.

But to return to the heat of the Sun, which is a very near cause, it is for this purpose two wayes considered.

One way, as it is mean and temperate; Otherwise, as it is vehement and burning. The mean, is by which he draweth vapors out of the water, and exhalations out of the earth, and not only draweth them out, but also lifteth them up very high from the earth into the air, where they are turned into divers kinds of *Meteors*.

The burning heat of the Sun is, by which he burneth, dissipateth and consumeth the vapors and exhalations before he draweth them up, so that of them no *Meteors* can be generated.

These two heats proceed from the Sun, either in respect of the place, or the time; but most properly according to the casting of his beams either directly or indirectly.

In places where the Suns beames strike directly against the earth and the water, the heat is so great, that it burneth up the *Exhalations* and *Vapours*, so that there are no fiery *Meteors*, much less watery: as it is in the South parts of the world, under and near to the Equinoctiall line.

But in places where the beames are cast indirectly and obliquely, and that where they are not too nigh to the direct beams, nor too far off from them; there is a moderate heat, drawing out great abundance of matter, so that in those Countries many *Meteors* of many sorts are generated, as in the far North parts are few but watry impressions. Also in *Autumn* and *Spring* are oftner *Meteors* seen than in Summer and Winter, except it be in such places where the Summer and Winter are of the temper of the *Spring* and *Autumn*. Let this be sufficient for the Efficient causes of impressions, as well first and principall, as second and particular. Concerning the formall and finall cause, we have little to say, because the one is so secret, that it is known of no man: the other so evident, that it is plain to all men. The essentiall Form of all substances, Gods wisdome comprehendeth; the universall chief and last End of all things, is the glory of God. Middle Ends (if they may be so called) of these impressions are manifold profits to Gods creatures, to make the earth fruitfull, purge the air, to set forth his power, to threaten his vengeance,

to punish the world, to move to repentance; all which are referred to one end of Gods eternall glory, ever to be praised,
Amen.

Of the places, in which they are generated

The places in which *Meteors* are caused, be either the air or
the earth: in the air be generated rain, hail, snow, dew, blazing
stars, thunder, lightning, &c. In the earth be wells, springs,
earthquakes, metals, minerals, &c made, as it were, in their
mothers belly begotten and fashioned. But for the better understanding hereof, such as have not tasted the principles of *Philosophy*, must consider that there be four elements, Earth, Water,
Air, and Fire, one compassing another round about, saving that
the waters by Gods commandment are gathered into one place,
that the land might appear. The highest is the sphear of the Fire,
which toucheth the hollowness of the Moons heaven: the next is
the air, which is in the hollowness of the fire: the air within its
hollowness comprehendeth the water and the earth, which both
make but one spheare or Globe, or as the common sort may
understand it, one ball. So each element is within another, as
scales of a perch are one above another: or (to use a gross similitude) as the peeles of an Onion are one within another: after the
same sort from the highest heaven to the earth that is lowest,
one part that is greater compasseth round about another that is
lesser. But for this present purpose it is to be known, that the
aire is divided into three regions, the highest the middle and the
lowest. The highest because it is next to the region of the fire, is
exceeding hot: the lowest being next the earth and waters, is
temperate, and by repercussion or striking back of the Sunne
beames waxeth hot, and by absence of them is made cold, being
subject to winter and summer. The middle region of the aire is
alwayes exceeding cold, partly because the Sunne beames cannot
be cast back so high, and partly because the cold that is there
between the heat above, and the heat beneath it, is so kept in,
that it cannot get out, so that it must needs be excessively cold:
for the water and the earth being both cold Elements, after the

Sun setting in the night season do cool the air, even to the middle
region. But in the morning the Sun rising warmeth the air, so
far as his beames which are beaten back from the earth and the
water, can extend and reach; which is not so high as the middle
region, and by heat on both sides is inclosed and kept, saving
that a little thereof falleth down in the night, which the next day
with much more is driven back again. Wherefore this region being so cold, is dark and cloudy, in so much that some doting
Divines have imagined purgatory to be there in the middle
region of the air. In the highest region be generated Comets or
blazing Stars, and such like, of divers sorts. In the middle
region clouds, rain, storms, winds, &c. In the lowest region,
dew, frost, hoar-frost, mists, bright rods, candles, burning about
graves, and gallowses, where there is store of clamy, fatty, or oily
substance, also lights and flaming fires seen in fields, &c. And
thus much for the general causes of all Meteors.

Of Fiery Meteors

A Fiery impression is an *Exhalation* set on fire in the highest
or lowest region of the air, or else appearing as though it were
set on fire and burning.

They are therefore divided into flames & Apparitions. Flames
are they which burn indeed, and are kindled with fire. These are
discerned by four wayes; by the fashion of them, by their place,
by the abundance of their matter, and by the want of their matter. Their placing is after the abundance and scarcity of the
matter whereof they consist: for if it be great, heavy, and gross,
it cannot be carried so far as the middle region of the air, and
therefore is set on fire in the lowest region: if it be not so great,
light, and full of heat, it passeth the middle region, and ascendeth to the highest, where it is easily kindled and set on fire.

According to their divers fashions, they have divers names:
for they are called burning stubble, torches, dancing or leaping
Goats, shooting or falling starres, or candles, burning beames,
round pillars, spears, shields, Globes or bowles, firebrands,
lampes, flying Dragons or fire drakes, painted pillars, or

broched steeples, or blazing starres, called *Comets*. The time
when these impressions do most appear, is the night-season: for
if they were caused in the day-time, they could not be seen, no
more than the stars be seen, because the light of the Sun which is
much greater, dimmeth the brightness of them being lesser.

Of the generation of the impression called burning stubble or sparkles of fire

The generation of this *Meteor* is this; when the matter of the
Exhalation is in all parts alike thin, but not compacted or knit
together, then some part of it being carried up into the highest
Region, by the fiery heat is set on fire before another part that
cometh up after it, and so being kindled by little and little, flieth
abroad like sparkles out of a chimney, insomuch that the common
people suppose, that an infinite number of Stars fall down, whereas it is nothing else but the *Exhalation* that is thin, kindled in
many parts, sparkling as when saw-dust or cole-dust is cast into
the fire.

Of shooting and falling Stars

A Flying, shooting, or falling Star, is when the exhalation being gathered as it were on a round heap, and yet not throughly
compacted in the highest part of the lowest region of the air,
being kindled by the sudden cold of the middle region, is beaten
back, and so appeareth as though a Star should fall, or slide from
place to place. Sometime it is generated after another sort; for
there is an exhalation long & narrow, which being kindled at
one end burneth swiftly, the fire running from end to end, as
when a silk thred is set on fire at the one end. Some say it is not
so much set on fire, as that it is direct under some Star in the
firmament, and so receiving light of that Star, seemeth to our
eyes to be a Star. Indeed sometimes it may be so; but that it is
not so alwayes, nor yet most commonly, it may be easily demon-

strated. The Epicureans, as they are very gross in determining the chief goodness, so they are very fond in assigning the cause of this Meteor. For they say that the Stars fall out of the firmament, & that by the fall of them, both thunder and lightning are caused: for the lightning (say they) is nothing else but the shining of that Star that falleth, which falling into a watery cloud, and being quenched in it, causeth that great thunder, even as hot Iron maketh a noise if it be cast into cold water. But it is evident, that the Stars of the firmament cannot fall, for God hath set them fast for ever; he hath given them a Commandment which they shall not pass. And though they should fall into the clouds, yet could they not rest there, but with their weight being driven down, would cover the whole earth.

For the least Star that is seen in the firmament, is greater than all the earth. Here will step forth some merry fellow, which of his conscience thinketh them not to be above 3. yards about, and say it is a loud lie; for he can see within the compass of a bushel, more than 20. Stars. But if his bushel were on fire 20. mile of, I demand how big it would seem unto him? He that hath any wit, will easily perceive that starres being by all mens confession, so many thousand miles distant from the earth, must needs be very great, that so far off should be seen in any quantity. Thus much for the shooting or falling starres.

Of flying Dragons or fire Drakes

Flying Dragons, or as Englishmen call them, fire Drakes, be caused on this maner. When a certaine quantity of vapors are gathered together on a heap, being very neere compact, & as it were hard tempered together, this lump of vapors ascending to the region of cold, is forcibly beaten back, which violence of moving, is sufficient to kindle it, (although some men will have it to be caused between two clouds, a hote and a cold) then the highest part, which was climing upward, being by reason more subtill & thin, appeareth as the Dragons neck, smoking, for that it was lately in the repulse bowed or made crooked, to represent the Dragons belly. The last part by the same repulse turned upward, maketh the tayle, both appearing smaller, for that it is both further off, & also, for that the cold bindeth it. This dragon thus being caused, flieth along in the ayre, & sometime turneth to & fro, if it meet with a cold cloud to beat it back, to the great terrour of them that behold it: of whom some call it a fire Drake: some say it is the Devill himselfe, and so make report to other. More than forty-seven yeeres agoe, on May day, when many young folke went abroad early in the morning, I remember by sixe of the clocke in the forenoone, there was newes come to London, that the Devill, the same morning, was seene flying over the Thames: afterward came word, that he lighted at Stratford, and there was taken and set in the Stockes, and that though he would faine have dissembled the matter, by turning himselfe into the likenesse of a man, yet he was knowne well enough by his cloven foote. I knew some then living, that went to see him, and returning, affirmed, that he was indeede seene flying in the ayre, but was not taken prisoner. I remember also, that some wished hee had been shot at with Gunns or shafts, as he flew over the Thames. Thus doe ignorant men judge of these things that they know not. As for this Devill, I suppose, it was a flying Dragon, whereof wee speake, very fearefull to looke upon, as though hee had life, because he mooveth, whereas it is nothing else but clowds and smoake: so mighty is God, that he can feare his enemies with these and such like operations, whereof some examples may be found in holy Scripture.

Of lights that go before men, and follow them abroad in the fields, by the night season

There is also a kind of light that is seen in the night season, & seemeth to go before men, or to follow them, leading them out of their way into waters, and other dangerous places. It is also very often seen in the night, of them that sail on the Sea, and sometime will cleave to the mast of the Ship, or other high parts, sometime slide round about the Ship, and either rest in one part till it go out, or else be quenched in the water. This impression seen on the land, is called in Latin *Ignis fatuus*, foolish fire, that hurteth not, but only feareth fools. That which is seen on the Sea, if it be but one, is named *Helena*; it it be two, it is called *Castor* and *Pollux*.

The foolish fire is an *Exhalation* kindled by means of violent moving, when by cold of the night, in the lowest region of the air, it is beaten down; and then commonly, if it be light, seeketh to ascend upward, and is sent down again; so it danceth up and down. Else if it move not up and down, it is a great lump of glewish or oyly matter, that by moving of the heat in it self, is enflamed of it self, as moist Hay will be kindled of it self. In hot and fenny Countries, these lights are often seen, and where is abundance of such unctuous and fat matter, as about Church-yards, where through the corruption of the bodies there buried, the earth is full of such substance: wherefore in Church-yards, or places of common buriall, oftentimes are such lights seen, which ignorant and superstitious fools have thought to be souls tormented in the fire of Purgatory. Indeed the Devil hath used these lights (although they be naturally caused) as strong delusions to captive the minds of men with fear of the Popes Purgatory; whereby he did open injury to the blood of Christ, which only purgeth us from all our sins, & delivereth us from all torments both temporall and eternall, according to the saying of the Wise-man, The souls of the righteous are in the hands of God, and no torment toucheth them. But to return to the lights, in which there are yet two things to be considered. First, why they lead men out of their way. And secondly, why they seem to follow men and go before them. The cause why they lead men out of the way, is, that men, while they take heed to such lights, and are also sore afraid, they forget their way, & then being once but a little out of their way, they wander they wot not whither, to waters, pits, and other very dangerous places. Which, when at length they hap the way home, will tell a great tale, how they have been led about by a spirit in the likeness of Fire. Now the cause why they seem to go before men, or to follow them, some men have said to be the moving of the air, by the going of the man, which air moved should drive them forward if they were before, and draw them after if they were behind. But this is no reason at all, that the Fire which is oftentimes three or four miles distant from the man that walketh, should be moved to and fro by that air which is moved through his walking, but rather the moving of the air and the mans eyes, causeth the fire to seem as though it moved, as the Moon to children seemeth, if they are before it, to run after them: if she be before them, to run before them, that they cannot overtake her, though she seem to be very near them. Wherefore these lights rather seem to move, then that they be moved indeed.

Of Comets or Blazing Stars

A *Comet* is an exhalation hot and dry, of great quantity, fat and clammy, hard-compact like a great lump of pitch, which by the heat of the Sun is drawn out of the Earth into the highest region of the Air, and there by the excessive heat of the place is set on fire, appearing like a Star with a blazing tayl; and some-time is moved after the motion of the Air which is circular, but it never goeth down out of the compas of sight, though it be not seen in the day-time for the brightness of the Sun, but still burneth until all the matter be consumed. An argument of the greatness is this, that there was never any *Comet* yet perceived, but at the least it endured 7. dayes; but much longer they have been seen; namely forty dayes long, yea fourscore dayes; and some six moneths together. Wherefore it must needs be a won-derfull deal of matter than can give so much nourishment for so great and fervent fire, and for so long a time.

There are considered in a *Comet* specially the Colour and Fashion, which both arise of the disposition of the matter.

Their Colours be either white, ruddy, or blew. If the matter be thin, the colour is white; if it be meanly thick, then is the Comet ruddy, after the colour of our fire; but when the matter is very thick, it is blew, like the burning of brimstone. And as the matter is more or less after this disposition, so is the Comet of colour more or less like to these three principall colours: some yellowish, some duskish, some greenish, some watchet, &c.

In Fashion are noted three differences; for either they seem to be round, with beams round about, or with a beard hanging downward, or else with a tayle stretched out sidelong in length. The first fashion is when the matter is thickest in the midst, and then round about the edges; the second is when the Exhalation is upward thick, and in length downward also meanly thick; the third form is like the second, saving that the tayl hangeth not down but lyeth aside, and is commonly longer than the beard.

The time of their generation is oftenest in Autumn or Harvest: for in the Spring there is too much moisture, and too little heat to gather a Comet; in Summer is too much heat, which will disperse and consume the matter that it cannot be joyned together; as for Winter, it is clean contrary to the nature of a Comet, which is hot and dry, Winter being cold and moist: therefore no time so meet as Autumn.

Now for so much as many learned men have gone about to declare the signification of Blazing Stars, we will omit nothing that hath any shadow of Reason, but declare what is written of them.

Such things as are set forth of the betokening of Comets are of two sorts: The first is of natural; The second of Civil or Politick Effects.

They are said to betoken Drought, Barrenness of the Earth, and Pestilence.

Drought, because a Comet cannot be generated without great heat; and much moisture is consumed in the burning of it.

Barrenness, because the fatness of the Earth is drawn up, whereof the Comet consisteth.

Pestilence, for so much as this kind of Exhalation corrupteth the Air, which infecteth the bodies of men and beasts.

The second sort might well be omitted, saving that *Aristotle* himself disdaineth not to seek out Causes for some of them.

Generally it is noted of all Historiographers, that after the appearing of Comets, most commonly follow great and notable Calamities. Besides this, they betoken (say some) Wars, Seditions, Changes of Commonwealths, and the Death of Princes and Noble men.

For what time Comets do shine, there be many hot and dry Exhalations in the Air, which in dry men kindle heat, whereby they are provoked to anger: of anger cometh brawling: of brawling, fighting and war: of war, victory: of victory, change of Commonwealths: then also Princes living more delicately than other men, are more subject to infection; and therefore die sooner than other men. If it were lawfull to reason in this sort, we might induce them to betoken not only these few things, but all other things that chance in the world.

Yet these predictions have a shew of Reason, though it be nothing necessary; but it is a wonder to see how the Astrologians dote in such devices; they are not ashamed to an earthly substance to ascribe an heavenly influence, and in order of judgment to use them as very Stars. Surely, by as good reason as to the celestiall Stars they attribute divine influences and effects. But this their folly hath been sufficiently detected by divers godly and learned men, and this place requireth no long discourse thereof. Wherefore this shall suffice, both for the natural Causes of Blazing Stars, and also for all Flames in general. It followeth therefore, that with like brevity we declare the Causes of Ayry Apparitions.

Under the name of ayry impressions, be comprehended such *Meteors*, whose matter is most of the aire. Of this sort be windes, earthquakes, thunder, lightnings, storme-winds, whirlewinds, circles, rainebowes, the white circle, called of some, Watling street, many sunnes, many moones.

Of Winds

The Wind is an Exhalation hot and dry, drawn up into the Air by the power of the Sun, and by reason of the weight thereof being driven down, is laterally or sidelong carried about the Earth. And this Definition is not to be understood of generall Winds that blow over all the Earth, or else some great Regions; but besides these there be particular Winds which are known but only in some Countries, and them not very large. These Winds oftentimes have another manner of generation, and that is on this manner;

It must needs be confessed, that within the globe of the Earth be wonderfull great holes, caves or dungeons, in which when Air aboundeth (as it may by divers Causes) this Air that cannot abide to be penned in, findeth a little hole in or about those Countries, as it were a mouth to break out of, and by this means bloweth vehemently: yet that force and vehemency extendeth not far; but as the wind that cometh forth of bellows, near the coming forth is strong, but far off is not perceived: so this particular Wind, in that particular Countrey where it breaketh forth, is very violent and strong, in so much that it overthroweth both trees and houses, yet in other Countries not very far distant, no part of that boisterous blast is felt. Wherefore this Wind differeth from the generall Winds both in Qualities and Substance or Matter: for the Matter of them is an Exhalation, and the Qualities such as the nature of the Exhalation is, very Airy, but not Air indeed: but of this particular Wind the Matter and Substance is most commonly Air.

There is yet a third kind of Wind, which is but a soft, gentle, and cool moving of the Air, and cometh from no certain place (as the generall Wind doth) yet it is felt in the shadow under trees, when in the hot light and shining of the Sun it is not perceived. It cometh whisking suddenly, very pleasant in the heat of Summer, and ceaseth by and by; this properly is no Wind, but a moving of the Air by some occasion.

As for the general Winds, they blow out of divers Quarters of the Air, now East, now West, now South, now North, or else inclining to one of the same Quarters: Among which the East-wind following the nature of the Fire, is hot and dry; the South-wind expressing the quality of the Air, is hot and moist; the Western blast agreeing with the Waters property, is cold and moist; the North that never was warmed with the heat of the Sun, being cold and dry, partaketh the condition of the Earth. The middle Winds have middle and mixed qualities, after the nature of those four principall Winds, more or less, as they incline toward them, more or less.

Generally the profit of all Winds, by the wonderfull wisdom of the Eternal God, is very great unto his Creatures. For besides that these Winds alter the Weather, some of them bringing rain, some driness, some frost and snow, which all are necessary: there is yet an universal commodity that riseth by the only moving of the Air, which were it not continually stirred as it is, would soon putrifie, and being putrified would be a deadly infection to all that hath breath upon the Earth. Wherefore this Wind, whose sound we hear, and know not from whence it cometh nor whither it goeth (for who can affirm from whence it was raised, or where it is laid down?) as all other Creatures beside, does teach us the wonderfull and wise providence of God, that we may worthily cry out with the Psalmist, and say, *O Lord, how manifold are thy works! in wisdome hast thou made them all,* &c. Let this be sufficient to have shewed the generation of the Winds.

Of Earthquakes

An Earthquake is a shaking of the Earth, which is caused by means of wind and *Exhalations,* that be enclosed within the caves of the Earth, and can find no passage to break forth, or else so narrow a way that it cannot soone enough bee delivered. Wherefore, with great force and violence it breaketh out: and one while shaketh the earth, another while rendeth and cleaveth the same: sometime it casteth up the earth, a great height into the ayre, and sometime it causeth the same to sinke a great depth downe, swallowing both Cities and Townes, yea and also mighty great Mountaines, leaving in the place where they stood, nothing but great holes of an unknowne depth, or else great lakes of waters.

Also the Sun, certain dayes before it, appeareth dim, because the Winds that should have purged and dissolved the gross Air, that causeth this dimness to our eyes, is enclosed within the bowels of the Earth.

The Water in the bottome of deep wells is troubled, and the savour thereof infected, because the pestilent *Exhalations* that have been long enclosed within the Earth, do then begin a little to be sent abroad. For thereof cometh it, that in many places where Earthquakes have been, great abundance of smoak, flame, and ashes, is cast out, when the abundance of brimstone that is under the ground, through violent motion is set on fire, and breaketh forth. Finally, who knoweth not, what stinking Minerals, and other poysonous stuff do grow under the Earth? wherefore it is no wonder, if Well-water, before an Earthquake, be infected: but rather it is to be marvelled, if after an Earthquake there follow not a grievous Pestilence, when the whole mass of infection is blown abroad.

Last of all, there is heard before it, in the time of it, and after
it, a great noise and sound under the Earth, a terrible groaning,
and a very Thundring, yea, sometimes when there followeth no
Earthquake at all, when as the wind, without shaking of the
Earth, findeth a way to pass out at. And these for the most part,
or at least some of them, are forewarnings, that the most fearfull
Earthquake will follow, than the which there is no naturall thing
that bringeth men into a greater fear.

Of Thunder

Thunder is a sound caused in the Clouds, by the breaking out
of a hot and dry Exhalation, beating against the edges of the
Cloud. It is often heard in Spring and Summer, by reason that
the heat of the Sun then draweth up many Exhalations, which
meeting in the middle region of the Air with moist and cold
Vapors, are together with them enclosed in a hollow Cloud: but
when the hot Exhalation cannot agree with the coldness of the
place; by this strife being driven together, made stronger, and
kindled, it will straight break out, which sudden and violent
eruption causeth the noise which we call Thunder. A Similitude
is put by great Authors, of moist wood that cracketh in the fire:
we may adde hereunto the breaking of an egge in the fire, of an
apple, or any like thing; for whatsoever holdeth and withholdeth
inclosed any hot wind, so that it can have no vent, it will seek it
self a way by breaking the skin, shell, or case. It were no ill comparison to liken Thunder to the sound of a Gun, which be both
caused of the same, or very like causes.

The sound of Thunder is divers; after which men have divided
the Thunder into divers kinds, making first two sorts, that is,
small Thunder and great. But as for the diversity of sounds,
generally it comes of the divers disposition of the clouds, one
while having more holes than at another; sometime thicker in
one place than in another.

The small or little Thunder is, when the Exhalation is driven
from side to side of that Cloud, making a noise, and either for
the small quantity and less forcibleness, or else for the thickness

of the Clouds walls, is not able to break them, but rumbleth up and down within the cloud, whose sides be stronger than the force of the Exhalation is able to break, it runneth up and down within, and striking against the cloud and moist sides, maketh a noise not unlike the quenching of hot iron in cold water.

And if the Exhalation be meanly strong, and the cloud not in all places of like thickness, it breaketh out at those thin places with such a buzzing, as wind maketh blowing out of narrow holes.

But if the cloud be so thin that it cannot keep in the Exhalation, although it be not kindled, then it bloweth out with like puffing, as wind cometh out of a pair of bellows.

A great Thunder is when the Exhalation is much in quantity, and very hot and dry in quality; the clouds also very thick and strong, that easily will not give place to the wind to escape out.

Wherefore if the Exhalation do vehemently shake the cloud, though it do not at the first disperse it, it maketh a long and fearfull rumbling against the sides of the cloud, untill at the last being made stronger by swifter motion, it dissolveth the cloud, and hath liberty to pass out into the open Air; the cloud dissolved droppeth down, and then followeth a showr of Rain.

Otherwhiles it shaketh the cloud not long, but straightway rendeth it a long space and time, whose sound is like the rending of a Broad-cloth, which noise continueth a pretty while.

And sometime it discusseth the cloud at once, making a vehement and terrible crack like a Gun, sometime with great force casting out stones, but most commonly fire, which setteth many high places on fire. As in the year of our Lord 1561. the fourth day of June, the steeple of St. *Pauls* Church in *London* was set on fire, as it hath been once or twice before, and burned.

The noise of Thunder though it be great in such places over which it is made, yet is not heard far off, especially against the wind; whereof we had experience also in the year of our Lord, 1561. on Saint *Matthias* day in February, at the evening, when there was a great flash of Lightning, and a very terrible crack of Thunder following; they that were but 15. Miles from *London* Westward heard no noise nor sound thereof; the Wind that time was Western.

The effect of Thunder is profitable to men, both for that the

sweet showr doth follow it, and also for that it purgeth and puri-
fieth the Air, by the swift moving of the Exhalation that breaketh
forth, as also by the sound, which dividing and piercing the Air,
causeth it to be much thinner: which may be verified by an History that *Plutarch* in the life of *Quincius Flaminius* reporteth, that
there was such a noise made by the Grecians, after their liberty
was restored, that the Birds of the Air that flew over them were
seen fall down, by reason that the Air divided by their cry, was
made so thin, that there was no firmity or strength in it to bear
them up.[1] And let this suffice for Thunder, which Lightning suc-
ceedeth in treaty, that seldom is from it in nature.

Of Fulgur

Fulgur is that kinde of Lightning which followeth Thunder,
whereof we have spoken before. For when that violent Exhalation breaks forth, making a noise as it beateth against the sides
of the Cloud, with the same violence it is set on fire, and casteth
a great light, which is seen far and near. And although the Lightning appear unto us a good pretty while before the Thunder-clap
be heard, yet it is not caused before the noise, if any Thunder at
all follow, but either is after it, or with it. Wherefore that we
see it before we hear the Thunder, may be ascribed either to the
quickness of our sight that preventeth the Hearing, or else to the
swift moving of the fire, and the light thereof to our eyes, and
the slow motion of the sound unto our ears and hearing.

These three kinds of Lightnings are more fearfull than hurtfull, but the fourth seldom passeth without some dammage doing.

Of the fourth kind, called Fulmen

The most dangerous, violent, and hurtfull kind of lightning is
called *Fulmen*, whose generation is such as followeth: What time

[1] 'Unless we will rather say, that it was the violence of the cry, which strook the
birds passing through the air, as they had been hit with arrows, and so made them
to fall down dead to the earth.' Plutarch, *Life of Flaminius*.

a hot *Exhalation* is enclosed in a Cloud, and breaking the same, bursteth forth, it is set on fire, and with wonderfull great force stricken down toward the Earth.

The crack of Thunder that is made when this Lightning breaketh out, is sudden, short, and great, like the sound of a Gun. And oftentimes a great stone is blown out with it, which they call the Thunder-bolt, which is made on this manner.

In the *Exhalation* which is gathered out of the Earth, is much earthly matter, which clottering together by moisture, being clammy by nature, consisting of brimstone, and other metalick substance, by the excessive heat is hardened as a brick is in the fire, and with the mighty force of the *Exhalation*, strongly cast toward the Earth, and striketh down steeples, and high buildings of stone, and of wood, passeth thorow them, and setteth them on fire; it cleaveth trees, and setteth them on fire: and the stronger the thing is that resisteth it, the more harm it doth to it. It is sharp-pointed at one end, and thick at the other end, which is caused, by reason that the moister part, as heavier, goeth to the bottome of it; so is the top small, and the bottome thick.

Men write, that the thunder-bolt goeth never above five foot deep, when it falleth upon the Earth: which standeth with reason, both because the strength of it is weakened before it come so near the ground, and also because the continuall thickness of the Earth breaketh the force, were it never so great.

Both *Aristotle*, *Seneca*, and *Plinius*, divide the lightning into three kinds. The first is dry, which burneth not to be felt, but divideth & appeareth with wonderfull swiftness: For being subtile and pure, it passeth thorow the pores of any thing, be they never so small; and such things as give place unto it, it hurteth not; but such things as resist, it divideth and pierceth. For it will melt money in mens purses, the purses being whole and unharmed. Yea, it will melt a sword in the scabberd, and not hurt the scabberd at all. A wine vessel it will cleave, and yet the wine shall be so dull, that by the space of three dayes it will not run out. It will hurt a mans hand, and not his glove. It will burn a mans bones within him to ashes, and yet his skin and flesh shall appear fair, as though nothing had come to him. Yet otherwise the whole man in the moment of an hour shall be burned to ashes, whereas his clothes shall not seem to have been touched. It will also kill the child in the mothers belly, and not hurt the mother: And all because the matter is very subtile, and thin, burning, and passing thorow whatsoever it be that will not give it free passage.

THE PLANETARY INFLUENCES

From *The Dial of Destiny*
by John Maplet, 1581

When I consider every thing that growes
Holds in perfection but a little moment.
That this huge stage presenteth nought but showes
Whereon the Stars in secret influence comment.
When I perceive that men as plants increase,
Cheared and checkt by the selfe-same skie:
Vaunt in their youthfull sap, at height decrease,
And were their brave state out of memory. . . .

Sonnet xv

Of the Concord and common felowship of the seven Planets, and also of their dreedeful debate and discorde

It is manyfest and approved by argumentes of force, and reasons of more secret and hid philosophy, likewise by demonstration and conclusions Mathematicall, that all Creatures whatsoever whych have their being essence, and preservation upon the face of the whole Earth, or els be contayned within the Regions or Precinct of the Ayre above, and subjected under the circle or Sphere of the Moone, have and receive their influence of the higher and more Celestiall bodies or Planets: and after a certayne sorte (saith *Proclus*) they rest and depend of them. And heerein his saying seemed not to bee amisse, for that experience playnly teacheth us, and also we see that there is nothing heere below so able, stronge, or riche of it selfe, that being voyde or destitute of the favour or furtheraunce of the celestiall bodies above, can be well pleased and contented with it selfe. *Agrippa* is in that opinion that at the former constitution or first breedinge of every ech thinge, both that which lyveth, as also that which is devoyde of lyfe (as likewise at the commixture or composition of the Elements for the increase of any baser kindes) the bountifulnes of certayne planets is such oftentimes, that besides the beneficialnesse of the owne nature of the thinges themselves (which worketh always liberally) there is a further free gyft bestowed upon every the sayd thinges, and kindes by the Planets themselves: and the same more rightly or preciously when as they meete together in more happy signe, or be in higher Horoscope or Ascendent. *Plato* with his Consectaryes doe affyrme, that all these Daughters or progeny of Dame Nature, are every one of them first sealed and (as it were) marked of the starres and Planets above, whereby in every thing they have to chalenge their owne. And even as by God the greatest and mightiest of all, and the first and principall cause of all things, all creatures are disposed generally to a like frame and customable order of the selfe same kinde: so in lyke sorte by the second causes the Planets although inferiours yet working causes, all things here underneath are in more speciall sorte sealed and ensampled. Easy it is to see that there is no one parte in all the whole proportion and workmanship of mans body, that is not ruled or disposed by some one Planet or other, to affectate that most of all other thinges which the superior force doth frame them and enclyne them unto: so that unto me all the whole body of man, as also the bodies of all other creatures here below, seeme to be possessed, busied, and as it were incensed and set on worke by them. As for example. To begin with *Sol* or the Sunne, it is apparant how he holdeth, governeth, and hath in possession the Braynes and forepart of the head, the heart, the marrow, the right Eye, the vitall Spirite or breath of life: likewise the Mouth, the tongue and all other the Organes or instruments of sense, or feeling: besides this, he chalengeth the hands, the feete, the Synewes, the Imagination, and the whole operation of the power phantasticall.

The Moone likewise hath in her subjection and ordreth after

a certayne sorte all the whole body, in such wise as both the humors and moysture both naturall and accidental: doth either abounde in them or dyminishe and lessen, according to her prime and wane. And whereas shee thus worketh generally in all sortes according to her owne variation, so in the speciall members and partes of the body shee especially ruleth in the Lunges, and dealeth also with a great portion of the Brayne. Hers is also the Marrow of the Backbone, as also the stomacke, the left Eye, with all other partes that yeelde forth and avoyde the excrementes, and superfluities of the body, with the powre and vertue increasinge. *Saturne* is lord over the Lyver, and hath to doe with the bottome or lowest parte of the stomacke. *Jupiter* chalengeth a righte in the Belly, as likewise in the Navell: insomuch that in the Temple of *Jupiter Hammon* in Lybia, the figure or lykenesse of a Mans Navell was hanged up, to signifie thereby that the thorough closing and fastning together of the Belly belongeth onely to *Jupiter* himselfe. Likewise hee holdeth the Ribbes, and the place about the privities, as also the Bowels, and Entrailes within. Moreover the best and more principall bloude is his, as also both the armes, and both the handes, as well the righte as the left, with all the whole powre and vertue Nutritive, whereby the whole body is nourished and maynteyned. To *Mars* appertayneth and belongeth the seconde and more base Bloude, as also the Vaines, the Kidney, the Celles or placinges of the Chest, the Backe, the Buttockes, the Corse and abundance of Seede, as also all that full powre of the Stomacke wherein Choler is ingendred. Proper to *Mercury* is the Spleene, the Mylte, the Bladder, the Matrix, and all those places within the Body which are naturally appoynted to the onely use and office of nourishing. *Venus* ruleth the Secret partes, and ordereth the naturall Seede, and also causeth and provoketh to the Lust and Appetite of thinges. It may be perceyved also that in some one parte of the body, they will all seven beare a sway.

Hermes sayth, that in the head of man there are seven Pores or holes, allotted to dyverse and sundry offices, of the which every one of them is subject to a sundry Planet. As that Pore or hole which is in the righte Eare apperteineth to *Saturne*: that in the left to *Jupiter*: *Mars* also hath the government of that which is in the right side of the nose: *Venus* the contrary: *Sol* is maister over that which holdeth the stringes of the Eye: *Luna* over the other in the left Eye: and all the whole workmanship of the mouth is proper alone to *Mercury*. Great and graciouse also are all such Benefites as Mankinde, as also the other baser kyndes doe eftsoones receive of the Planets, especially when as those of like condition, nature and quality doe meete together in gracious signes of like house. And contrariwise heavy and hearde is their happe, fortune, and chaunce, which have and obtayne any thing of them as they be in battlement, stryfe, and contencion among them selves: . . . in so much that it was not without juste cause and occasion that *Heraclitus* sayd, that al things were perfited and made by a proportion fetched from friendship and discord.

By these Planets also happeneth better chaunce and fortune, as also mischaunce and misfortune. Insomuch that some of them are tearmed the Gods of grace and fortune: as is *Jupiter* whom they name *Fortuna major*, the greater or more gracious. Likewise *Venus*, who in the rules of Astrologie is named *Fortuna minor*, as if you woulde say lesse gracious, and yet a Lady of grace. The others are called the Gods of mishap or casuall chaunce, of the which sort is *Saturne*, whom they name *Infortuna major*: As also *Mars* who is called *Infortuna minor*. And *Mercury*, which is called the God of indifferency, who is for al companies, for with the good, he is good, and with the bad, he is as bad. *Sol* by his shyning Sunne beames, and amiable aspecte or countenaunce is cheareful to al things: but being in conjunction with other or eclypsed, both hindreth much for the present time, and prognosticateth, and threatneth more for the future time comming. The moone is sent in message from one to another, and hath hir recourse and passage by them all: so that she hurteth or benefiteth as occasion serveth by them, and from them. By Astrologie also they have all theyr determynate kinde: As *Venus* and *Luna* are feminyne or of the woman kinde: And all the other are accompted Masculine, or after men. They are also devided into Planets of the day, and Planets of the nyghte. The day Planets are *Saturne*, *Jupiter*, *Sol*, and *Mercurie*. The night Planets are *Mars*, *Venus* and *Luna*. Againe they be devyded as that certaine of them be holden for heavy and Massie, of the which sorte are *Saturne*, *Jupiter*, and *Mars*: other are as subtile and light, as are *Venus*, *Mercury* and *Luna*. But *Sol* or the sunne is partaker of neither of both these properties.

Amongst the elementes these do also contend for the superiority. For *Jupiter* dealeth with that commixture whych partely is of the ayer, and partely of the Water. *Luna* or the Moone exacteth that which consysteth and commeth of the Water alone. *Sol* also helpeth forwardes the meanes, or maner in doing or accomplishing of things. *Luna* or the Moone, as it were ministreth matter in such behalfes. *Mars*, and *Mercury*, labour their proceeding and going forward, and doe geve them speedy and quick expedition: the firste by the meanes of his force, and might, and the other by his aptnesse and Dexterity in deliveraunce. The plenty and store of matter commeth from *Venus*, and the continuation or wayght of any businesse whatsoever, is proper alone to *Saturne*. Moreover all the Sygnes in the Zodiacall Circle doe participate, and injoy the qualities of the seven Planets. As *Taurus*, and *Capricornus*, bee Saturnine: *Virgo*, and *Libra*, are after *Jupiter*: *Aries*, and *Scorpio*, be after *Mars*: *Cancer*, and *Leo*, be after *Sol* or the Sunne: *Gemini*, and *Sagittarius*, be after *Venus*: *Aquarius*, and *Pisces*, bee after the Moone. And accordinge to the course of the Sunne, *Aries*, *Taurus*, and *Gemini*, doe procure a warme and moyst Springtime, very good for the Sanguine Complexion, and for tender age. *Cancer*, *Leo*, and *Virgo*, likewise cause a hoat Summer and a dry: very good for the Cholericke complexion and men of middle age. Likewise *Libra*, *Scorpio*, and *Sagittarius*, cause a colde and moyst Autumne, agreable to the Phlegmaticke complexion, and young age. And *Capricornus*, *Aquarius*, and *Pisces*, cause the winter naturally to be cold and dry, aunswerable to the Melancholicke complexion, and to olde Age. But of these thinges we are to speake of, as Occasion shall serve more particulerly, as hereafter followeth. . . .

Of Venus *the thirde Planet*

Venus is a faeminine Planet very placable and pleasaunt: a pacifier of *Mars* in his great fury, and malice, and fiery fervency, quieting him with friendly and amiable Aspect, in such wise, as a beautifull and lovinge Woman doth appease and still the rage, and anger of her Husband being incensed. Shee alwayes accompanieth the Sunne: and when shee goeth before him, and sheweth in our Horizon before the sun she is called *Lucifer* the bright morning light or day star: but when she followeth the Sunne, and is seene of us after the Sunne set she is called *Hesperus* the star of the night: and so howsoever or whensoever she doth appeare shee is the Sunnes Messenger, either that hee is already comming, or that hee is already gone. . . .

This *Venus* is of a bright shyning colour, being therein of al other starres most acceptable and pleasaunt to the eyesight: and shee is called *Venus* for venustie and beautiful countenaunce: or (as some ymagine) for that through these qualities and contemperature, which shee naturally planteth in the body (that is to say) heate and moysture, shee causeth burninge Love, and provoketh to tickling Lust. . . .

Those that be borne under *Venus* are amiable, and of a merry and smylinge Looke or Countenaunce, great laughers, very wanton, and such as do greatly delight in Musicke: they have also a very perfect smell and taste, and their voyce is very sweete or delectable. They are also geven much to the composing and making of sweete oyntments and Odoures: Their bodies are wel set, and be of proper features: their Faces and vysages are round: their hayre yellow, their Eyes glittering and rowling. In conditions they be gentle, curteous, fayre spoken, milde, and modest, meete for all companies: whereupon for such her deserving towards Mankinde, they of olde time pictured *Venus* after these sorts following. First they drewe her out in the similitude or lykenesse of a Woman, upon whose heade stoode a Byrd, which purporteth Love his force: and her Feete were after Ægles feete, signifying the swyftnes of the same: and this woman held in her hand an Arrowe or Darte, noting forth the forcible stroke or persifeness thereof. Another Image of her they were wont to engrave in the Precious stone Lazulus, which represented a fayre and beautifull mayde all uncovered and naked, whose hayre hunge downe a long all over her body, who also had a lookinge Glasse in her hande, and a Chayne tyed or fastened to her Necke, by whom stoode a fayre younge stripling and beautifull, who with his left hand held her fast by the sayd

chayne, and with his right hand held her by the hayre: herein peradventure noting forth the circumstaunce of Suiters and Woo-
ers, and so forth. Shee had also another manner of Image other
wheres: for there were that drew her forth in the habite of an
Handmayden or Damsell, whose hayre lay scattering aboute her
necke, and whose garment hung downe to her shooe, which were
all white and milky coloured: who helde in her right hande a
Lawrell braunch, and sometimes an Apple, or els a Posie of
sweete and fresh flowers, in her lefthand she held a Combe,
whereby is signified that al such as are borne under her, are
naturally geven to bee lovers of civilnesse and cleanlinesse, and
to delight much in pleasant smells and sweete Odours.

Under her government or rule are al such bruite beastes
which are delicate and leacherous, and which are geven to excesse of lust: as the Cony, the lesser kinde of Dogs, the Goate
and goatebucke, the bull and al other which are of like set and
disposition. Over birds or fowles she hath the rule of the Swan,
the Wagtayle, the Swallowe, the Sparrow, the Partrich, the Bergander, the Crow, all kindes of Doves, and likewise the she
Eagle, which is of such immoderate lust that being trod xiii.
times in a day, yet at the call of her Mate is ready to take it
agayne. Amonge fishes *Venus* ruleth over the gylthead or Golde-
ney, the Merling, the Whiting, and the fishe Cancharus which
is jelous over her Mate, and striveth often for him. Among
Plants or Hearbs subject to her is the Violet, the Malow, the
herbe Venus hayre or goldy lockes, the Lylly, likewise the
hearbe Lada or Ledum whose Gum is called Ladanum and most
commonly Labdanum and is used in Pomanders: furthermore al
and every odiferous thing as is Ambra, which is englished Am-
bergrise: it is found on the sea shore by a countrey called Zingi
in the East part of the world, and is for his gray colour commonly called of the Apothecaries Ambergrisia, hereof are made
very precious and cordiall medicines: hetherto belongeth also
the sweete smelling Time, and the spice Saunders: furdermore,
all such fruits as are pleasant, and of good taste, as the Apple,
the Pare, the fig, the currant, the date, the Pomgranet and so
forth. Amonge Precious stones shee chalengeth the Beril, the
Chrusolyte, the Saphyr, the Jasper, the Cornellys, the pretious
Ætites, the stone Lazulus, the Coral and al such as be beautifull,

and of mylke white or grassy greene colour: Among Mettalls she
requireth a right in Copper and brasse, and partly in silver; and
among savours that which is sweetest, delicious, and unctuous is
hers; and among humors a part of bloude, as also the whole
course of naturall seede is at her disposicion: among the Elements she holdeth a porcion in the ayre and also in the water. . . .

Agrippa saith that *Venus*, in all kindes of Creatures, pur-
chaseth and procureth Love betwixte Mate and Mate: and that
she laboureth chiefly in the multiplication and increase of seede,
to the continuance and preservation of the whole kinde, coveting
alwayes as nigh as she can, and thereto with mighte and mayne
labouringe, to abandon and remoove Barraynesse out of the way,
which coveteth to cut off the Race and continuance of all. . . .

Of Sol, *or the Sunne, the fourth Planet*

Sol, or the Sunne, is the fourth in place and preheminence
amonge the seven, and is among them as it were a Kinge in the
midst of his Throne, Trayne, and Guarde. For under him he hath
Luna or the Moone, *Mercurius*, and *Venus* of whom we have
already spoken: and above him in position and place he hath as
many, that is, to weete, *Mars*, *Jupiter*, and *Saturn*. And it should
seeme it was not without great cause and consideration that the
mighty *Jehovah*; the Maker of Heaven and Earth placed the
Sunne in such a proportioned equality along them all: notwithstanding through his excellency he deserveth the highest roome
of prerogative and dignity. For if the Sunne which is the most
universall cause, and the very beginning and fountayne of light
and influence, and also of vitall heat, of whom all the other
starres doe receave their light, and al things lyving their life,
were placed nexte to the Earth, it woulde come to passe that the
Earth by his excessive heate must needes be brent up and consumed, and all things and creatures also upon the earth, not able
to abide and suffer that his heate, must needes dye and pearishe:
and likewise the starres on high, which now receive their light
at his hands, should not so commodiously enjoy such their illu-
mination. And contrariwyse, if the Sun had the highest place

and were in that roome where *Saturne* continueth, the Earth
heere belowe should be voyde and destitute of sufficiente heate;
all things living should periclitate and be in daunger of decay: as
also the Planets far belowe could not sufficiently have illumina-
tion of the Sunne, being so farre distant from them. Which inconveniences to meete withall the preserver and maker of all,
the mighty and provident God, would have the same so placed
in such degree as that from the superior and inferior Planets, hee
should be alike distant, by that meanes providing that neither
the Sun sould be too nigh the earth, nor els too far of from it.

This property also hath *Sol* wyth *Mars* in common and alike,
that as *Mars* is whot exceedingly, so also is the sun, but herein
they differ, for that the heate of the sun not going beyond his
temperature, doth produce and bring forth to life such things as
are apt to take life, and is also perfiter of al those things which
are endowed with life, and such things as get and grow on by litle
and litle, towards their perfection: as experience teacheth us in
al things having life, even in the very fruites wee behold it how
all of them ripen and come to their maturity and perfection by
the sunnes heate: but contrariwise the heate of *Mars* is an utter
destroyer and Consumer. Besides, *Mars* procureth speede of
death through his such extremity, as we see in the heate of
Choler, and experience whereof we perceive in those that bee
troubled with hot burning Agues: but contrariwise the sunnes
heate is kindly, whose operation we beholde in that heate of the
heart, called the natural of life heate, which giveth and preserveth the life of the body. These two also differ manyfestly in
their effects: for where *Sol* with a good and favorable aspecte
hath rule, he geving them temperate heate of hearte, maketh
them to bee of a courage in deede right manly, and verye
valiant: so contrariwise *Mars* mynistring to his intemperate
heate of heart, maketh them in stomacke to be rather wylde and
savage, rather then properly Puissant: and more venturouse
rashe, and bolde, then considerate and Polliticke. For it is the
excesse of heate, which burning and boyling within a man that
bringeth boldnesse and rashnesse, when as the bloude about the
heart is immoderately and to much set on fire. . . .

Such as be borne under *Sol*, are for the most parte of a browne
colour, and of smal stature, yet well and comely knit and pro-

porcioned: they be also of a very thin haire and curled Head,
Gray eyed: they be also hawty stomacked, and they are advanced often to great honours and dignities. And the Disposition of their minde is such that they be studious of difficult and
hard matters, being very desirous of glory and renowne. They
bee also fast and faythfull in friendship, and constant in Fact and
worde. They bee likewise, Wise, and Polliticke touching common wealth affayres, and are given much to procure the profit of
their country.

Under his government among the kindes of Beastes are also
all such as be of bigge stature, and of hawty stomacke: likewyse
such as are desierous of superiority, and have naturally a pryde
in themselves: Of which sorte is the Lyon, the Crocodile, the
wilde and untamed Lynx, the Ramme, the Oliphant, the Tyger,
likewise the Wolfe whom the aunciente Gentils dedicated to
Apollo and *Latona*: among Fowles hee hath as his owne the
Phoenix, which chiefly keepeth about the Coastes of Arabia,
and is in bignesse about the greatness of an Eagle, which shyneth
like Golde aboute her necke, and in other partes of her she is
purple coloured, saving that her Tayle being blew is distinguished with rose coloured feathers. She lyveth a long time,
even six hundred and three score yeares: and when she waxeth
olde and is weary of her lyfe, shee getteth slippes of Casia, and
Frankinsence, and maketh her Nest on hygh as nigh the sun as
she can, and in the same she dieth being brunt and consumed into
Ashes by the suns heat: out of whose bones and ashes there ingendreth first as it were a litle smal worme, which in shorte
time after proveth to become a young Phoenix. There is no man
that ever seeth the Phenix eating.

Likewise to *Sol* appertayneth the Eagle which keepeth most
in mountaynes, and which almost of all Fowles is without her
cry, and is also very ravenous, so that whatsoever pray it
catcheth, it carieth it away swiftly. But one good property it is
not without herein, for that it seeketh after his pray a far of
alwayes, never spoyling about the place where she abideth and
breedeth. They never commonly dye upon death,[1] nor sicknesse,
but upon famine: for that when they wexe old, their bill growing out at length in the upper part thereof onely, and the neather

[1] *i.e.*, natural death by old age.

parte of the same rather shrynking then still continuing at his olde stay, doth cause that she cannot commodiously receive her Foode. Her flight and travaylinge is onely in the after Noone, sitting still idle all the foore Noone eyeing the assemblies of men, and will not remoove till she have had wearinesse therein.

In her Neast is onely found the Precious stone Ætites which is very Medicinable and which no fire can doe harme unto. Her feathers being put amonge other Birdes Feathers will eate and consume up the other: this hath a great and mortall hatred to the Dragon, which very greedely hunteth after the Eagles Egges. . . .

Of Jupiter *the sixt Planet*

Next in place above *Mars* is *Jupiter*, which tempereth and allaieth the malice of *Mars* and sinister conditions of *Saturne*. For this *Jupiter* is in his qualities very temperate (that is to say) hoate and moyste, and causing heate and moysture. Whereupon he is sayd to be the father and worker of the Sanguine Complexion. For it is proper to bloude to bee hoate and moyst. Hereupon for such benefite wrought by him, he hath often ben called the Original Lyfe Planet. And they were wont to draw him forth in the Royal likenesse of a Kyng, holding a Scepter or golden Mace in his hand: geving to understande thereby his rule and Empyre over all Creatures lyving. The Poets affirme him to bee Sonne to *Saturnus*, and *Rhea*, which *Saturne* understandinge by a Prophesie that it should come to passe that his owne Sonnes should thrust him out of his Kingdome, provided with him selfe to slea them all as soone as ever they shoulde be borne. So hee began to deale heerein, first with *Ceres*, then with *Neptunus* whom he had by the aforesayd *Rhea*. Who when she perceived his purpose herein, being great with childe of *Jupiter* and delivered of him, sent him forthwith very privily into Lycton a place of Creet, where he was hidden in a Denne: and when *Saturne* came to have devoured him also, she cast him a stone in steede of her childe. . . .

Such as are under the government of *Jupiter* are outwardely of

merry Countenance, and of comely and seemly behaviour and
gesture: they be also lovers of clenlinesse, and such as be fayre
speached. Their colour is commonly white, yet stayned here and
there with some red among: their body is well set and proportioned, and their stature and height is indefferent: they be also
of thyn haire, of great eyes, and the pupill or ball of their eye
exeedeth and is after a black: they bee moreover of shorte Nose,
curled Bearde, and their fore teeth are great and long. And inwardly concerning the frame or qualities of their minde, they be
studuous, quiet, and well affected towards all men, but their love
is sodainely got and quickly lost againe. Moreover as concerning worldly benefits *Jupiter* advanceth his to great Prosperity,
good successe, much Riches, high Honoure, and getteth them
Favour and friendship in the Worlde, and preserveth them from
the assaults of their enemies.

Among bruite beastes all such kyndes are his whych in pryde
of stomacke, contende and strive one with another for and concerning the prerogative of their kynde: as the Elephant and
Dragon betweene whome there is continuall and deadly discorde as they that travaile the wildernesses of Affrica, and
Mauritania can witnesse. For the Dragon and the Elephant in
their meeting purpose the death and destruction of ech other.
And in theyr first sighte thay malice one anothers being. In so
much that the serpent twyning about the other with the greate
length of his body and tayle styngeth him round aboute, at
which deadly strokes, the other extreamely payned doth fall
downe to the ground presently, with the waight or force of
which fall he both killeth hymselfe or at leaste wise hurteth hymselfe very grievously, and is thereby in daunger of dying himselfe, as also he presently kylleth the Dragon which is so wounde
and twynde about his body, and crusheth hym all to pieces. So is
the Tyger also subjecte to *Jupiter* in that respecte that he like
wise beareth a naturall grudge and most mortall malice to the
Horse. And his swiftnes also in running is nothing inferiour to
the others. This kinde is bred most often in Hyrcania and India,
a wylde beast of marvailous swiftenes in running, as also terrible
with all in the same. And the smel of the females of this kynde
is also exceding wonderfull: For so often as shee being forth at
purveying for her younge, and for her owne pray (for the Male

kynd hereof doth never a whit regard either her or her yong all this whyle) and in the meane time (as it cannot other wise be) it falleth so forth that she be robbed of any of her whelpes, at her returne home againe to her Den, when she perceiveth that she hath lost any of her littour, she goeth forth out of her den by and by, and smelleth about which waies these should be taken, and after shee pursueth that waies hastely. And to avoyde the daunger of her which is but present death the partye that hath robbed her, being on horsebacke (for on foote he may not be, for he wil then be quickly overtaken of her) turning one of them downe, he must yet make away as fast as ever he can, and not stay til he be got on the other syde of some greate Water, unto whych place shee can not approach, and she in this time makyng after, at the finding of that one so caste in her way, seemeth to be so glad thereof, as that she presently returneth again withal home and there having bestowed the same, taketh againe after the other that she misseth, and never staying till shee come at the Water where the robber in passing through escaped her fury and revenge, shee standeth at the brym or bankes of the same and roreth out very straungely. So is the Unicorne in subjection to *Jupiter*, which is also a heavy and a sore enemy to the Elephant, whych with her one horne whetted and filed upon some flinte, prepareth her selfe to encounter with him. And alwayes in her fighte shee striveth and laboureth very busily to pushe at the belly of the Elephant, which she knoweth to be the most tender place.

And as concerning fowles, all such kyndes be hys, as are of tender and softe meate, and of moste temperate bodies, As is the Pheasaunt, the partrich, which was sometimes dedicated to *Jupiter* and *Latona*: Of all fowles the most lecherous. . . . Under *Jupiter* also are the Plover, the Quaile, the Larke, the hen, the capon. Amonge fishes hee challengeth great a do in the Dolphin called Philiotechnos for that she loveth her yong dearely. The female of this kynd hath both milk and breastes and geveth her younge sucke with the same. As their younge beginne to learne to swim, they set them in a ranck or rowe one afore another, and the elder Dolphins aswell hee as shee, to keepe them in theyr ray or order, do swym by them on ech side, the other on the other side: But as her younge waxe great, this ranke is broken. The Whalefish is also pertinent to *Jupiter*. This kynde bryngeth forth no spawne but a younge fish at the first, and geveth her younge milke. This is very heavy and slowe in swimminge. The Indian Sea is full of these which are in quantity and bignes five times as big againe as the Dolphin.

Over Trees hee ruleth over the Popular tree, the Oke, the wyllow tree, the beeche, the Damascen tree, the Pare and Ipple trees. Likewise he requireth the fruite of the Almond tree, date tree: and among sweete leaves and rootes Mirabolanum, Rheubarbarum, Cassia. Among herbes he hath Mynt, Jupiters beard, Sage, Time, Hemlocke, Helicampane. Amonge gems or precious stones he retaineth the Jacinct, the Berill, the Saphy, the Turkys, the Emerald, the more dusky kind of Jasper, and all other sortes whych declyne towardes a dusky or darke colour. In Mettalles he is chiefe maister of Tyn, which (as *Plynie* sayth) being over layde on such vessels as are of Brasse, maketh them savour more sweetely, and preserveth them from rusting. All wholsome moysture also proceedeth from him, which cause good increase or nourishment in the body. And as concerning the Elements he ruleth and dealeth as him lysteth in the Ayre.

Of Saturne *the seventh Planet*

Saturne is a Planet cold and dry, masculine, malicious and hurtfull in many such Effectes as hee worketh: for when he Raygneth, lyghtlye those that bee borne under him, either dye shortely, livinge no longe time to accompt of, or els if they live any long time, they have for the most part an heavy and hard fortune. Thereupon for this his pernitious condition of hurting and destroying, hee was wont to be set out as a Mower or Harvest man, having and holding a Scythe or Sickle in his hand, as one which by his owne will was fully bent and geven to accelerate and hasten the ruine and decay of all living things; and were it not but that *Jupiter* placed betwixt him and us, did temperate and bridle him much in his aforesayd heavy qualities, and condicions: nothing here beneath almost coulde eyther lyve longe, or prosperously endure. Wherein we have to consider the

G

unspeakable and wonderfull wisedome of the almighty that as in all other thinges, so in this hee hath most especially and wisely provided: that, that enemy of life so ernestly labouring the death and decay of all thinges, shoulde have hys place appoynted him there so far off from the earth, where all creatures lyving make their abode, that of all other Planettes he the cruellest should be most remote and furthest of. For how should any creature lyving sustain, help, and defend it self against the force of such extreame cruelty: If this mortall enemy of all were bestowed and placed any thinge nighe: yea, or any nearer then he is now, to the earth here below, the place of our aboade: yea and how shoulde any thinge continue oute his appoynted and determinate Time, if this fearse and furious harvestman as it were, every day labouring to downe with all, were not let and hyndered by other more friendly and gracious powers, staying him from such hys force. See therefore the truth of holy writ, and how truely it is there sayde, God the whose perfecte wisedome hath disposed all things in their just number, measure and waighte. It is not therefore for his owne worthinesse or dignity that *Saturne* hath the highest place amonge the other Planets, for his deserts deserved: but rather the contrary, upon other effects and occasion: as that all things living might by that meanes be the further of from so frowning, froward, and fatall Foe. He is of a pale and wan colour, and disposeth to the Melancholicke complexion. . . .

Such as are borne under *Saturne* commonly called Saturnystes, are lumpish, heavy and sad, dull witted, full of Melancholy, hard and straunge, a long time to receive understandinge and learninge, but yet after they have once with much adoe apprehended and taken the same, they after become fast Keepers and Retayners thereof . . . as that Seale doth better Imprinte and keepe his Marke which Sealeth in Waxe, and so forth: then that which is bestowed upon Water. The greatest desire of the Saturnistes also is for the most part to addresse them selves to become sole or solitary in theyr life, and to allow of the religious estate or condition chyefly. Their Phisiognomy is altogether blockish, their countenance cruell and stronge, theyr head hanging downe, theyr eyes ever bent and caste upon the ground. Theyr property is such that they be ever almost either musing or murmuring

with themselves. And in their sleepe they are much troubled:
For they dreame oftentimes that they be buried alive and put
into the earth quycke, or else they dreame of deade men, and
thynke they see such sights which make them astonished, and to
cry out in theyr sleepe, as when they dreame of devils which they
do often, and of hel and helfier, and of cruell persecution and
tyrannye and such like. . . . They are also very ready and prone
to civill dissention and discorde. They be also for the most part
shorte lifed, because the exceeding cold in them is a shortner of
their Dayes, as we see it cometh to passe in old men, which
through coldnes of nature are chopte up of a sodaine: for olde
men as they grow on towards death becom very colde and dry,
all heate and moysture whych are the preservatives of Lyfe then
forsakyng them and bidding them farewel. . . .

And they also are geven to bee sodainely moved and angred:
And solitarynes is a great part of their desire, and the pryvate
kind of life: as Experience gave forth in the Dayes of *Diocle-
tianus* and *Maximinianus*, Noble Prynces or Emperours: which
forsakyng theyr royall roomes and publique, and pryncely preheminence: for to obtayne a quietnes of lyfe, which they hoped
to have in exempting themselves from worldly affaires, gave
over all. . . . Such an other was *Timon* of Athens, for solitarines
of lyfe, but not to a like ende: for the other for desyre onely of
knowledge in heavenly thinges separated themselves from the
society of men, but this other through a waywardnes and croked-
nes of nature, abhorred and shunned all mens companies. Therfore in the field *Atticus* he got him a Den and was gladdest when
he was furthest of from the sight of al men. . . .

Amonge the Elementes *Saturne* hath most a doe with the
Earth whose Qualities are also after the maner of *Saturnus*, that
is most colde and drye: which Earth the Phylosophers not wyth-
oute greate cause, called the Nourse or Graunde Mother of all
lyvinge thinges here with us, for that she conceyved and brought
forth so many distinct and divers kindes of things as make nowe
to the enriching and beautifying of the whole Worlde. And as
the Earth serveth to bring forth such variety of fruites and provision, as wherewithall al thinges lyving are richly sustayned:
so doe all other things in the Worlde by Gods special apoynt-
ment serve to the commodity and use of Mankinde, whom God

hath made Lord and maister of all. So that the Fyre (as saith *Lactantius*) which serveth to heate and to geve light: the Fountaynes which out of the Earth and sides of hylles geve forth water: the floudes which water our grounds: the Hilles that bring forth Vynes and other deliciouse kindes of fruite: the Fennes, and Marishes, which bringe forth Reede and Sedge: the sea which both storeth us with variety of Fishes, as also serveth to the passage of Marchauntmen, and marchaundize: the Sun which altreth and chaungeth the times and seasons of the yeare: the Moone who is a Guide and governour in the darke night, and also a Distinguisher of the yeare into severall Moneths: the starres which serve greatly to the travayling of the sea faringe men; the windes which preserveth the Ayre from corruption: all these, as all thinges els which the Earth produceth of her self any wayes beneficially (which are Infinite) serve all to the commodity, behofe, and use of Man.

OF UNIVERSAL PROPORTION

From *The Courtiers Academy*
by Annibale Romei
translated by J. Kepers, 1598

What time this worlds great workmaister did cast
To make al things, such as we now behold,
It seemes that he before his eyes had plast
A goodly Paterne, to whose perfect mould
He fashioned them as comely as he could;
That now so faire and seemely they appeare,
As nought may be amended any wheare.

That wondrous Paterne wheresoere it bee,
Whether in earth layd up in secret store,
Or else in heaven, that no man may it see
With sinfull eyes, for feare it to deflore,
Is perfect Beautie which all men adore,
Whose face and feature doth so much excell
All mortal sence, that none the same may tell.

SPENSER, *An Hymne in Honour of Beautie*

H is Highnesse, according to his wont, being the last
yeere towards the end of Autumne in the said place,
and the most famous Duchesse, accompanied with
thrise noble Gentlemen, and gratious Dames, besides the Gentlewomen of the renowmed Duchesse, desirous to
go down to the sea side, made it knowne to the Gentlemen and
Gentlewomen, that while they were abroad, his minde was, that
every one might lawfully betake himselfe to that contentment,

which was to him most acceptable. Whereupon one part of the Gentlemen, the Lady *D. Marfisa* and *Bradamante*, and other Gentlewomen of the Court, accompanied his Highnesse, and the Duchesse to the sea side: but the greater part, especially of women, unto whome the sea winde in the end of Autumne was not pleasing, went to the Pallace, to the end that with some delightsome entertainement, they might passe the time till the returne of his Highnesse. The Countesse of *Sala* for her quiet, had retired her selfe into her lodging apart, unto whome all the Gentlemen and Ladies resorted, to manifest unto her their favour and good will, as also to bee partakers of her most gratious conversation. The Lady Countesse therefore, seeing so faire and honorable an assembly in her chamber, as she that is the inventrice of fresh and honest contentments, me thinkes said she smiling, that souldiers can hardly keepe their ranckes without an head, and therefore, I would advise, so it be pleasing to you Lords and Ladies, that by lot we chuse out amongst our selves (to avoid envy) who ought to commaund, and that her empire may continue til the returne of his Highnes. This motion by the Countesse propounded, was of all the whole company commended. The lotte fell to the Lady Countesse of *Scandiano*, and with great joy she was crowned with a garland of Lawrell leaves. This vertuous Lady, the Queene, peradventure of more than one heart, considering that in this noble concourse, there were the most learned and flourishing wittes of all the Court, desirous to heare them discourse of some matter that might be contenting, and acceptable to the whole company, spake thus: Amongst all the things which administer delight and wonder, it seemeth Beauty holdeth the chiefest place, the which is so much the more admirable, in that she by few being perfectly knowne, is notwithstanding by every one beloved, which thing I with my selfe having oftentimes considered, it maketh me enter into a singular desire to understand, what maner of thing this is, which we terme Beauty; whether truely she be to be found in the world, or that we forge such a matter, in our fantasie, perceyving every day, by experience, that what to one seemeth deformed, to another appeareth beautifull. Seeing therefore a favourable starre and gentle fortune have exalted me to so great Empire, and that I may commaund over the divinest wittes, I determine to satisfie my honest desire: I enjoyne you therefore Signior *Francesco Patritio*, under paine of the losse of my favour (the which hitherto I have vouchsafed you) to discourse upon Beautie, endevoring in the best manner you can to give me satisfaction.

This *Signior Patritio* is a Gentleman of *Dalmatia*, a man very learned, but especially in Platonicall philosophie, who having bene a little buffeted by Fortune, in the end retiring himselfe into the sanctuary of men literate (for so is the court of this Prince) he was with honorable regard, by his Highnesse embraced. Rising up therfore, and making reverence: This curtesie of your Majestie, thrice famous Queene (said he) hath beene great and singular, having before any desert on my part vouchsafed me so great a reward, as to bee made woorthy of your Majesties favour. And whatso greevous punishment can be imagined, that to the losse of this, may be compared; but as with so gratious a gift I remaine comforted, so upon some further consideration, I finde my selfe altogether perplexed & doubtfull, because in obeying your commandement, I am sure not to satisfie your desire, knowing my owne insufficiencie to intreate of so high a subject, as is Beautie: and by disobedience I should incurre the penaltie set downe, the which I much more feare than death it selfe. To avoyde therefore so greevous punishment, I will make no doubt to expose my selfe to so great an enterprise, hoping, that as those blessed intelligences, in their spheres, illuminations and motion, infuse that, whereof the beautiful of-spring of Nature in this inferior world is derived, so that these resplendant intelligences which are heere placed so neare our hearts, reverberating upon me their most glittering beames will kindle light, and stirre up motion in my obscure and dull understanding: from whence conceits and words may spring, apt not only to discover that participated of, but even essentiall and true beauty.[1] Notwithstanding we (most famous Queene) having Beauty before our eies, leaving the first demand, pertaining onely to the blind, and searching out what thing this is which we call Beauty, I will affirme, that it is no other but a most pretious qualitie, which shineth in the universall frame, growing from proportions or colours, or from the one and the other together, brought foorth

---

[1] 'capable of discovering not only beauty as manifested in particular objects, but also the archetypal beauty in which they participate.'

by the chiefe Creator, to no other end, but with wonder and delight, to kindle love in those mindes, which can comprehend it. Desiring therefore to make knowne, that this my definition is perfect, and under it that all things else be comprehended, it is necessary, that discoursing somewhat more deepely, I do shew the proper and particular beauty of all those things, which in the universall frame of this world are of beauty capable. I say then, that as this great worke which we call the world, is known by sense, and by understanding conceived, so is it divided into two partes, the one of which we terme the sensible, and the other the intelligible world: the sensible world hath two parts one subject to vicissitudal generation and corruption, & it is this world which wee enjoy, being so deare to us, the other is the celestiall world, subject to no other transmutation, but onely locall motion: the corruptible worlde is contrived of the foure Elements, Earth, Water, Ayre, and Fire, as likewise of all things mixed: whereof some be perfect, and others unperfect, and of the perfect some be living, other some without life: of living things, some have onely the soule vegetative, others have vegetation, and sence: and the third sort enjoy both vegetation, sense, and also reason. Imperfect mixtions, so called, because they want little of being simple; are the vapours, whereof all those imperfect mixtions are generate in which moisture beareth sway, as deaw, frost, mistes, clowds, rayne, snow, tempests, and such like; and exhalation the mother of all such things, in which heate and drynesse prevaile, as are lightnings, thunders, thunderbolts, windes, falling starres, comets, and other like impressions, which are ingendred in the highest region of the ayre; the perfect mixtions without life, are stones, pretious gemmes, and minerales: living things, retaining vegetation, are plants, hearbes, and all sortes of fruites: living things having both vegetation & sense, be unreasonable creatures, of which som be imperfect, others perfect, the imperfect be those which have no other sense, but feeling and imagination confused: and therefore they living halfe a life, are recounted betweene plants and living creatures, as oysters, muscles, sponges, and other such like creatures, fastening unto stones: creatures perfect be all the other sorte, whether they be beasts on the earth, fish of the sea, or foules of the ayre; the living creature possessed with a soule vegetative, sensible, and reasonable is onely man. The celestiall world, although it be al of one selfe same substance, and that it seemeth at the first sight one heaven alone, yet notwithstanding by divers motions wee learne, that it is distributed into ten spheares: the first of which ascending upwarde, is the spheare of the moone, the second of Mercurie, the third of Venus, the fourth of the Sun, the fift of Mars, the sixt of Jupiter, the seventh of Saturne, the eight of the starrie firmament, the ninth and tenth, the one of which (if the position of Astrologers be true) giveth motion trepedative, and the other motion diurnall, called therefore the first mover. The intelligible world is comprehended by many and divers orders of blessed soules and spirits, the lowest of which is mans soule, and after that ensueth the not erring intelligence, called the soule of the world and Nature, for the three effects, she produceth in this universall frame, for in as much as she giveth life & preserveth the world, she is tearmed the soule of the world, and in that she imprinteth into matter with the seale of divinitie, al formes generative and corruptible, she is called nature: lastly because she directeth everie thing deprived of understanding, to their ende, shee is tearmed intelligence never erring. This is she (most famous Queene) that procureth the birds with so great industrie to build their nests, she imprinteth naturall desire of generation in all creatures, and contemning their own proper commodity, with great care and labour to bring uppe their yong. She maketh the Bee and Ant to provide in summer, for the future wants of winter, and to conclude, it is shee that is alwaies intentive to the good of the whole world. The Angelical spirits follow, being the most noble ornaments of the celestial spheares, divided into many Hierarchies: the first of which wholly enflamed with divine love, is that of the Seraphins, the second of the Cherubins, all replenished with incomprehensible knowledge, in the third be the thrones faythfull secretaries of the celestiall minde: then follow Dominations, Powers, Principalities, the Angels and Archangels: above whome sitteth as perfect, the first understanding, being the most excellent & great God, who immovable, draweth and conjoyneth all the other understandings, as of them beloved & desired, to himselfe. As this universall worke is divided into two parts, the one corporeall and sensible, the other incorporeal

G2

and intelligible, so be there two beauties, the one sensible, the other intelligible. But in that the beginning of all our knowledge, is derived from sense, we will first intreate of Beauty sensible: the which is no other but that most gratious qualitie, which shineth in bodies sensible, springing from proportion or colors or together both from the one & other, which administring delight, produceth love in those minds that can comprehend it. And because bodies sensible are of two sortes, that is, simple, as the heaven and foure elements be, or compounded as al bodies mixed are, we must observe, that of all bodies simple, Heaven onely may bee termed beautifull, for the elements being incapable of proportion, light & colors, they cannot properly be called beautifull. Leaving them therefore apart with the mixed bodies, that com not much short of being elements, we will affirme, that sensible beauty only in heaven, and bodies perfectly compounded is comprehended, which notwithstanding is not all one, but as compounded bodies be divers, so are there beauties distinct and different: in that some are compounded of like partes as stones, pretious gemmes and mineralles, others of parts unlike, and in themselves dissenting, as plants, and living creatures. We wil then averre, that both the beautie of heaven, and of compounded bodies of partes unlike consisteth only in colours, for though the beautie of things compounded of partes different, consisteth in proportion and colours; yet of some the beautie consisteth principally in colors, as likewise of other some in proportion. The beauty therefore wherewith heaven is adorned, is no other but his most bright and shining colour, which doth not onely make heaven beautifull, but further, is an occasion, that al other sensible beautie is faire and apparant. The beautie of stones consisteth in their colours, as of marble, porpherie, alabaster, and such like. That of the diamond in his white and excellent colour, like to the starres, as also the beautie of the rubie is in his red and cleere colour. The beauty of mineralles also consisteth in colours; for gold in colour like to the Sunne, receiveth his brightnesse; and silver in whitenesse resembleth the Moone, and so all other mettalles by their proper colours are esteemed faire and beautifull. Plants have their beautie in proportion, and colours; but more specially in proportion. That of hearbs and floures, consisteth rather in colour than proportion: but the beautie of creatures irrationall, is placed principally in the proportion and correspondencie, that the partes betweene themselves, have with the whole, and farre lesse depending on colour. Mans beautie consisteth in proportion, and in splendor of his proper and well placed colours: But in that I reserve the discussion of humane Beautie, to the end of this my discourse, we wil now leave it. And that no Beautie may remaine untouched, before we passe over to the Beautie of the world intelligible, we will speake somewhat of artificiall Beautie, seeing things artificiall also are termed beautifull: and amongst those artificiall, I place Poesie, and Speach or Oration, the one being governed by Arte Poeticall, the other by the Art of Rethorike. And as we find quantitie both in the one and other, so in them both proportion, and colours Poeticall and Rethoricall are comprehended; yet these are not knowne by sense, but by the minde and understanding, wherefore the beautie of Poesie and Oration, ought to bee called an artificiall intelligible Beautie, differing from other beauties artificiall, which by the sense of seeing onely are comprehended. The beautie therefore of things artificiall, being as it were the image of those naturall, consisteth as well in colour as proportion; yet in some we consider only proportion, as in statues, buildings and other like, which proceede from manuall Artes, in which there is little reckoning made of colours. In some other things the beautie remaineth in colour; and these bee such as depend on the Arte of Weaving, as clothes of silke, wooll, linnen, and such like. The beauty of plants is respected both in one and other, that is, in proportion and colors: And let this spoken, be sufficient for Beautie artificiall.

Now passing over to that Beautie which onely with the eyes of the soule is comprehended (being Beautie intelligible) beginning from the lowest, and is that which is found in the soule of man. I saye, that as the Beauty of humane bodie (as we wil shew) is placed principally in the superiour part, which regardeth heavenly light; so the Beautie of mans soule is found in the more eminent parte of the same, the which is exposed to divine light. This is called understanding, by which our soule conceiveth and knoweth, not only the being of things corporeall & sensible, but also by meane of thinges visible, raiseth it selfe to the knowledge of those invisible, so that as we observe the soule of man to be compounded of parts and divers parcells, so the same soule from the consent of partes and colours, receiveth his excellencie: colours are no other than intelligible kinds, placed in the understanding, which with colours have the like similitude, as the visible colours themselves, and these may be termed intelligible; for as colours are not actually visible, neither can their beauty by bodily eie be seene, if first that eie, and those colours, be not by some light, and especially by the light of the first visible (which is the Sunne) illuminated, so the forms and intelligible kindes of our understanding (which is the eie of the soule) cannot be comprehended, if first that understanding and those intelligibles, bee not by the light of superior understanding cleered and illumined. These intelligibles, which placed in understanding, do make it absolutely perfect and beautiful, be of two sortes: some be intelligibles of trueth, others intelligibles of good: those of good be decking our soules with prudence, fortitude, temperance & justice, make them most beutiful: those of truth apparel them with two pretious habites, wisedom & sapience, throgh which habites, our souls becom like to divine beuty: proportion, by which one parte of the soule with admirable symetry answereth to the other, is no other but a famous vertue, which maketh our soule so faire & beautiful, that if with bodily eyes it might be contemplated, it would produce in us incredible love, and wonderfull affection: this by the eie of the mind is onely discovered, being more excellent than a thousand bodily eyes; and therefore in those whose minde is not blinde, it bringeth foorth affections not onely wonderfull, but out of doubt such, as neither by the tongue can be expressed, nor by the mind comprehended.

According to order, the Beauty of the worldly soule followeth, called Nature, and intelligence not erring, whose beauty in like manner is observed in colours and proportion. Colours are no other, but divine Ideaes infused in the same soule: and proportion is nothing else, but an exemplar forme, of superior understanding imprinted in the said soule, after whose image by the seale of divinitie, it maketh matter deformed, beautifull. The beauty of Angelles divided into divers Hierarchies, as wee have saide, is no other but Angelicall understanding, garnished, and replenished with all formes intelligible by understanding divine.

These of all understandings, have the greater proportion to receive celestiall splendor, as those who beeing alwayes present, do face to face beholde divine Beauty: and therefore those Angelicall understandings, are alwayes in action of intelligence, and are made beautiful, after suche a sort, as of deformitie they are uncapable, which is not in humane intellect, by reason it is not ever in action of intelligence, and is capable as well of deformitie as beauty: For when the soule abaseth it selfe with cogitations, and intimation in the obscuritie of sensible delights, the conceit of Beauty remaineth extinct and darkened; but when it is exalted to the contemplation of things supernall, exposing it selfe to celestiall light, then procureth shee her owne native beauty, to be cleere and excellent. Hitherto (most famous Queene) we have intreated of sensible and intelligible Beautie, in as much as it is Beautie participated of.

Now remaineth it unto us to discourse of true & essential Beauty, by mean of which al things created are so much the more fayre, by how much the more they are partakers of it. This is found in the first understanding, beeing the most mighty and excellent God, creator and giver of all Beauty: because he alone is absolute perfection, perfect wisedome, and incomprehensible Beauty: especially not to be comprehended by our understanding: the which at contemplation of divine essence, remaineth no lesse obfuscate, then is the eye of a Bat in beholding the sun. Having therefore to discusse upon so high a subject, I will endevour to the uttermost of my wit and capacity, to direct your majestie to the contemplation of essentiall and true divine Beautie, by those meanes which are granted unto us by the Creator: For he hath not equally distributed his Treasures. Angelicall understanding is replenished by the chiefe creator, essentially with all formes intelligible, and to it is permitted the contemplation of divinity face to face. Intellect humane, in as much as it is united to the material body, deprived of all intelligibles, (as a plaine & smoothe boord) is yet in potential power to receive all the formes & intelligible representations, the materiall & sensible, by theyr own Ideas, and the immaterial and insensible by anothers, or in anothers likenes & similitude: & therefore al our knowledge proceedeth from sence, things sensible being the true meanes which guide to the knowledge of those intelligible, being as it were similitudes and representations of them. By these representations therefore & similitudes, I wil seeke to make known divine & true Beauty, the which consisteth, though in a most supereminent manner, in colour & proportion, for it is a thing most certaine, that this sensible light is no other but a bright colour, colour being likewise nothing els, but a shadowed & obfuscate light, seeing it is generate, not only by the mixtion of the first qualities, but also by light and shadow: there is this difference, that the shadowie light is not of it selfe in visible act, but to that is procured by bright colour, wheras bright colour is not only of it self, alwaies in visible act; but further, is an occasion that al other things be visible, seene, & by al mens eyes beheld. And therefore the sun adorned with this bright colour, is the first visible, the first seene, and first seeing, deservedly called by *Heraclytus* the eie of the world.

This bright sensible colour, which is the sunnes beauty, easily guideth to the knowledge of brightest colour intelligible, which is the Beautie of the first understanding, being as it were the Image and similitude of it: for as sensible colours can neither bee visible nor seene, without the most bright colour of the sun, so intelligible colours, which be those intelligible forms, cannot have actual intelligence, nor be conceived, without the presence of most bright color divine: And as the eies should not be actually seeing without celestial light, so Intellects, which be no other but incorporeal eyes, should not actually be intelligent without divine splendor & brightnes: for as the light of the sun is of it selfe visible, & by it selfe seene, so the most bright colour divine is of it selfe intelligible, and by it selfe understood. And as the sun by his most bright color is the first visible, first seen, and first seeing, so the first understanding, which is god, most mighty and excellent, with his most glittering shining colour, and light essentiall, is the first intelligible, first understoode, and first intelligent. The Sunne by his resplendant light, exceedeth all the celestiall bodies in Beauty: the first intellect (excepting alwayes, it it bee lawfull to make comparison, betweene the finite and infinite) through his divine splendor, and most glittering light is in the intelligible world, of al intellects the beautifullest, and most supereminent: and as the light of our material fire, in these inferiour parts, representeth the Sunne; so

is the light of the sunne in the worlde celestiall, the true similitude of divine light and brightnesse. And therefore the divine
Philosopher, defineth light to be no other than an influence of
divine essence, into al worldly things infused, not being any
thing throughout the universall woorke, wherein some shadow of
light doth not appeare and shine. These be the meanes and
similitudes (renowmed Queen) which shew that the Beautie of
the first Intellect consisteth in his proper colour, being the same
light which beautifieth, and is diffused throughout the whole
world. It remaineth that I procure you to understand the other
part of divine and essentiall beauty, which is proportion. Yet let
not your highnesse imagine, that these beauties which I place in
God, be in themselves divers, as also distinct, from divine essence, as wee see in other understandings. For in God there is
nothing which is not divinity of it selfe, and therefore in God
Idea, light, wisedome, justice, be no other but God himselfe;
notwithstanding they are divers by our unperfect manner of
understanding: because therefore we understand proportion as
divers from his light, we will so expresse it. Proportion then,
which is in God parte of his Beauty, is no other but the Idea and
exemplar forme of the whole world, in that divine intellect, in
which universall frame, al the parts being togither, within themselves wholly correspondent, they are in the divine understanding with greater proportion then in the world. As in the Architects understanding, the modell and exemplar forme of buylding
is much more fayre and excellent, then in the buylding it selfe:
In that the forme of Building may receive impediment from matter which ever resisteth Ideall reason, but that which is in the
Soule being pure and Immateriall, can have no defect. So that as
the Beautie of the buylding and of al parts thereof, dependeth
on the exemplar forme, which ⟨is⟩ in the understanding of the
Architect, and therefore this in the Building is called Beautie
participated of, and that in the Architects understanding, Beautie
essentiall.

So the Beauty of this worldly Frame, and al the parts thereof
dependeth on Ideal form, in minde divine comprehended, and
therefore that is tearmed Beautie participated of: and this in the
minde of the divine Architect, is true and essentiall beauty,
which consisteth as I have sayd, in Ideall proportion, and his

shining light, which is not onely the true light, that illuminateth man comming into this world, but further, is that which causeth the universall frame to be resplendant and beautifull. The divine Prophet sheweth (and it is true) that God having created in five dayes all other things which are comprehended in the whole world, he finished his labour the sixt day in the worke of man. I having therefore dilated of the whole world in the first part of my discourse, as also of the parcels thereof, and in the second of the corporeal Beauty sensible: in the third of Artificial beauty: in the fourth of the Beauty of Intellects, and in the fift of essentiall Beauty divine, in imitation of divine wisedome, I determine in this sixt and last part, to conclude with the Beauty of the shape humane. Throughout the whole world divine Beauty obscureth al other pulchritude. The Sun exceedeth in beauty al bodyes celestiall, and Beauty humane excelleth all the other of this inferiour world, and therefore we may say with the holy scripture, that God created man after his owne Image, seeing that in man the beame of divinity doth appeare and shine. This heavenly creature whome we call man, was compounded of soule and body, the which body, having to be the harbour of a most fayre and immortall soule, was created without covering of hide, bristles, feathers, skales, brutish tusks, or hornes, neyther with bil, or clawing talents, but most exquisite, with his eyes towards heaven, and was placed in the midst of the world, to the end that as in an ample Theater, hee might behold and contemplate the workes of the great God, and the Beauty of the whole world: as also there was granted unto him a perfect tongue & speech, that enflamed with love divine, and replenished with admiration, he might praise, and with words extoll divine beauty. In humane body we find proportion & colours, more then in all other bodies compounded of parts unlike, because in it that proportion is comprehended, which representeth the whole corporeal sensible world, as also the colours that beautifie this sensible world; the one of which is white, like to heavenly light, and the other is red, like to the shining colour of material and visible fire: and therefore man was worthily called a little world, seeing the body of man is no other but a little modell of the sensible world, and his soule an Image of the world intelligible. The beauty therefore of humane body, consisteth in due measure of proportion, that is, in fayre and goodly lineaments, and in colours wel disposed: and further, which falleth not out in any other body compounded of parts unlike, his beauty principally is discovered in one part alone: & this is in the superiour part, which regardeth towards the light of the Sunne: whose beautie is that, which by meane of the eye procureth Love. Moreover (which likewise in no other kind of creature is founde) Beautie humane is in women, in farre greater excellencie observed, then in men, which was thus dispensed with great providence by the cheefe creator. For having graunted woman unto man for a companion, he endowed her with excellent beautie, for production of Man, and to enflame in him a desire to generate that fayre and beautifull. This *Anacreon* confirmeth, saying, that as running is the ornament of an horse, and wisedome of a man; so beautie is the proper honour of a woman: And the Philosopher in the first of his Rhetoryke, doth in such sort appropriate beauty to a woman, as he setteth it downe principally amongst feminine vertues, saying, that the vertues of a woman be beauty, honestie, and desire to take paines, without avarice. And in the same booke speaking of the beautie of man, he placeth in the visage of man, togither with the aspect, terrible regard and countenance, to the ende that, provoked in fighting, he might be a terror to his enemies, which doth clearly manifest that beautie is not in man in so great perfection as in a woman, because his beautie procureth as wel terror as love, wheras Beauty in women doth alwaies generate love, & never procureth feare. If I were willing to describe the beauty of visage humane, I might much more easily poynt it out with my finger, then expresse it by my tong. Yet for al this I wil not forbeare to affirme that to form perfect Beauty in humane visage, foure things fitly concur, proportionable feature, color wel disposed, favor and presence: to goodly feature & color, fair & comly presence addeth such excellencie, as without it al other Beauties languish & weare away.

Whether this be a beame of the soule, which glittereth in the countenance after the same sort as the beames of the intelligences shine in their proper heavens & spheares, or that it be an harmony of shadowed colours & lineaments, I dare not affirme, but confesse my self to be ignorant, & wil remain bound to him, that shal make me capable hereof. How much favor importeth to the perfection of beauty humane, from hence we easily conceive: for without favor, beauty would neither be gracious, nor accepted of: for she accompanied with favor, hath force to draw to hir self, al those minds which can comprehend her; & without favor beauty may be sayd to be unperfect: therfore the ancients fained the Graces to be the waitingmaids of *Venus*; by this inferring, that beauty ought ever to be accompanied by favor, & from hir never to be seperate. Presence principally is discovered in the sweet and comly motions of the body, for the body standing immoveable, is not apparant, and for my part I would say that presence is no other then a certaine faculty and agilitie, which the body hath to obey the soule.

It remaineth unto me (most excellent Queen) for conclusion of this my discourse, that I declare unto your highnesse, that humane beuty to no other end, hath by the chiefe creator bin produced, amongst al beauties sensible, most excellent, but to kindle this honest & holy love divine, which uniteth humane creature with his creator. For man wholly astonished in beholding humane Beauty, raiseth up his mind to the contemplation of Beauty true & essential, whereof this is a shadow and similitude.

The maner of handling this controversie pleaseth me well, replied the L. Duchesse, seeing every one may reason to their owne minde: yet give you the onset, and begin first from proportion, the which out of doubt naturally exceeds colors, as do the elements things mixed. When *Partitio* therfore, had a litle pawsed with himself, he said: Among al beuties sensible, that seems the most perfect beuty, which is neerer to beauty intelligible, as also of that most participating. Proportion is such: therfore amongst all beuties sensible shee is the greater: and consequently where she is found, is that, which to beauty, giveth greater perfection. Proportion questionlesse hath greater similitude wyth intelligible beautie, because it can not bee proportion without order, and order is proper to reason, which reason is no other, but a similitude of beautie intelligible, and of the selfe divine intellect: but further it is the more principall parte of beautie sensible, which reacheth delight, not onely to sense, but also to the minde, and such proportion: for by the order and disposition of parts, the footesteps of reason do in hir appeere, and therefore shee is very conformable to the nature of the minde,

being apt to delight, and ravish it, with unspeakeable contentment: Further, proportion is the principal cause of beuty,
throughout the universal frame, aswel of the world corporeal
and sensible, as of the intelligible: considering that by proportion, it is created, and by the same preserved; therfore it deserveth the chiefest place in the beauty of humane body, which
is no other but a model of the great world. Except we should
foolishly beleeve, that the worlde was made by chance, we must
necessarily conceive, that with speciall providence, it was built
by the divine architect, as also it is necessary to place in the
same divine mind, the Ideal forme, as we have said of the world,
by others termed the worldes Archtype, even as it is necessary
that the model and Idea of the building, should be in the minde
of the Architect. Now the principal and most perfect part, as
well in the minde of divine, as humane Architect is proportion,
because in it order and disposition are comprehended. According to this Ideall proportion therefore was the whole worlde by
God created, and first of figure circular; because to containe this
universall worke, that of al other figures was most proportionable, and the heavenly spheares were with so great proportion
framed, as likewise to every one, motion, with so singular proportion dispensed, that in mooving (as the divine Philosopher
affirmeth) they procure celestiall harmony: every starre hath his
proportion to receive light from the Sunne; and the Sunne pro-
portionably to every one of them, dispenseth & infuseth of his
light; and both the stars, and Sunne, with so great measure and
proportion, doe infuse their light and heate into these inferiour
bodies, as with marvel, and wonder from them, springeth the
beutie of this inferior world. Such proportion we finde in the
elements, as well in quantitie as qualitie, as if of this their proportion, the least part were but disproportioned, one element
would convert al the other into his proper Nature, or els the
world would be confounded into Chaos. Proportion causeth harmonie in number, in bodies beautie, in humours health, in minde
vertue; as contrariwise disproportion procureth in numbers discord, in bodies deformitie, in humors infirmity, and in the minde
vice: But who is it that wil doubt proportion to be the cause of
all delights, as well sensible, as intelligible, in that the good
which delighteth, is no good, if it bring not with it proportion,

neither is there any thing that desireth to be united with good simply, but with a good to it selfe proportioned; and from hence proceedeth the saying of *Heraclytus*, that every thing is ravished with his own contentment, the which standes in union of good, to it selfe proportioned: and this is that which properly of all things is beloved and desired.

GLOSSARY

ability: financial resources.
abrogation: doing away with.
absides: apsides; points in the orbit of a planet when it is either
    furthest from or closest to the body it revolves about.
accident: adj., incident (to), liable to happen (to).
        sb., symptom.
accidentary: inessential.
acronycal: happening in the evening.
admiration: astonishment.
adust: parched.
adustion: dryness.
adustive: fiery.
adventure: risk.
advisement: consideration.
affect: desire.
affectate: inclined, disposed.
affection: passion, state or power of being affected or acted upon.
affects: effects.
affluence: plenty.
ague: malarial fever.
alegar: malt vinegar.
aliment: food.
Almain: German.
amaze: astound.
ampliation: enlarging.
Antipodes: dwellers at the other side of the globe.
apparently: visibly, obviously.
approvable: demonstrable.
approve: prove.
artificer: craftsman.
assimulate: absorb.
asunder: apart.
aver: assert as a fact.
avoid: eject, evacuate.

back-friend: pretended friend.
baggage: rubbishy.
balancer: one who rides on a coach to keep it steady.
ballassed: filled.

bawd: procuress.
bear in hand: manage, assure, lead to believe.
beck: call, command.
beeregar: vinegar made from beer.
behoof: use, benefit.
bent: inclination.
bergander: sheldrake; a duck with variegated colouring.
beseeming: suiting.
bewray: expose.
blain: blister.
bolt: sift.
botcher: patcher, cobbler.
botches: boils.
brackish: salty.
bragget: fermented honey and ale.
brent: burnt.
brigandine: body armour, corslet.
broached: pierced through.
brook: endure, tolerate.
brunt: burnt.

camarine: fetid swamp.
careful: burdened with worries.
casque: helmet.
catholic: universal.
celebrated: resorted to, thronged.
chafe: heat.
chamlet: camlet; a costly oriental fabric.
cheer: countenance towards; entertainment.
chevisance: provision.
chilum: chyle; a fluid which assists digestion.
chirurgeon: surgeon.
choplogic: sophistical arguer.
churlish: surly, grudging.
cleft: split.
clotter: coagulate.
coaction: force, compulsion.
cogging: cheating.
coleworts: cabbages.
collation: comparison.
colour: outward appearance, semblance.
colourably: plausibly.
coozinage: cozenage; deception.

commission: committing crime.

commixion: mixture.

commodity: advantage, profit.

commonalty: the common people.

complexion: combination of qualities or humours, constitution, temperament.

composure: composition.

comprehend: contain.

conceit: notion, conception.

conceptory: vessel, cavity.

concoction: digestion.

conditions: character, disposition.

conferred: compared.

congruency: agreement, correspondence.

contiguity: nearness, being in contact.

consectary: corollary.

contemn: scorn.

contentation: strife, dispute.

convenience: agreement, accordance of nature.

convenient: suitable, consistent.

cony: rabbit.

cordial: reviving the heart, hence invigorating.

cordwainer: worker in Cordovan leather, shoemaker.

corned: salty.

cornellys: cornelian.

cosmical: at sunrise.

covert: shelter.

covet: desire.

crudity: indigestible matter.

cuirass: breastplate.

cuisses: armour for the thighs.

cunning: skill.

curious: elaborate, exquisite.

curiosity: undue refinement.

currier: leather-dresser.

cursitor: courier.

damascen: damson.

damnified: injured.

dapper: trim, smart.

decked: arrayed, clothed.

defecate: clarify.

deflore: deflower, spoil.

defluxion: discharge.
delicacy: luxuriousness.
delicate: effeminate, self-indulgent.
delicious: voluptuous, luxurious.
demonstrate: demonstrated.
desert: deserted.
derive: convey.
dingthrift: spendthrift.
discrasie: discrasia; bad temperament of body or air.
discreet: discerning.
discuss: drive away, disperse.
distemper: disorder.
distemperature: ailment.
divination: prophecy.
dotage: feeble-mindedness.
drift: aim, purpose.
drossy: worthless.
dryth: drought.
dumpish: slow-witted, dejected.

ecliptic: the great circle of the sun's apparent orbit.
edify: build.
eftsoons: again, afterwards.
elect: choose.
emmet: ant.
engrosser: monopolist.
ensampled: modelled.
entertain: maintain.
entertainment: treatment, accommodation, provision.
ephemerides: tabulated positions of a heavenly body for a series of
    successive days.
epicycle: orbit of any of the seven planets.
equinoctial: pertaining to the equinoxes.
Equinoctial line: the Equator.
eschew: shun.
espial: spy.
exasperate: irritate.
excoct: extract by heat.
excrement: outgrowth, secretion.
exemplaries: archetypes.
exonerate: unload.
extol: boast.
exulcerate: irritate, aggravate.

fabrifacture: construction.
fact: deed, action (usually crime).
fain: glad, gladly.
fantasy: imagination, hallucination.
fasting: binding.
fastness: firmness.
favour: charm, attractiveness.
fear: frighten.
fearful: terrible; timid.
feces: sediment.
feign: invent, make up a story.
fell: fierce, ruthless, dreadful.
fellmonger: dealer in skins.
fet: fetched.
fetched: drawn from, derived.
firmity: firmness.
fleame: v. *fleume.*
fleume: phlegm; one of the four humours.
flowers: discharge.
foist: sb., light galley or barge.
　　　vb., cheat at dice.
fomentation: encouragement.
fond: foolish.
forecast: estimate, conjecture.
franked: enclosed.
fret: chafe.
froward: perverse.
fuller: one who cleans cloth.
fulsome: abundant, offensive.
furbisher: one who burnishes metal.
furniture: provisions, equipment.

garnished: decorated, embellished.
generate: generated.
Genes: Genoa.
glazer: polisher.
godsforbod: obscure, but probably the translator's rendering of *Gottesverbot,* God's commandment.
goldfiner: refiner of precious metals.
gorgets: throat-armour.
graff: graft.
gratulation: feeling of gratification.
greaves: armour for the lower leg.

grogram: coarse fabric.
gurmandize: gluttonous eating.
gymnosophist: naked philosopher.

handfasted: joined, betrothed.
haskardly: vulgar, base.
headiness: rashness, violence.
heliacal: said of a star visible just before sunrise or just after sunset.
hemorrhoids: small veins discharging into the lower bowel.
hicket: hiccups.
holigarcical: oligarchical.
historiographer: chronicler, historian.
honest: virtuous, reputable.
horoscope: ascendant; the degree of the ecliptic (q.v.) that is rising at any given time.
house: one of the twelve parts of the heavens as divided by great circles through the north and south points of the horizon.
huissier: usher.
humorous: capricious, moody, fantastic.

imbecility: weakness.
impanelled: entered on an official list.
impair: injury.
impatible: incapable of being acted on.
impeach: impediment.
impermixt: unmixed, pure.
impolluted: clean.
import: signify.
imposthume: abscess.
impression: atmospheric phenomenon (possibly restricted to the visible ones).
inclinable: favourably disposed.
indeed: in fact.
indeficient: incessant.
indifferency: impartiality.
indifferent: unbiased.
ingenerate: self-existent, inborn.
ingluviously: gluttonously.
inordinate: immoderate.
insolency: arrogance.
intelligencer: informer.
intentive: attentive, heedful.

interchangeable: changeable, subject to change.
interlard: mix, mingle.
intermeddle: mix together.

knapped: snapped or broken smartly.

labdanum: laudanum, opium.
lazulus: lapis lazuli.
leiger-du-maine: legerdemain, sleight of hand.
let: obstruct.
libidinous: lustful.
ligature: tying up an artery.
lightly: easily.
lightness: wantonness, lechery.
lineage: ancestry.
lineaments: features.
list: wish, desire.
lively: lifelike, vivid.
look big upon the matter: assume a pretended importance.
lumpish: heavy and clumsy.
luxation: dislocation.
lye: water impregnated with salts.

malice: to hate.
Malvesey: malmsey, a sweet Spanish wine.
maniable: easy to handle.
manuring: working on.
marchpane: marzipan.
marish: marshy.
marron: sweet chestnut.
match: wick.
maugre: in spite of.
mean: adj., moderate, middling.
    sb., middle, centre.
meanly: moderately.
meath: mead; fermented honey and water.
mediocrity: middle position or course.
meet: fit.
mensuration: measurement.
mercer: dealer in textiles.
mere: sheer, absolute.
merry pin: gay humour.
mesaraic: mesenteric; situated in the abdomen.

metheglem: metheglin, mead.
minion: favourite, mistress.
moe: more.
morion: vizorless helmet.
motion: inner prompting, mental agitation.
murr: a severe form of catarrh.
musculous: muscular.
must: unfermented grape-juice.

naughty: wicked, inferior.
navets: root vegetable similar to parsnips.
ne: nor.
nether: lower.
newfangled: fond of novelty.
next: nearest.
nilling: refusing.
nomotechnic: study and interpretation of law.
notary: clerk.
notice: intimation, warning.

obfuscate: darkened.
oblivious: unmindful.
opinion: belief, judgment.
ordnance: large guns.

painful: painstaking.
pantoffles: slippers.
parcel: portion.
partisan: long-handled barbed spear.
paste: pastry.
patrimony: inheritance.
pauldron: shoulder-armour.
peaking: shrinking.
peakish: slothful, spiritless.
pedotribe: gymnastic master.
pellicles: membranes.
peradventure: perhaps, by chance.
perbrake: parbreak, vomit.
percifeness: persiveness, power of penetration.
periclitate: be endangered.
perfited: perfected.
perfused: diffused.
permutation: barter.

perturbation: mental agitation, disorder.
pestilence: plague.
platform: outline, plan.
plight: condition.
policed: regulated.
policy: polity, constitution.
Polonia: Poland.
pomander: aromatic ball; often an orange stuck full of cloves.
ponderosity: heaviness.
Portingal: Portugal.
posset: hot milk curdled with ale.
predestinate: fore-ordained.
pretermit: omit, neglect.
prevent: anticipate.
proclivity: propensity, tendency.
progenitor: ancestor.
promiscuous: indiscriminately mixed.
properness: suitability.
propone: set forth.
propose: present to the mind.
prosecute: pursue.
pruse Byer: Prussian beer.
puissant: powerful.
pulse: peas, beans and so forth.
pursy: corpulent.
purvey: procure food.
put to plunges: bring into difficulties.

queachy: dense, thicketed.

rampire: rampart.
ray: array.
raunge: range, reduce, change.
reacheth: hands on, gives.
recognisance: acknowledgement.
recounted: accounted.
recourse: gathering together; course.
reduce: set down, record in writing.
regiment: regime, rule.
regrater: retailer, middleman.
replication: answer.
repining: fretting, complaining.
replenished: filled with.
repugn: oppose, resist.

repugnancy: antipathy, distaste.
revisitor: inspector.
rifely: plentifully.
right: straight.
rochet: cloak, mantle.
rout: disorderly crowd.
roving: straying.
rude: untutored.

sad: serious, steady.
salad: light armoured headpiece.
sallet: salad.
sarsenet: fine silk material.
saunders: sandalwood.
saving: excepting.
scantlines: scantlings, measuring-rods.
scarify: wound, make sore.
schiff: skiff.
sconce: hide, shelter.
scutcheon: badge.
searcher: customs officer.
seclude: exclude.
seculent: succulent, full of juice.
segmentary: in the form of an arc.
self: (as prefix) very.
sentence: aphorism.
service: sorb; a small pear-shaped fruit.
set all upon six and seven:⎫
set up one's rest:⎭ hazard one's entire fortune.
sever: distinguish.
shamefast: modest.
sherman: cutter.
shoutes: chutes.
silly: naif, defenceless.
similitude: simile.
simple: medicinal plant or herb.
sithence: since.
snevilly: snuffly.
sodden: boiled.
softly: gently.
solicitor: prompter.
sorted: consorted, associated.
spettle: spit.

splenetic: irascible.
spoiling: marauding, seeking prey.
spurging: throwing off impurities during fermentation.
squeamish: reluctant.
squier: square.
stability: fixity.
stagger: waver, hesitate.
stand in hand: behove.
stillatory: distillery.
stomach: sb., disposition, pride.
        vb., resent, feel as a grievance.
strainable: coercive.
straitly: strictly.
subalternation: succession by turn.
subtle: rarified, delicate.
succour: help.
superficies: surface.
supernal: celestial.
supputation: calculation, reckoning.
sustentation: nourishment.
swarfie: swarthy.
swath: track left by scythe-strokes.
sway: momentum, influence.
Sweathland: Sweden.

tabernacle: movable dwelling.
talent: talon.
tallage: taste, savour.
tapesters: tapestry-makers.
tarriance: delay.
tasses: thigh-armour.
tedious: irksome.
temperature: temperament.
tenuity: thinness.
testy: short-tempered.
then: than.
theoric: theory.
throughly: thoroughly.
tick: mattress-case.
tillage: cultivation.
tires: female headdress or clothing.
touching: concerning.
traffic: trade between distant countries.

travail: work.
trencher: wooden plate.
tuition: protection, care.
turkys: turquoise.
turning: casting.
turn the cat in the pan: change sides.
turn up: make appear.

uliginous: waterlogged, swampy.
unapt: unsuitable.
unconcoct: undigested.
unkindly: unnatural.
unmeet: unfitting.
unhosed: barelegged.
utter: outer.

vauntbrace: vambrace, armour for the forearm.
vegetation: power of growth.
venerous: lustful.
venison: game.
venusty: grace, beauty.
vertue: power, faculty.
vessel: plate.
vicissitudal: subject to change.
vinewed: mouldy.
vintner: wine-merchant.

watchet: blue.
watching: sleeplessness.
wayless: pathless.
well-favoured: handsome, good-looking.
wesandpipe: windpipe.
wex: increase, grow.
wexkernels: enlarged glands.
wheel and string: driving mechanism.
whenas: when.
whittled: drunk.
wimple: garment covering head and neck.
without: beyond.
womb: belly.
wot: know.
wry: twisted.

THE END